The United States Change and Challenge

The Colonial Period to the Present

Senior Consultant
Dr. Judith Irvin
Florida State University

HOLT, RINEHART AND WINSTON

A Harcourt Classroom Education Company

Austin · New York · Orlando · Atlanta · San Francisco · Boston · Dallas · Toronto · London

Staff Credits

EDITORIAL

Manager of Editorial Operations
Bill Wahlgren

Executive Editor
Patricia McCambridge

Project Editor
Victoria Moreland

Component Editors: Carolyn Logan, Pamela Thompson

Assistant Editor: Tracy DeMont

Writers: Claire Colombo, Mara Rockliff

Copyediting: Michael Neibergall, *Copyediting Manager;* Mary Malone, *Copyediting Supervisor;* Christine Altgelt, Joel Bourgeois, Elizabeth Dickson, Emily Force, Julie A. Hill, Julia Thomas Hu, Jennifer Kirkland, Millicent Ondras, Dennis Scharnberg, *Copyeditors*

Project Administration: Marie Price, *Managing Editor;* Lori De La Garza, *Editorial Operations Coordinator;* Heather Cheyne, Mark Holland, Marcus Johnson, Jennifer Renteria, Janet Riley, Kelly Tankersley, *Project Administration;* Ruth Hooker, Joie Pickett, Margaret Sanchez, *Word Processing*

Editorial Permissions: Susan Lowrance, *Permissions Editor*

ART, DESIGN AND PHOTO

Book Design
Richard Metzger, *Design Director*

Graphic Services
Kristen Darby, *Manager*

Design Implementation
The Format Group, LLC

Image Acquisitions
Joe London, *Director;* Jeannie Taylor, Tim Taylor, *Photo Research Supervisors;* Rick Benavides, Terry Janecek, Cindy Verheyden, *Photo Researchers;* Sarah Hudgens, *Assistant Photo Researcher;* Michelle Rumpf, Elaine Tate, *Art Buyer Supervisors,* Gillian Brody, Joyce Gonzalez, *Art Buyers*

Design
Isabel Garza Design

Cover Design
Curtis Riker, *Director;* Sunday Patterson, *Designer*

PRODUCTION

Belinda Barbosa Lopez, *Senior Production Coordinator;* Beth Prevelige, *Prepress Manager;* Carol Trammel, *Production Supervisor*

MANUFACTURING/INVENTORY

Shirley Cantrell, *Supervisor of Inventory and Manufacturing;* Wilonda Ieans, *Manufacturing Coordinator;* Mark McDonald, *Inventory Planner*

Cover Photo Credits: (Guadalupe Mountains National Park, *El Capitan Peak with Boulders*), © Laurence Parent; (steam train), © Kim Todd/Picture Quest; (train track), Digital Imagery © 2001 Photodisc, Inc.; (launch of the space shuttle *Discovery*), NASA/Roger Ressmeyer/CORBIS; (stars in the night sky), © Digital Art/CORBIS.

All art, unless otherwise noted, by ArtToday.com.

ISBN 0-03-065036-4

5   043   05 04

Contents

CHAPTER 6
American Issues: The United States from 1914 to the Present 185

CHAPTER 1

A City Upon a Hill
The Colonial Period   1608–1775

Oops! Just a Misunderstanding . . .

Captain John Smith's heart beat faster as his captors surrounded him. Chief Powhatan spoke, and they raised their clubs above Smith. Suddenly a girl rushed forward and shielded his body with her own. It was the chief's favorite daughter, twelve-year-old Pocahontas.

Generations of Americans have heard and retold John Smith's tale of his rescue by the princess Pocahontas. However, many historians today believe Smith wasn't near death at all—just dead wrong.

In fact, they say, the whole scene was a traditional initiation ceremony, and Pocahontas was simply playing her part. Smith was in no more danger than if he'd been kneeling before the king of England, with a sword raised over his head to knight him. When the ceremony was done, Chief Powhatan and the others welcomed Smith as the newest member of their tribe.

My Teacher Lives at School

When you were younger and just starting school, did you think your teacher slept in the classroom at night?

If you'd gone to a dame school in early New England, you would have been right. Its "classroom" was in the teacher's home, and she went about her household chores while the students worked.

Dame schools had no rows of desks and chairs, no chalkboards, and often even no books. Children learned their ABCs from a horn book, a piece of paper protected on both sides with a thin, transparent layer of horn. (This was before plastic was invented.)

▲ Captain John Smith.

Memorable Quote

"For we must consider that we shall be as a city upon a hill, the eyes of all people are upon us."

—John Winthrop, governor of Massachusetts Bay colony

▲ Page from a horn book.

INVESTIGATE: What other stereotypes about Pilgrims or Puritans can you disprove?

▲ A Puritan couple.

The Granger Collection, New York

VOCABULARY MATTERS

The word *colony* was used long before English settlers came to the Americas. It comes from a Latin word that means "settlement." It was used to describe a group of Roman citizens who lived in a newly conquered territory to guard it for Rome. The English colonists in America, however, were more independent; they left England to find new freedoms and to build a new society.

Loud and Clear

If you've got a voice that can be heard a block away, you could have been a colonial town crier. With no radio, no TV, and no Internet, the only way to spread late-breaking news was by word of mouth—and the town crier had the loudest mouth in town. He walked the streets bellowing "Oyez, Oyez" (ō´yes´) or "Hear ye, hear ye." (In other words, everybody, LISTEN UP!)

Fashion Statements

Picture a Puritan. If you're like most people, you probably see a man or woman draped head-to-toe in black, with maybe a little bit of white. Actually, only important government officials and village elders dressed that way. An ordinary Puritan who wore black would have been viewed as a "showoff."

The Puritans did insist on dressing in "sadd," or serious, colors: violets, blues, deep reds and greens, earthy browns and oranges. You'd never catch them decked out in Massachusetts Bay Magenta or Puritan Pink.

Freedom for Me, and Even for Thee

The young Puritan preacher Roger Williams had dangerous ideas. He agreed with his fellow Puritans that the beliefs about God found in the Bible were the only true ones. He wanted to change people's minds by talking to them, though, not by driving them out or punishing them if they refused to convert.

Unlike most other colonists, Williams went to the trouble of learning the language of the Wampanoag and Narragansett people who lived nearby. He recognized their tribal ownership of the land and said only they—not the king of England—had the right to sell it to the settlers.

Williams's friendship with local tribes saved his life. In January 1636, fed up with his radical preaching, colony officials decided to send him back to England. Williams fled. Lost and freezing in a "howling wilderness," he was overjoyed to run into his friend Massasoit, the chief of the Wampanoags. With his help Williams survived the winter. Then Williams went on to found Rhode Island, the first colony to offer true religious freedom for all.

Recently, a group of scientists and historians turned to trees in their quest for more information about North America's first two British colonies, Roanoke and Jamestown. In the following article, you'll discover exactly what they learned.

Droughts Played Major Role in Jamestown, "Lost Colony" Tragedies

from *William and Mary News*

by PEGGY SHAW

Tree-Ring Evidence Suggests Worst Droughts in 800 Years Led to Settlements' Decline

▲ Narrow rings from this centuries-old tree reveal times of drought.

Photographers Consortium/eStock Photography/Picture Quest

The worst droughts of the past 800 years likely played a major role in the mysterious disappearance of Roanoke Island's "Lost Colony" and in the "starving time" endured by colonists at Jamestown, researchers from the College of William and Mary and the University of Arkansas have concluded after studying growth rings of ancient trees in the Tidewater area. The findings appear in the April 24, 1998 issue of the journal *Science*.

"If the English had tried to find a worse time to launch

You Need to Know...

Historians have always known that both Roanoke and Jamestown faced severe challenges during the first years of their existence. Roanoke, founded in 1585 at the urging of Sir Walter Raleigh, had completely disappeared within five years. Jamestown, founded in 1607 by a group of businessmen, struggled through a period of disease and death known as the "starving time" before it eventually flourished. However, the details of the colonies' first difficult years have never been known for certain. So when thousand-year-old trees from the area were allowed to tell their stories, historians were thrilled to have many of their suspicions confirmed.

their settlements in the New World, they could not have done so," said Dennis Blanton, director of the William and Mary Center for Archaeological Research. "From 1387 to 1589, the most extreme drought in 800 years is implicated in the disappearance of the Lost Colony, and the Jamestown settlement was later plagued by the driest seven-year episode in 770 years. These droughts make the dry summer of 1997 pale in comparison."

"If the English had tried to find a worse time to launch their settlements in the New World, they could not have done so."

The researchers' findings were based on an examination of ancient trees in the nation's southeastern Tidewater region. The project was funded by the National Park Service as part of the Jamestown Archaeological Assessment project, a cooperative project among the College of William and Mary, the Colonial Williamsburg Foundation and the National Park Service.

Soon after the Roanoke Island Colony was established near the end of the 16th century, the settlers mysteriously disappeared, leaving only the enigmatic word "Croatoan" carved on a tree. More is known about the hardships at Jamestown, which was founded in 1607 but nearly failed in 1609 and 1610—historically known as "the starving time"—when the colony suffered an appallingly high death rate. According to historians, 43 percent of the 350 colonists alive in June of 1610 were dead by the end of that summer.

Blanton, who has long been intrigued by the events at Jamestown, asked University of Arkansas climatologist[1] David Stahle to undertake the tree-ring study after hearing of his work. Several years ago, a team of researchers from the tree-ring laboratory at Arkansas had conducted general climate studies along the East Coast by taking

Try and Try Again

Roanoke, the first British colony in the Americas, seemed doomed from the beginning. It was originally settled in 1585, but conflicts with American Indians and a shortage of food soon sent the defeated colonists back to England. Within a year, though, 150 new settlers gave the colony a second try. Its governor, John White, discovered that the American Indians had not forgotten past troubles. Still, he befriended one tribe, the Croatoans, before sailing for England for supplies. When White returned, he was greeted by one of the great mysteries of colonial history: a deserted village and one word, "Croatoan," etched into a nearby tree. The mystery of Roanoke's ruin has never been solved.

---

1. **climatologist** (klī′mə•täl′ə•jist): scientist who studies the climate.

nondestructive core samples from selected trees. Blanton asked them to examine the core samples taken specifically from centuries-old bald cypress trees in swamps along the Blackwater and Nottoway rivers on the Virginia-North Carolina border.

"I had read articles about their work and thought we could use the data in archaeology," Blanton explained. "I was trained as a prehistoric archaeologist, and we routinely look at environment to see what role it has played. You don't do any study in prehistoric archaeology without first understanding the limitations of the environment."

At Blanton's request, Arkansas climatologists spent several months analyzing the existing core samples, which covered the period between 1185 and 1984, for information about rainfall and temperatures during the Tidewater growing season. Archaeologists from William and Mary's Center for Archaeological Research did extensive historical and archaeological research into past Tidewater climate conditions. The groups then correlated and interpreted the data.

archaeology (är′kē·ôl′ə·jē): a branch of science that studies past human cultures by looking at the clues they left behind.

▲ Bald cypress trees like these were analyzed in the drought study.

"The tree-ring data indicate the extraordinary drought conditions that attended the settlement of both the Roanoke and Jamestown Colonies," the *Science* article says. A tree growth anomaly map for the period 1587–1589, for example, shows that the Lost Colony drought affected the entire southeastern United States, but was particularly severe in the Tidewater region near Roanoke. The cypress growth anomaly map for the Jamestown drought, 1606–1612, reveals that the most severe drought conditions during that period occurred in the Tidewater region near Jamestown. (An anomaly map illustrates specific conditions—in this case growing-season precipitation—over a certain geographical area.)

subsistence (səb·sis′təns): existence; life.

decimated (des′ə·māt′id): destroyed; killed.

"The Roanoke and Jamestown colonies have both been criticized for poor planning, poor support, and for a startling indifference to their own <u>subsistence</u>," concluded the writers in *Science*. "But the tree-ring reconstruction indicates that even the best planned and supported colony would have been supremely challenged by the climatic conditions of 1587–1589 and 1606–1612."

The Jamestown drought, for instance, <u>decimated</u> corn crops on which the colonists depended and aggravated tense relations with the native Powhatan Indians. Blanton speculated that when the Indians could not supply food to the colonists as promised, hard feelings followed and conflict erupted. The dates of at least two Anglo-Indian wars correlate perfectly with the droughts, he said.

Drought also affected the quality of the colony's critical water supply. "Poor water quality is another factor implicated in the ill health suffered at Jamestown, and water quality at Jamestown is poorest during drought," said the *Science* article. "The lower James River is a brackish estuary, and there are archival references to foul drinking water and associated illnesses among the settlers, particularly before 1613."

During the drought, many people starved, and some of the Jamestown colonists eventually resorted to cannibalism. Citing a staggering death toll that nearly forced abandonment of the colony, the *Science* article notes that "only 38 of the 104 original settlers were still alive after the first year at Jamestown, and 4,800 out of the 6,000 settlers sent to Jamestown between 1607 and 1625 died during this extraordinary period.

"The colonists were expected to live off the land and off trade and tribute from the Indians. But this subsistence system would have left the colonists extremely vulnerable during drought."

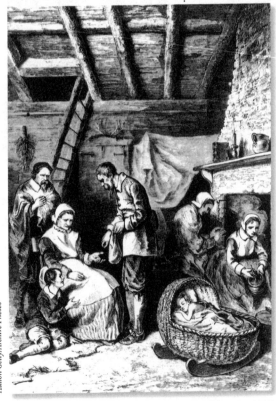

Hulton Getty/Archive Photos

▲ A Jamestown settler shares corn with neighbors in 1609.

Members of the Roanoke Colony—last seen in August of 1587—are thought to have been similarly afflicted by extreme drought from 1587 to 1589, the area's driest three-year period in 800 years.

"I am not an environmental determinist,"[2] said Blanton. "Other factors clearly played a role in the demise of the Roanoke Island settlers and the hardships of those at Jamestown, but the droughts were certainly among the most serious problems both groups faced.

"Only multidisciplinary research could lead to such exciting discoveries as these," he added. "History, archaeology, or climatology alone could not have reached these conclusions, but a combination of the disciplines enabled us to discover these significant patterns."

---

2. **determinist** (dē·tʉr′mi·nist): someone who believes that everything that happens can be traced to a certain specific set of causes.

✓ Reading Check

1. When did the most extreme drought in 800 years occur?

2. What kind of information did climatologists look for when they studied the tree-ring samples?

3. Identify two ways in which the drought of 1606–1612 affected the colony of Jamestown.

4. Researchers from what three disciplines, or areas of study, worked together on this project?

5. Paraphrase the conclusion drawn by Dennis Blanton in the last paragraph of the article.

The *Mayflower* Pilgrims—were they cheerful, hearty people who lived in log cabins and shared cozy meals with nearby Indian tribes? Probably not. Read on to find out what the Pilgrims' first winter was *really* like.

from "The Time of Most Distress"

from *William Bradford: Rock of Plymouth*

by KIERAN DOHERTY

"But that which was most sad and lamentable was, that in two or three months' time half their company died. . . ."[1]

On December 16 the *Mayflower* headed across Cape Cod Bay. By the time the Pilgrims left their anchorage at the northern end of the cape, they may well have decided to name their settlement Plymouth, perhaps because Plymouth was the last harbor they had seen in England or perhaps because they knew that was the name given to the harbor and the land around it by Captain John Smith when he visited the region in 1614.

In any event, they arrived too late in the day on December 16 for any on board to go ashore. Since the next day was the Lord's Day, they again put off their landing. Finally, on December 18, an exploring party made its way to shore.

You Need to Know...

William Bradford, a passenger on the *Mayflower* and Plymouth's second governor, kept many records describing events in the colony. Kieran Doherty uses these records to paint a telling picture of the harsh conditions the first Pilgrims faced after they arrived in 1620. The records also tell us that the *Mayflower* really *did* land near a large boulder known as Plymouth Rock and that the Pilgrims *did* live lives of adventure.

1. All quotations in this selection are from William Bradford and Edward Winslow, *Mourt's Relation* (Boston: Applewood Books, 1986).

The Pilgrims' first order of business was to determine exactly where to build their settlement. The spot they chose was near a freshwater brook that emptied into the harbor. This brook, now known as Town Brook, provided them with a supply of fresh water. Better yet, as they had discovered on their first visit, it was bordered by land that had been cleared by Indians and apparently abandoned, ready for planting. Of equal importance, the place chosen by Bradford and the others was at the bottom of a small hill where guard could be posted and cannon mounted for protection.

The Pilgrims must have been particularly pleased when they noticed that the brook formed a natural channel through the mudflats near shore, and that a large boulder stood just outside the mouth of that channel. This boulder provided the Pilgrims with something like a natural pier or landing stage. In all likelihood, one of the first things the Pilgrims did was build a walkway of squared logs running across the mudflats between the rock and the shore. With that walkway in place, the Pilgrims were able to hop from the shallop or the *Mayflower's* longboat to the boulder and cross the wooden walkway to the beach without getting soaked.

Mark E. Gibson/Folio Inc.

▲ The *Mayflower II,* a replica of the original *Mayflower,* was built in 1955. It is moored at Plymouth, MA, near Plymouth Rock.

This boulder is famous as Plymouth Rock. Although there is no evidence that there was ever a large-scale landing of the Pilgrims on Plymouth Rock, the rock still was important to the settlers of the colony. In fact, when the first town wharf was built in the mid-1700s, it was built directly over Plymouth Rock.

While the Pilgrims were in a hurry to get to work on their settlement—and the crew of the *Mayflower* wanted nothing but to dump their passengers on shore so they could return to England—bad weather delayed any work on Plymouth Town for several days. Finally, on December 23, twenty men came ashore with tools to start building homes. Soon the sound of axes and saws filled the air as the Pilgrims began constructing rough shelters. One of the most enduring myths about the Pilgrims of Plymouth is that they lived in log cabins. The fact is that there were no such cabins in America until about 1640 when settlers from Denmark arrived on the banks of the Delaware River and used logs to build homes like the dwellings in their homeland. The Pilgrims' very first homes were one-room cottages built of twigs covered with mud—the same "wattle-and-daub" construction that was used for peasant cottages in England until the early seventeenth century. These tiny, rough shacks had fireplaces and chimneys made of clay-covered logs and roofs thatched with rushes that grew in the low lands near the shore.

The Pilgrims' very first homes were one-room cottages built of twigs covered with mud.

Later, more permanent homes were made of squared timbers. To make these timbers, the Pilgrim men would dig a pit about 6 feet (2 meters) deep and lay a pine log across it. One man would stand in the pit, another outside on its edge. By pushing and pulling a two-handed saw they would rip the pine log into squared boards. These boards would then be placed side-by-side, vertically, to cover a frame made of stout oak beams. The inside walls of most homes were covered with clapboards, made by splitting cedar logs using an iron wedge known as a beetle, and a maul, or heavy hammer. These cedar clapboards were also popular in England and were exported by the Pilgrims as a way to pay off their debt to the Merchant Adventurers.

The Pilgrims quickly set to work building their homes, for they knew they must have shelter or they would perish in the New England cold. Even on Christmas Day—which the Saints did not celebrate because they believed that no one knew the exact date of Christ's birth—the Pilgrims, both Saints and Strangers, worked. "Monday, the 25th

Day, we went on shore," Bradford said, "some to fell timber, some to saw, some to rive,[2] and some to carry, so no man rested all that day."

While some of the men worked building shelters, others cleared a road from the waterfront to the foot of the hill that overlooked the harbor. That road is now called Leyden Street. The hill, first known simply as the Mount, was later called Fort Hill and known still later as Burial Hill, since it became the site of Plymouth's burial ground.

Lots just 8 feet (2.4 meters) wide and about 50 feet (15 meters) deep were laid out on both sides of Leyden Street. Each person was <u>allocated</u> one lot, so that a family of four would have a parcel of land 32 feet (10 meters) wide and 50 feet deep. Single men were asked to attach themselves to a family, so the Pilgrims figured that they only needed nineteen houses to shelter everybody in the young colony. As things worked out, they needed far fewer.

Before construction started on any permanent dwellings, the Pilgrims set about building a common house, about 20 feet (6 meters) square, where supplies could be stored. By the end of the first week of January, this storehouse was almost completed, and families were busy building their own houses on both sides of Leyden Street.

As the Pilgrims struggled to gain a foothold in the New World, they suffered terribly. During the four months

allocated (al′ō·kāt′id): given out in portions according to a plan.

---

2. **rive:** to split.

Saints and Strangers Set Sail

In this case, Saints and Strangers don't refer to famous holy people and unknown others. Below you'll find a brief description of each of these groups, plus some others whose names you may see.

Puritans wanted to "purify," or simplify, their religion. They believed that the Church of England was too much like the Roman Catholic Church.

Separatists believed that the Church of England would never change and so formally separated themselves from it. Both the Puritans and the Separatists were persecuted by King James I.

Saints—The name the Separatists gave themselves.

Strangers—The name given by the Separatists on the *Mayflower* to colonists from London who were not Separatists.

Pilgrims—A name given to the Saints and Strangers who sailed for the Americas in 1620.

▲ The Pilgrims worked hard to establish new homes. **? What other challenges did they face?**

since their departure from England, they had had no fresh fruit or vegetables to eat. Now, on land, they had to get along on a diet largely of shellfish and game birds. While they had food, it was unappetizing to men and women used to hearty meals of beef, wheat bread, and beer. As a result, they were plagued by scurvy.[3] Drenched by almost constant cold rains and weakened by the rigors of the ocean voyage, the change in their diet, and the scurvy, many came down with pneumonia. Others, it is thought, caught typhus,[4] spread by lice on the *Mayflower*. Soon, almost everybody in the little settlement was sick.

In fact, during the early months of 1621, Plymouth was almost wiped out by disease. Of the one hundred and two passengers who arrived in Cape Cod, four died before the *Mayflower* anchored in Plymouth Harbor. In January and February, Bradford later said, "there died some times two or three of a day. . . ." By the summer of 1621, fifty Pilgrims had died. Only a dozen of the original twenty-six heads of families survived; and just four of the original twelve unattached men or boys. Almost all the adult

---

3. **scurvy:** a disease caused by a lack of Vitamin C.
4. **typhus:** an infectious disease which causes a rash and fever and is spread by fleas, lice, etc.

women perished. The younger boys and girls, perhaps because they were cared for by adults, fared better, and most survived. Conditions on the ship were no better than those on land. Indeed, many of the sick Pilgrims remained on board the ship, waiting for shelter to be completed ashore. In the ship's close quarters, the sickness that was killing Pilgrims on shore also ravaged the *Mayflower's* officers and crew.

During these months, the storehouse was filled with the sick. Of the settlers, Bradford wrote, ". . . in the time of most distress, there was but six or seven sound persons" to care for the sick and dying. Among those who nursed the ill, changed their filthy bedding, and fed them as best they could were William Brewster, Bradford's old mentor from Scrooby, and Myles Standish, the rough-and-tumble military man.

One of the chores the few healthy men had was to bury those who died. While there was no contact with the Indians who inhabited the region near what the Pilgrims called Plymouth Town, Bradford and the others felt certain that the local Native Americans were watching them carefully. To hide the fact that the little settlement was being scourged by disease, burials during these early months were done in secret, late at night, without any ceremony. Graves were unmarked, probably covered with brush, so the Indians could not tell how many of the settlers had died.

scourged (skʉrjd): punished; made to suffer.

During this period, Bradford himself was laid low by illness. On January 11, while working in the fields, he was "vehemently taken with a grief and pain" so severe that it was feared he might die. Moved to the common house, which by that time was crowded with the sick, he slowly started to recover.

vehemently (vē'ə•mənt•lē): forcefully; with intensity.

Two nights later a spark from an open fire set the thatch roof of the makeshift[5] hospital ablaze. Burning reeds and embers cascaded into the room where Bradford and other patients lay helpless, surrounded by open barrels of gunpowder and loaded muskets.[6] Somehow, the few healthy

---

5. **makeshift:** used as a temporary substitute.
6. **muskets:** guns with long barrels used in the seventeenth century.

Meeting the Neighbors

During the following spring the Pilgrims of Plymouth became well acquainted with the American Indians that they feared. One afternoon in March, much to the Pilgrims' surprise, an Indian armed with a bow and arrows entered town, strolled up Leyden Street, and said, in English, "Welcome." His name was Samoset, and he was a guest of the chief of the Wampanoags, the most powerful tribe in the area. Several visits later, Samoset brought with him a friend known as Squanto. His tribe, the Patuxets, had once lived near the Plymouth settlement. During Squanto's absence, they had perished in an epidemic. Squanto befriended the Pilgrims—William Bradford, in particular—and eventually took up residence in Plymouth.

men in the settlement managed to get the patients and the armament[7] outside to safety. Though the building was saved, clothing and other valuable goods stored in the common house were lost.

Even as the Pilgrim colony was ravaged by illness, the handful of healthy men worked on permanent dwellings and struggled to prepare against the likelihood of an Indian attack. Slowly, the little community of Plymouth took shape. Houses were raised along Leyden Street, and the top of the hill overlooking the town was leveled.

In Bradford's history, nothing is said of the role that children played in these early days in Plymouth. However, in the seventeenth century, even three-year-old children were given easy chores—if for no other reason than to keep them busy and out of mischief. By the time boys and girls reached the age of six or seven, they were considered little adults. Boys undoubtedly were set to work gathering rushes to be used as thatch or shellfish from the shallows near the beach. Bigger boys, strong enough to handle a musket, probably hunted. Girls helped their mothers prepare meals, mend clothing, and do other household chores. There was no school in Plymouth for many years, but, knowing the Pilgrims, we can be sure there were home-taught lessons—at least in reading the Bible—when there was no work to do.

There were adventures, as well. Two of the young Pilgrim men, John Goodman and Peter Browne, set off in search of rushes, taking with them the settlement's spaniel and a mastiff.[8] Suddenly, the dogs took off in pursuit of a deer. Goodman and Browne followed and soon were lost in the woods. After wandering for a day and night, they made it back to the settlement, but not before Goodman's feet were so swollen from the cold that his shoes had to be cut off. Just a few days later, he limped into the woods again with the spaniel. "A little way from the plantation," Bradford later wrote, "two great wolves ran after the

---

7. **armament:** weapons.
8. **mastiff:** a large, very strong breed of dog used for hunting in the seventeenth century.

dog. . . ." Unarmed, Goodman kept the wolves at bay with a stick while they, according to Bradford, "sat on their tails grinning at him. . . ."

While the Pilgrims had been left alone by the Indians around Plymouth Town, Bradford and the other leaders knew it would be foolish not to be prepared in the event of trouble. In mid-February, Myles Standish was formally placed in charge of defense and authorized to command the other men. At the same time, the *Mayflower's* captain, Christopher Jones, brought ashore several of the ship's large cannons and helped the Pilgrims <u>install</u> them on top of the Mount.

And so, with work and adventures and dying, the New England winter passed. . . .

install (in•stôl′): to secure in the correct position to be used.

✓ Reading Check

1. How was the boulder now known as Plymouth Rock actually used by the Pilgrims?

2. Briefly describe the Pilgrims' first homes.

3. What two purposes did the common house, or store-house, serve?

4. Why were burials done in secret, late at night?

5. What kinds of chores did Pilgrim boys and girls perform?

MEET THE *Writer*

Kieran Doherty is a journalist and a business writer, but he also enjoys writing nonfiction books for young people. In addition to his book about William Bradford, Doherty has published a biography of William Penn and a book about the southeastern colonies. In 2000, *William Bradford: Rock of Plymouth* was named a Notable Social Studies Trade Book by the Children's Book Council and the National Council for the Social Studies.

In colonial times, doctors and scientists often had to face down fear and prejudice as well as dangerous diseases. Read on to learn about the risks that Cotton Mather and Benjamin Franklin encountered when they promoted an African practice used to protect people against disease.

from Smallpox

from *Invisible Enemies: Stories of Infectious Disease*

by JEANETTE FARRELL

W e do not know the full story of the worldwide history of inoculation, because in many places no written records were kept of its practice. In Africa, for instance, knowledge of inoculation was passed from generation to generation by word of mouth; it was not written down. We do know that just as inoculation came to England from Turkey, it came to America from Africa in the person of Onesimus, slave to the famous colonial clergyman Cotton Mather. But all we know of what Onesimus knew about Africa's practice of inoculation is his owner Cotton Mather's written words.

Most probably the man who would later be given the slave name Onesimus was from the Gurumanche people, who lived in West Africa, although of his real home and even of the name of his tribe we have no clear record. Slave traders branded him with their mark,

You Need to Know...

This selection tells how colonists in Boston learned to protect themselves from a deadly smallpox virus. The method they learned, known as inoculation (i•näk'yə•lā'shən), had for many years been a common practice in the distant lands of India, China, and Africa. Shortly before American colonists began to inoculate, members of British society had discovered the practice, too. In the early 1700s, Lady Mary Montagu, a British aristocrat, had witnessed inoculation while visiting the Ottoman Empire (modern-day Turkey). When she became convinced that it worked, she had her own six-year-old son inoculated. She also urged her friend, the Princess of Wales, to inoculate her own children and the other children of England. Read on to discover why, in Boston, the inoculation of children outraged many of the city's citizens.

chained him by the ankle to another slave, and stuffed him and hundreds of others in the four-foot-high space between the decks of a slaving ship, to be carried as cargo. There, for the endless weeks of travel, Onesimus heard the moans of men dying from fever and dysentery, and watched as others chose to die, refusing to eat, until the slavers pried open their mouths to shove food down their throats. Somehow, Onesimus kept his mind and spirit alive. In surviving, he brought to the people that enslaved him the secret to saving thousands of lives.

▲ The first vaccination by Dr. Edward Jenner in 1796.

This Gurumanche man was purchased for forty English pounds[1] for Cotton Mather by Mather's congregation. He was a valued slave: Cotton Mather called Onesimus a "smile of heaven upon our family." When Mather asked if Onesimus had had smallpox—an important question, as an <u>immune</u> slave who could survive an <u>epidemic</u> was much more valuable—the slave gave the curious answer of yes and no. He showed Mather a round, dark scar on his arm, and explained that he had been given a small case of smallpox so that he would not get the full-blown disease.

This is how Cotton Mather recalled the incident (when he describes what the slaves told him, he imitates the pidgin English that they spoke):

> *Enquiring of my Negro-Man* Onesimus, *who is a pretty Intelligent Fellow, Whether he ever had ye Small-Pox, he answered* Yes *and* No; *and then told me that he had undergone an Operation, which had given him something of ye Small-Pox, and would forever preserve him from it, adding, That it was*

immune (i·myōōn′): unable to contract a disease.

epidemic (ep′ə·dem′ik): an outbreak of a disease that spreads quickly among many people in a given area.

---

1. pounds: the basic monetary unit of England.

Big Voice Against Smallpox

Cotton Mather was born in February, 1663, to Increase Mather and Maria Cotton Mather. After earning both a B.A. and an M.A. from Harvard University, Mather followed in both his father's and his grandfather's footsteps and became an ordained minister. In many ways, Mather was a crusader for change in society. He argued strongly for the humane treatment of slaves, and he urged people to overcome their fear of the smallpox inoculation. Today, though, Mather is remembered mostly for involvement in the Salem Witch Trials of 1692.

---

distraction (di·strak′shən): a state of mental agitation and disturbance.

intervening (in′tər·vēn′iŋ): coming between.

virus (vī′rəs): a disease caused by a tiny living particle that reproduces inside cells.

---

often used among ye Guaramantese, *and whoever had ye Courage to use it, was forever free from ye Fear of the Contagion. He described ye Operation to me, and showed me in his Arm ye Scar. . . I have since mett with a Considerable Number of these* Africans, *who all agree in one Story; That in their Countrey* grandy-many *dy of the Small-Pox: But now they Learn This Way: People take Juice of* Small-Pox; *and cutty-skin, and putt in a Drop; then by'nd by a little* sicky, sicky, *then very few little things like Small-Pox; and no body dy of it; and no body have Small-pox any more. Thus in* Africa, *where the poor creatures dy of the Small-Pox like Rotten Sheep, A Merciful God has taught them an* Infallible Preservative. *Tis a* Common Practice, *and is Attended with a Constant Success.*

Cotton Mather was so impressed by what this slave told him that he recorded it in his letters, his diaries, and the book he wrote about medical practices. When he also read accounts of inoculation in Turkey, he resolved to use this practice to protect Bostonians from smallpox.

Mather soon had his chance: in mid-April of 1721 the smallpox epidemic that inspired the British princess to inoculate arrived in Boston harbor, carried aboard the ship *Seahorse* from the West Indies. It was to be the worst smallpox epidemic in eighteenth-century Boston. By July so many people were dying that the constant ringing of funeral bells drove the living to distraction and terrified the sick. The city ordered that only one bell could be tolled at a time, and then only at designated hours.

The fact that the last smallpox epidemic had been nineteen years before allowed this one to be so fierce: all those born in the intervening years had had no chance to be exposed to the disease and to become immune. The city was full of potential victims. The smallpox virus could spread by the millions in the air exhaled by the infected. Inhaling as little as one virus particle could be enough to cause disease. Despite the city's efforts to isolate the infected by hanging red flags at the doors of their houses so that the uninfected would know to stay away, six thousand Bostonians contracted smallpox. Those who could fled the town, leaving their businesses and homes boarded up; the half-empty town seemed full of death.

In the American colonies, as in England, the pioneers of inoculation experimented on their children. On June 24, as the epidemic began to gather force, Mather wrote to a friend of his, the doctor Zabdiel Boylston, to say that now was the time to try inoculation. It was a terrifying prospect to take the deadly disease into one's home. But in the streets the terror was just as great. Zabdiel's wife and other children had left the city, leaving only six-year-old Thomas with his father. On June 26, 1721, Boylston inoculated him, as well as his thirty-two-year-old slave Jack and Jack's two-and-a-half-year-old son.

It was a terrifying prospect to take the deadly disease into one's home. But in the streets the terror was just as great.

Long before their pustules[2] rose, before even night had fallen on the first day, news of the inoculations spread through Boston. The city was horrified: a doctor had infected his own son with a deadly disease! Around many an inn table, men seethed about what they would do with Dr. Boylston. Someone tarred the saddle of a horse mistakenly thought to be his. Boylston went into hiding for two weeks, while men threatened to hang him. But nevertheless, as his child and slaves healed, Boylston was convinced inoculation worked. The fever and pustules passed quickly, leaving nothing but the inoculation scars to show for them. The doctor continued to inoculate, demanding that the critics come and view the health of his patients.

Mather, however, while a brave promoter of the cause, found his heart weak when it came to his own son. In June, Samuel came home from college at Harvard terrified

---

2. **pustules:** small swellings on the skin filled with pus.

because his roommate had died of smallpox. Samuel had not yet had it and therefore was not immune. His father was tormented. On August 1, he wrote in his diary:

Full of Distress about Sammy; *He begs to have his life saved, by receiving the* Small-pox, *in the way of* Inoculation, *and if he should after all dy by receiving it in the common Way, how can I answer it? On the other Side, our People, who have Satan remarkably filling their Hearts and their Tongues, will go on with infinite Prejudices against me and my Ministry, if I suffer this Operation upon the child.*

Mather had reason to worry. Like Lady Mary's child, Mather's son had a one-in-fifty chance of dying from the inoculation, and, until his pustules healed, he could give the disease to anyone else who was not immune. That August, Mather finally chose to risk inoculation and more community ill will. Sammy survived inoculation, and the epidemic, and became the only one of Mather's sixteen children that was to live longer than his father.

Cotton Mather, like Zabdiel Boylston and Lady Mary Wortley Montagu before him, had gambled with and for his child's life and had won. But in the story of inoculation, there was also a brave person who feared to risk inoculating his child, and was still brave enough to admit to and advise others against the mistake he thought led to his son's death.

Benjamin Franklin was a very young man when Zabdiel Boylston began inoculating in Boston. In 1721 he was apprenticed at his brother James's newspaper, the *New England Courant.* It was in the pages of the *Courant* that James published such fierce criticisms of inoculation that Mather referred to them as the work of the devil.

Fifteen years later, however, as editor of his own newspaper in Philadelphia, *The Pennsylvania Gazette*, Benjamin Franklin promoted inoculation. Therefore, when his four-year-old son, Francis, died of smallpox, it was all over the city that it was inoculation that had killed him.

Hearing this, the mourning Franklin was filled with even more anguish. Not only had he failed to inoculate his son but now his example, misinterpreted, could lead others to make the same mistake. Again, he took to the pages of his newspaper, and bravely he wrote (referring to smallpox as distemper):

> *Understanding 'tis a current Report, that my Son Francis, who died lately of the Small Pox, had it by Inoculation: and being desired to satisfy the Publick in that Particular; inasmuch as some People are, by the Report . . . deter'd from having that Operation perform'd on their Children, I do hereby sincerely declare, that he was not inoculated, but receiv'd the Distemper in the common Way of Infection; And I suppose the Report could only arise from its being my known Opinion, that Inoculation was a sage and beneficial Practice; and from my having said among my Acquaintances, that I intended to have my Child inoculated, as soon as he should have recovered suffi-cient Strength from a Flux with which he had been long afflicted.*

The flux Franklin speaks of was probably dysentery,[3] which was a common affliction of children in those days. Presumably, he had postponed inoculating the boy until he was well, and then never had the chance.

With the help of Franklin's promotion, inoculation did catch on in Philadelphia as well as in the rest of the colonies. It was common to prepare for the practice by days of rest and special diet and then to remain isolated while the infection subsided. High society made this the occasion for a party, like the inoculation parties in Turkey, a chance to invite friends in for a week so they could all get a minor case of smallpox together. Here's an invitation to one such party, dated July 8, 1776:

> *Mr. Storer has invited Mrs. Martin to take the small-pox at his house: if Mrs. Wentworth desires to get rid of her fears in the same way we will accommodate her in the best way we can. I've several friends that I've invited, and none of them will be more welcome than Mrs. W.*

High society made this the occasion for a party, like the inoculation parties in Turkey, a chance to invite friends in for a week so they could all get a minor case of smallpox together.

---

3. **dysentery** (dis'ən•ter'ē): a disease which causes abdominal pain and diarrhea.

As you might imagine, inoculation was not a party to which everyone was invited. All this elaborate preparation, plus time off work for isolation and rest, made it a luxury. As a result, mainly the rich were inoculated, and the poor, the slaves, and especially the Native Americans continued to die of smallpox at very high rates. It was not until an epidemic in 1764 in Boston that inoculation was for the first time made available to the poor anywhere in North America.

✓ Reading Check

1. How did Cotton Mather learn about inoculation?

2. Describe inoculation as it was practiced in colonial times.

3. Why was the smallpox epidemic in Boston so severe?

4. When Benjamin Franklin's four-year-old son died of smallpox, why did many people believe Franklin was to blame? Why were they wrong?

5. Why was inoculation considered a luxury in the American colonies?

MEET THE *Writer*

Jeanette Farrell wrote *Invisible Enemies: Stories of Infectious Diseases* while in medical school. Before studying to become a doctor, Farrell worked for six months with leprosy patients in India. It was during this time that Farrell became aware of the fear and prejudice directed toward people with some diseases—even curable ones.

Farrell enjoyed the research and the writing that went into her book. "It's a rich subject," she said. "You can just scratch the surface and come up with wonderful stories." The book has been called "a riveting read" by the *School Library Journal*. It has also been chosen as a selection by the Junior Library Guild.

How could normally rational, intelligent people in a small New England village be responsible for the torture and death of innocent citizens? The following article answers that question.

The Young Witch Hunters

from *Muse*

by RHODA BLUMBERG

When nine-year-old Betty Parris and her 11-year-old cousin Abigail Williams played a fortunetelling game, they thought it would be harmless fun. Even though fortunetelling was forbidden by the church, they decided to look into the future by playing the egg-in-water game: an egg white dropped into a glass of water formed a blob that would, supposedly, reveal something about their future. When they tried it, they were frightened out of their wits. The egg white looked like a coffin! To them this meant that they would be punished for dabbling in magic. Betty and Abigail were about to make history. What they did next started a terrifying witch hunt that would eventually lead to the hanging of 19 people. It all took place in 1692, at the Puritan village of Salem, Massachusetts.

> ## You Need to Know...
> In 1692, in the village of Salem, Massachusetts, 14 women and 5 men were convicted of practicing witchcraft—at that time, a crime punishable by death. Within days of their trials, these 19 individuals were hung. Meanwhile, over 150 other people who had been accused of witchcraft trembled in fear in the local prisons. This bizarre piece of American history becomes even more shocking when one considers how it all started— with two children, an egg white, and a glass of water.

Most of us think of witches as fairy tale characters, usually old women bent with age and intent on doing evil. Sometimes we picture them as Halloween hags riding broomsticks by the light of the moon. But when the rage against witches swept through Europe in the 1500s and

1600s, most people didn't think of witches as just fly-by-night storybook characters. They thought they were real people who were able to harm or help others through their <u>supernatural</u> powers. Witches were thought to use curses and spells to make storms, sink ships, spoil crops, and cause disease. They also were said to do minor mischief, such as souring milk, putting fleas in peas, causing nightmares, and creating lovers' quarrels.

Many people were falsely accused of witchcraft. Blaming witches for bad luck was an easy way of explaining everything from business failures to floods and fires. Most frightening was that anyone could be called a witch. According to popular belief, witches spent most of their lives looking and acting like ordinary people.

Settlers took the fear of witches with them from Europe to the American colonies. But outside of New England only one person was executed as a witch. She was Rebecca Fowler, hanged in Maryland in 1685. Usually, though, colonists were more concerned about real Indians than they were about imagined witches. A few witch trials did take place, but the accused was usually pardoned or spent only a short time in prison.

Puritan New England was different. Ministers constantly gave long sermons about the devil and the tortures of hell. Their warnings about sin and Satan were enough to frighten the wits out of anyone—or to make them suspect their neighbors had made pacts[1] with the devil and were witches.

It's no accident that the Salem witch scare began in the home of the Reverend Samuel Parris, the town minister. He was Betty's father, and Abigail, her orphaned cousin, lived with them. Both girls had been constantly warned that any sin—even neglecting daily prayers—could lead to eternal damnation and hellfire.

Because of the way the girls were brought up, playing a fortunetelling game probably made them feel very guilty. After the egg-white experiment, Betty started to have strange "fits." She barked, screamed, and cried out that

> **Blaming witches for bad luck was an easy way of explaining everything from business failures to floods and fires.**

---

1. **pacts:** contracts between people or groups of people.

someone was pinching and poking her body. Then Abigail started babbling and barking. Reverend Parris didn't know what to do.

Hoping that the Almighty would cure the cursed children, Reverend Parris led his congregation[2] in special prayers and fasting. However, prayers made the girls worse. Abigail stamped her feet, covered her ears, and screamed. Betty interrupted a church service by hurling a Bible across the room. When her fit was over, she sobbed and trembled because she was sure she was damned.

The girls' baffling sickness was <u>contagious</u>. Two friends who played with them imitated their symptoms, and added a few of their own. Twelve-year-old Ann Putnam kept screaming that she had visions of murdered people, and 17-year-old Elizabeth Hubbard claimed she was being tortured by an unseen hand. The madness soon spread to at least a dozen other girls, who brought attention to themselves by acting strangely. Some of them claimed to see visions of witches torturing and killing people.

In desperation Parris turned to William Griggs, a local physician, for help. After examining Betty and Abigail, Dr. Griggs declared, "The Evil Hand is upon them." He had no medical explanation for the ailment, and suspected that it was the work of witches.

The girls' insane actions came at a bad time. Within the past two years, the villagers had endured a drought that killed crops, a brutal winter that chilled them to their bones, a smallpox epidemic that brought death to their doors, and threats by hostile Indians ever ready to attack. It seemed obvious to the community that they were being doomed by the devil.

The people of Salem were terrified, and Reverend Parris decided to ask other Massachusetts ministers for help. After meeting in Salem to observe the girls, they decided that the girls must be ordered to identify their tormentors.

contagious (kən•tā′jəs): spreading from one person to another.

Bettmann/CORBIS

▲ Girl accused of being possessed by the devil.

---

2. congregation: a group of people who meet for religious worship.

CORBIS

▲ Witchcraft trial of George Jacobs.

bizarre (bi·zär′): very surprising and incredible.

accusations (ak′yoo·zā′shənz): formal statements finding a person guilty of wrongdoing.

torment (tôr′ment′): to cause physical or emotional pain; torture.

It was the courts' job to have suspects jailed and brought to trial. Those proven guilty would be sentenced to death. But finding the witches was a problem because they were thought to look like ordinary people. How could the courts tell who was a witch and who wasn't? Betty Parris and her cousin Abigail were the answer. They became town celebrities because they were thought to have the power to detect witches. Someone suspected of being a witch was brought before the girls and ordered to touch them. If the girls felt any pain, it meant that the person was a witch. Streams of fascinated visitors came to watch the girls' bizarre behavior, and hear them describe the witches they saw in visions. They accused three Salem women of witchcraft: a slave, a beggar, and a woman who supposedly had "loose morals."

Tituba, a Caribbean Indian slave who worked in the Parris household, was first on their list. She was shocked by the children's accusations because she had taken care of them with love and devotion. Tituba denied working for the devil. However, after being questioned and beaten by her master, Reverend Parris, she confessed that she could fly through the air, and that she obeyed Satan, who appeared "sometimes as a hog and sometimes like a great dog . . . [and sometimes as] a tall man from Boston." She declared that if she failed to torment children, the devil would throw her into a fire.

Tituba made up stories hoping that by doing so, she would be left in peace. Why were her accusers, Betty and Abigail, so cruel? Part of the answer is that by blaming Tituba and others for their own behavior, the girls were rewarded with praise and attention. And they might also have been so shocked by their own actions that they thought they really *were* possessed by the devil.

Sarah Good was the next victim. She was a pipe-smoking woman who begged for food, muttered to herself, and didn't attend church services—sure proof that the devil had taken her soul. Sarah Osborne was the third on the list. Because she had been married three times and was not a regular churchgoer, it seemed easy to believe that she dealt with the devil, too! Both Sarahs said they were innocent, but they were ignored. The three prisoners were immediately placed in jail, and then sent to a Boston prison to await trial for witchcraft.

Other girls—even some adults—became accusers. They named one person after another as a witch. Men, women, and children were arrested. Four-year-old Dorcas Good—Sarah Good's daughter—was thrown into a dungeon and chained to the wall because she was said to turn herself into a dog. Seventy-year-old Rebecca Nurse, accused of killing babies who had died years before, was hanged. No one was safe. Even a clergyman, the Reverend George Burroughs, was hanged on the gallows.[3] He was called a "black minister" in league with the devil.

The horrible witch hunt lasted from March to September 1692. It stopped when one of the girls accused Lady Phips, wife of the governor of Massachusetts, and Samuel Willard, president of Harvard College. The judges decided that these important people couldn't be witches, and therefore the young accusers were not reliable.

As a result of these "mistakes," 150 people were arrested. Two died in prison. One man who refused to plead guilty or innocent was pressed to death with stones. Nineteen were hanged. They were hanged not because they admitted to being witches but because they denied it! No one who confessed to being a witch went to the gallows.

During September 1692, most people still locked up were set free—but only after they paid the costs of being kept in prison. A few had to stay behind bars because they couldn't buy their way out. Reverend Parris refused to pay for Tituba. She remained jailed until April, when he made money by selling her as a slave to another master. The two

---

3. **gallows:** a structure used for hanging people who have been condemned.

Witch or Snitch?

Several factors probably contributed to the mass hysteria that swept through Salem during the summer of 1692. Two of the most powerful factors were the villagers' superstition and their fear. At that time many people believed in witches and witchcraft. When the villagers saw several girls whom they had known from birth acting in strange and violent ways, they became very afraid. If it could happen to *those* girls, they thought, it could happen to our children—or even to *us*! Once the accusations started to fly, some people may have felt it would be safer to accuse someone else of witchcraft than to risk being accused themselves.

others imprisoned at the same time as Tituba died: Sarah Osborne in prison, and Sarah Good on the gallows.

"To take the blame and shame" for the witch hunt that took the lives of innocent people the Commonwealth of Massachusetts set aside 14 January 1697 as a day of fasting and atonement.[4] In 1706, Ann Putnam apologized in church for causing the deaths of innocent people—but blamed the devil. In 1957 Massachusetts officially cleared the names of everyone who had been accused of witchcraft.

---

4. **atonement:** making up for a sin or wrongdoing.

✓ Reading Check

1. Name two examples of the mischief witches were thought to do in the 1500s and 1600s.

2. How did Betty Parris and Abigail Williams feel after they conducted the egg-white experiment? Why?

3. When the witchcraft scare occurred, the villagers of Salem were going through a "bad time" in other ways, too. Name two difficulties the villagers were facing.

4. Why did Tituba, the Parrises' Caribbean slave, make up stories about being possessed?

5. What finally stopped the witch hunt? Briefly describe the aftermath of the witch hunt.

MEET THE *Writer*

Rhoda Blumberg (1926–   ) writes nonfiction works for young people. Her writing has earned many awards, including a Newbery Honor and the 1997 Washington Post/Children's Book Guild Award for her broad contribution to nonfiction. Blumberg loves the true stories of history and hopes to spark the same passion in her readers.

Africans sold into slavery faced not only terrible hardships and abuse but also tremendous fear and uncertainty. In the following excerpt from his autobiography, a kidnapped African prince describes his experiences aboard a slave ship.

The Slave Ship

from *The Kidnapped Prince: The Life of Olaudah Equiano*

by OLAUDAH EQUIANO, adapted by ANN CAMERON

So I traveled both by land and by water, through different countries, till, six or seven months after I had been kidnapped, I arrived at the coast.

The first thing I saw was a vast ocean, and a ship, riding at anchor, waiting for its cargo. The ocean and the ship filled me with astonishment that soon turned to fear. I was taken to the ship and carried on board!

The crew had strange complexions and long hair. Their language was very different from any I had ever heard. Some of them thumped me and tossed me around to see if I was healthy. I was sure that I had got into a world of bad spirits and that they were going to kill me.

I was terrified. I wished I was anyone but me. I would rather have been even the lowest slave in my own country. If I had owned ten thousand worlds, I would have given them all to change my lot for his.

> **You Need to Know...**
>
> Olaudah Equiano was an African youth—a prince from the kingdom of Benin—who was captured and enslaved during the mid-1700s. Eventually Equiano was able to buy his own freedom. He then settled in London, married, and became an outspoken abolitionist—someone who campaigns against slavery. When he was about forty-five years old, Equiano published *The Interesting Narrative of the Life of Olaudah Equiano*. The book was a bestseller and influenced many later writers.
>
> *The Kidnapped Prince* is an adaptation, or an updated version, of Equiano's own book. Ann Cameron wanted young people to know about Equiano's amazing life. However, she thought the original book was difficult to read. Cameron simplified and shortened Equiano's long, detailed story. "I wanted to be entirely faithful to the adventures, meanings, and spirit of Olaudah Equiano," she says. "I did not add any ideas of my own."

complexions (kəm·plek'shənz): the appearance of the skin, especially the face.

lot (lät): a person's situation in life.

When I looked round the ship I saw a furnace boiling on the deck, and many black people all chained together, every one of their faces full of sorrow. I was overpowered by horror, and fainted. When I recovered, I saw some black people around me. They were some of those who had brought me on board, and they were receiving their pay. They tried to cheer me, but in vain.

I asked them if we were not to be eaten by those white men with horrible looks, red faces, and long hair.

"No," they said.

A white man brought me a little liquor in a wineglass. I was afraid of him, and wouldn't take it out of his hand. A black took it from him and gave it to me, and I swallowed a

SIDELIGHT

In the following preface to his autobiography, Olaudah Equiano explains why he chose to write about his life.

"It is dangerous to publish the story of one's life. People who do are often accused of being vain. If unusual things have happened to them, they are rarely if ever believed. But if their story is too ordinary and too obvious, readers turn away in disgust.

Almost every experience in my life has made an impression on my mind, and influenced the way I act.

Some events in my life have happened to very few people. Others may not seem important.

But what makes any event important? I think no event is really important unless we use it to become better and wiser. To people who think about their lives, almost everything that happens, or that they read, provides a way of learning. To those who don't examine their lives, all the experience of the ages is worthless.

If I were a European, I would say I had suffered a lot. But I am an African. Compared to many of my people, I have suffered very little, and I consider myself a particular favorite of Heaven.

I didn't write my memoirs because I am vain, or to gain immortality or fame. I wrote them for my friends, who thought the world should know my story, and to serve the interests of humanity."

little of it. I never had had alcohol before. The strange sensation it gave me threw me into the greatest consternation.

Soon after this the blacks who had brought me on board went off the ship, and left me abandoned to despair. I had no chance now of returning to my country—and not even the smallest chance of getting back to shore.

The crew took me down below decks, into the ship's stinking hold.[1] With the horribleness of the stench and my crying I was so sick and low that I couldn't eat. I wanted to die.

Two white men offered me food, but I refused to eat. Then one of them held me fast by the hands and laid me across the windlass.[2] He tied my feet, while the other flogged me.

When they let me loose I wanted to jump into the sea. Even though I couldn't swim and I was afraid of the water, I still wanted to do it. I couldn't. Nets were stretched all along the sides of the ship, and they were too high for me to jump. Besides, the sailors watched us all the time if we weren't chained down to the decks.

Days later, I saw some poor Africans severely whipped for trying to jump overboard. And every hour there were Africans whipped for not eating. It often happened to me.

That first day, among the poor chained men in the hold, I found some people of Benin.

"What are they going to do to us?" I asked.

"They are taking us away to work for them," a man from Benin explained.

"And do they only live here," I asked, "in this hollow place, the ship?"

"They have a white people's country," the man explained, "but it is far away."

"How can it be," I asked, "that in our whole country nobody ever heard of them?"

"They live *very* far away," another man explained.

"Where are their women?" I asked. "Do they have any?"

consternation (kän′stər•nā′shən): alarm; dismay; bewilderment.

flogged (flägd): beaten with a stick or whip.

---

1. **hold:** the cargo compartment in the belly of a ship.
2. **windlass:** a machine used for hauling or lifting by turning a crank to wind a rope around a drum.

Early Artisans Break the Mold

At the end of the 1400s, the Benin tribe was the largest in the region of present-day Nigeria. To please the tribe's royalty, Benin craftspersons created artworks known as bronzes. First, an object was carved from wax. A kind of plaster was then poured over the wax. When the plaster had hardened, the wax was melted, poured out, and replaced by melted brass. After the brass had cooled and hardened, the mold was removed. In the late 1800s, many Benin bronzes were seized by the British during an attack on Benin City. Although today these artworks can be seen in the museums of Europe and America, some people believe the bronzes should be returned to their homeland.

Burstein Collection/CORBIS

▲ Benin bronze, sculpture head of princess.

"Yes," the first man said.

"And why don't we see them?"

"They leave them behind."

"How can the ship go?" I asked.

"We don't know exactly," they said. "They put cloth on those tall poles with the help of ropes. Then the vessel goes. Besides that, they have some spell or magic they put in the water to make the ship stop when they want it to."

I was exceedingly amazed at this account and really thought the white people were spirits from another world. I really wanted to get away from them. But I felt a little less scared, knowing they were taking us to work. If that was all they did to me, I could stand it.

Despite what the men from Benin told me, I was often afraid I should be put to death, the white people looked and acted so savage. I had never seen such brutal cruelty.

At times while we were anchored off the coast I and many others were permitted to stay on deck. One day, to my great astonishment, I saw one of the ships coming in with its sails up. As soon as the whites saw it, they gave a great shout, at which we were amazed. The vessel got larger as it got nearer, and then the anchor was let go. I and my countrymen were convinced it was done by magic.

Soon after this the other ship got her boats out, and they came on board of us.[3] The people of both ships seemed very glad to see each other. Several of the strangers shook hands with us black people, and made signs with their hands. I suppose they were trying to tell us that we were going to their country, but we did not understand them.

At last our ship got in all her cargo. The crew made the ship ready with many frightening noises. We were all put under deck, so that we could not see how they managed the vessel.

In the hold of the ship many of us died, victims of the greed of our purchasers. All of us were penned up together, crowded so close that we could hardly turn around.

---

3. Small boats were stored on the ship to use in case of shipwreck, and to carry people and supplies from ship to shore and from one ship to another.

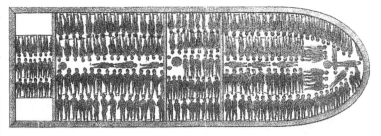

▲ Drawing showing people packed together on a lower deck of a slave ship.

🔆 **How do some of the slaves try to escape this terrible treatment?**

Our chains galled[4] us. Open tubs were used for toilets. Often children fell into them and nearly drowned. The heat caused heavy perspiration, and the air became unfit to breathe. It sickened us. It almost suffocated us. And in this thick, <u>fetid</u>, pestilential[5] air the shrieks of women and the groans of the dying vibrated hour upon hour.

fetid (fet′id): having a foul or rotten smell.

Fortunately, I was soon so near death that they kept me on the deck almost all the time, and because I was so young, I wasn't chained. Nearly every day some of my companions were brought upon deck at the point of death. I hoped that I would soon die too. Often I thought that the inhabitants of the deep were much happier than I. I envied the fish their freedom, and I wished I could have changed my lot for theirs.

In the hold of the ship many of us died, victims of the greed of our purchasers.

Everything I saw convinced me more of the cruelty of the whites. One day they netted a lot of fish. They killed and ate all they wanted. Those of us who were on the deck begged for some fish, but they threw the rest back into the sea. A few of my countrymen who were very hungry tried to take some fish when they thought no one was watching, but they were caught, and flogged severely. And

---

4. **galled:** rubbed the skin and created sores.
5. **pestilential:** likely to cause a disease; deadly.

the cruelty wasn't only toward us blacks, but also toward some of the whites themselves. Once I saw a white man flogged so unmercifully with a rope that he died; and they tossed him over the side of the ship like a dead animal.

During our trip I saw flying fish, which surprised me very much. They used to fly across the ship, and many of them fell on the deck. Also I saw the first use of the ship's quadrant.[6] I had often seen the sailors make observations with it. One of them let me look through it. The moving clouds looked to me like land that disappeared. But how could land disappear! I was sure that I was in another world, and everything around me was magic.

---

6. **quadrant:** an early instrument used to measure altitude, or height above the sea.

✓ Reading Check

1. How does Equiano feel when he first comes on board the ship? Describe some of the things he sees.

2. Why can't Equiano escape by jumping overboard?

3. What does Equiano believe the white people to be?

4. Describe the conditions below deck where the captives were kept.

5. What did the sailors do when the captives on deck begged for some fish?

MEET THE *Writer*

Ann Cameron (1943–   ) has written many books for children. Two of them, *The Stories Julian Tells* and *More Stories Julian Tells*, have been named ALA Notable Books. Another one, *The Most Beautiful Place in the World*, is the winner of the Child Study Book Award and is also a Jane Addams Children's Award Honor Book. Today Cameron lives in Guatemala, where she serves as the volunteer director of her city library.

Most Americans have heard of a field game called lacrosse. Many have even played the game or watched a match at a nearby school. What they may not know is that this popular game is older than the United States itself.

PHYSICAL EDUCATION •

HISTORY •

Lacrosse Yesterday and Today
from *Cobblestone*

by STANLEY A. FREED

The violent ball-and-racket game known in a highly modified form today as lacrosse was the favorite sport of the eastern North American tribes from Hudson Bay to the Gulf of Mexico. French settlers named it lacrosse because the racket resembled a bishop's staff. ("Lacrosse," translated literally from the French, is "the crosier," or shepherd's crook.) It is an ancient sport, predating the arrival of Christopher Columbus in the New World, and is probably the oldest team sport of American Indians in the United States and Canada.

As played by Indian men in early times, lacrosse was both a game and a festival that featured feasting, dancing, gambling, and religious activities. Broken bones, cuts, and head injuries were common. Even the occasional death on the playing field was considered normal. Violence was so

modified (mäd'ə·fīd'): changed or altered.

> ## You Need to Know...
> Lacrosse (lə·crôs') was first played by North American Indians hundreds of years ago. For these players a lacrosse game was an elaborate event that served several purposes. It was a form of entertainment, it helped to train warriors, and it was also an important way of worshiping the Creator. Although the game has changed dramatically over the years, American Indian players still approach it with reverence. They believe that the spirits of their ancestors are on the field with them, giving them strength. They also view the game as a symbol of bounty. "For all that the game provided," says one modern-day lacrosse player, "the Native Americans consider lacrosse to be a gift from the Creator."

▲ This illustration by George Catlin shows a large group of Sioux playing a game of lacrosse in the mid-1800s. ❓ **Why was this game called the "little brother of war?"**

agility (ə·jil′ə·tē): speed and grace-fulness of movement.

stamina (stam′ə·nə): staying power.

much a part of the game that the southeastern tribes called it the "little brother of war." The Iroquois used the sport as training for war, as it is extremely fast and requires great <u>agility</u> and <u>stamina</u>.

Today lacrosse is an international sport. Although it is still a fast and rough game, the violence is much reduced, and players wear protective equipment. As in all popular team sports, there are strict rules and referees to enforce them. It was not that way in early times among the American Indians. In those days, the length of the field varied, from perhaps one hundred to five hundred yards, and the number of players ranged from eight or ten up to several hundred. The rackets were of several different shapes, and balls were made of stuffed deerskin or wood. Southern tribes used two rackets, while the Iroquois and other northern tribes used only one. As in the modern game, the ball could be caught, thrown, or carried only with the racket. A point was scored when the ball crossed the opposing team's goal.

In modern lacrosse, a match lasts sixty minutes, but American Indians set no time limit. The teams agreed on a certain number of points, often twelve, as the winning score, and play continued until one team scored that many points. Games often lasted all day, although there was a break for lunch. Teams usually came from different villages; today teams often represent schools and colleges.

George Catlin, the famous nineteenth-century artist, attended a major Choctaw lacrosse game in 1834. He painted several dramatic scenes of the game and wrote an account of it. The game attracted thousands of spectators. The day before, the two teams measured the playing field, each team constructed its goal, and bets were laid. In the evening, a torchlight <u>procession</u> of men and women from the camp of each team assembled at its goal. Each party danced and sang through the night. (The players obviously had little rest.) Each side brought its medicine men, who used incantations[1] to strengthen their team and weaken the opponents.

Play was pure <u>mayhem</u>. Stomping, tackling, wrestling, tripping, and hitting were permitted. In another Choctaw game about the same time, an observer reported that three men were crippled and two died. Women did not play but were active, rushing about with hot coffee for the men and swinging quirts (riding whips) to spur on players who were not playing hard enough.

Lacrosse in North America has been dominated by Euro-Americans since about 1880. They control the rules, manufacture the equipment, and support the sport financially. But a turning point came in 1990 when the Iroquois Nationals went to Australia to compete in the World Cup Lacrosse Championship games. The team failed to win a match, but participation was a symbolic victory. It is a point of pride among American Indians that, after more than a century, they have returned to the "Indian game" at the highest international level.

---

1. **incantations:** chants.

procession (prō•sesh'ən): a group of people moving forward together in an orderly way.

mayhem (mā'hem): purposeful injury of another person; deliberate violence.

Sioux ball player Ah-No-Je-Nange, "He who stands on both sides," 19th century (litho) by George Catlin (1794-1872) (after), Private Collection/Bridgeman Art Library, London/New York

▲ The Sioux ball player in this Catlin portrait is dressed in a typical game uniform of the day. As you can guess, the headdress and breechcloth did not provide much protection.

1. From where did the sport of lacrosse get its name?

2. Name three ways in which early lacrosse and modern lacrosse are different.

3. Name two ways in which early lacrosse and modern lacrosse are the same.

4. Who painted pictures of an 1834 lacrosse game and wrote a story about it?

5. What important event in the sport of lacrosse occurred in 1990? Why was it important?

▲ Contemporary American Indian lacrosse players.

Lawrence Migdale

Cross-Curricular ACTIVITIES

■ SCIENCE/ART

A Day in the Life If you've ever had the flu, you've had a virus. The microscopic organisms—the tiny creatures—that invade your cells make you feel awful, but they're also fascinating life forms. Look in a science book or an encyclopedia to learn about viruses. What do they look like? How do they spread? What do they need to survive? Then, create a chart or a poster that shows how a virus works. Your poster should be informative *and* fun to look at. For example, you might want to give your virus human qualities and create a cartoon or a picture story about it. When you have finished, present your poster to the class.

■ HISTORY/DRAMA

Meeting the Neighbors With several class-mates, use books or Web sites to find out more about the colonists' relationships with neighboring American Indian tribes. What were the colonists' and Indians' first reactions to each other? What agree-ments did they make? What knowledge did they share? When you have finished your research, use what you know to plan a short skit about one of the colony's first meetings with neighboring Indians.

■ HISTORY/HEALTH

What's for Dinner? Alone or with a partner, plan and prepare a meal like one the colonists might have eaten. Using books or Web sites about colonial life, find out more about colonial cuisine. What were some typical colonial dishes? Write a menu describ-ing or giving the history of each dish.

■ HISTORY/ART

Sailing to Slavery Reread the description of the slave ship on pages 29–34. Then look in history books or an encyclopedia for more information about these vessels. When you have gathered enough information, create a diagram of a typical slave ship of the 1700s. You may want your diagram to be a cross-section of the ship. (A cross-section shows an object as if it had been cut in half, so the insides can be seen.) Label the different parts of the ship. Then write brief captions telling what each part of the ship was used for. If possible, add statistics or other interesting facts you find. Display your diagram in the classroom.

■ PHYSICAL EDUCATION/ SPEECH

"Play Ball!" Find out more about the history of a modern sport, such as basketball or hockey. What types of equipment were originally used? How were the original rules different from the rules of today? Create a chart that compares the historical game with the game of today. Include illustrations of equipment and uniforms. Use your chart as a visual aid and present your findings to the class.

■ ART/ HISTORY

Images of a New Nation Create a collage, mural, paper quilt, or other work of art that shows what you see as the most significant people and events (both positive and negative) involved in the formation of the American nation in its earliest days. Explain to the class the choices you made in select-ing images for your artwork.

READ ON: FOR INDEPENDENT READING

■ NONFICTION

The Double Life of Pocahontas by Jean Fritz (G. P. Putnam's Sons, 1983). Pocahontas has been a good friend to the English since they first set foot on her father's shore. Then one day they invite the teenage princess on board their ship—and kidnap her! This award-winning classic tells the *true* story behind the legend of Pocahontas, with plenty of humor and drama. Laura Ingalls Wilder Medal, Boston Globe Horn Book Award, ALA Notable Book.

The Many Lives of Benjamin Franklin by Mary Pope Osborne (Dial Books for Young Readers, 1990). You know Benjamin Franklin helped write the Declaration of Independence, but did you know that he invented a pulley system so he could lock and unlock his bedroom door without getting out of bed? That he drew the first American newspaper cartoon? That he was the best swimmer in the colonies? Read about all these accomplishments and more in this Orbis Pictus Notable book.

Science in Colonial America by Brendan January (Franklin Watts, 1999). What did the colonists know about medicine? nature? astronomy? electricity? Find out in this look at the scientists and discoveries of the colonial era.

Slumps, Grunts, and Snickerdoodles: What Colonial America Ate and Why by Lila Perl (The Seabury Press, 1975). Why did *johnnycake* mean "travelin' bread," and where was it going? What happened to the oysters in corn oysters? What did they *really* put in red flannel hash? Find the answers, and recipes for everything from succotash to shoo-fly pie, in this book about early American food from north to south.

They Came in Chains: The Story of the Slave Ships by Milton Meltzer (Benchmark Books, 2000). Not everyone left home and crossed the ocean to the Americas in search of freedom. Some came in chains, leaving freedom far behind. Pictures and primary sources help bring to life this tragic piece of America's past.

■ FICTION

The Journal of Jasper Jonathan Pierce: A Pilgrim Boy by Ann Rinaldi (Scholastic, 2000). Experience the voyage of the *Mayflower* through the eyes of Jasper, a fourteen-year-old orphan and indentured servant. Rather read about a *girl* Pilgrim? Try ***A Journey to the New World: The Diary of Remember Patience Whipple*** by Kathryn Lasky (Scholastic, 1996).

Roanoke: A Novel of the Lost Colony by Sonia Levitin (Atheneum, 1973). In 1587, Governor John White set sail for England to pick up supplies for his new colony. When he returned three years later the colonists had disappeared. What happened to them? No one ever found out. This novel, told in the voice of a teenage colonist, shows what might have been.

Tituba of Salem Village by Ann Petry (Thomas Y. Crowell Company, 1964). *She's a witch!* In Salem in 1692, all it took was an accusation to condemn an innocent woman—especially if she was a dark-skinned and gifted slave from Barbados. Petry's classic novel recreates the fear and suspicion that led to the notorious Salem witch trials and forever changed the life of a woman named Tituba.

CHAPTER 2

With Liberty and Justice for All
The New Nation   1776–1804

The Great Escape

In the United States' first naval battle in 1812, the USS *Constitution* won the nickname "Old Ironsides" when British cannonballs bounced harmlessly off her wooden hull. However, the ship and its crew almost didn't make it to that legendary battle. A month earlier, they'd met a squadron of British ships that outgunned the *Constitution* five to one, but both sailing ships were left motionless when the wind disappeared.

Then began what may have been the slowest chase in U.S. history. The crew of the *Constitution* struggled to stay ahead of the British. They rowed. They towed. Finally, on the third day, they tried "kedging"—ferrying an anchor out ahead, dropping it, and using it to draw the ship forward, then hauling it up and starting again. Bit by bit, the *Constitution* edged away until a breeze caught her sails and she escaped.

In 1905, schoolchildren helped save Old Ironsides by raising $154,000 in pennies. The USS *Constitution*, with new sails and new copper plating, can be seen today in Boston harbor.

Stars and Stripes (Not Quite) Forever

Although the Continental Congress approved a stars-and-stripes flag design in 1777, the army was not supplied with new flags until six years later. Revolutionary soldiers fought the war under flags embellished with eagles, pine trees, rattlesnakes, gold stars, or yellow stripes—even, sometimes, elements of the British flag. No wonder the British retreated in confusion!

CORBIS

▲ Photograph of the USS *Constitution* taken in 1905.

DONT TREAD ON ME

The Granger Collection, New York

▲ An early flag used by Revolutionary soldiers.

Sometimes new words come from simple descriptions. During the Revolutionary War, the British soldiers were called *redcoats* (red′kōts) because the invading soldiers of the British army wore bright red coats. The word made its first appearance in England in 1520 in the lyrics of *Song Lady Bess*. Words can also be derived from place names. *Hessian* (hesh′ən) troops were paid to fight alongside the British soldiers in the Revolutionary War. These men were from an area of Germany called Hesse-Kassel.

Memorable Quote

"I think this is the most extraordinary collection of talent, of human knowledge, that has ever been gathered together at the White House—with the possible exception of when Thomas Jefferson dined here alone."

—President John F. Kennedy, at a dinner for a group of Nobel Prize winners.

Teenage Celebrity

Any fourteen-year-old girl would be excited to see her poem printed in a newspaper, but for Phillis Wheatley the moment was truly historic. Kidnapped when she was a little girl from her home in West Africa, she had lost everything—even her name. *Phillis* was the name of the slave ship that brought her to America, and *Wheatley* was the name of the family that bought her at a Boston slave auction. The Wheatleys taught Phillis to speak English and provided her with an excellent education. She grew up to be the first published African American writer and an international celebrity. One of Wheatley's biggest fans was General George Washington.

Detail from The Pierpont Morgan Library/Art Resource, NY

The *Other* Constitution

Was the U.S. Constitution based on the Iroquois nations' Great Law of Peace? Some historians see parallels between the two constitutions—both guarantee political and religious freedom, checks and balances, and a federal union of separate states. However, look at what the U.S. Constitution could have borrowed from the Iroquois—and didn't.

- Under the Great Law, women had the power to elect male leaders. The United States didn't catch up until 1920, when the Nineteenth Amendment gave women the right to vote.
- Under the U.S. Constitution, slavery was legal until 1865. The Iroquois never allowed slavery.
- Instead of "majority rules," the Iroquois council made decisions by unanimous consent—everyone had to agree.
- Unlike the U.S. government, the Iroquois council met only when necessary. There were no full-time politicians!

The list of Benjamin Franklin's inventions is long. Find out why the invention of science itself should top the list.

from Inventor and Scientist

from *Benjamin Franklin: The New American*

by MILTON MELTZER

The Granger Collection, New York

To be forty-two in Ben Franklin's time was to be well beyond middle age. Life was much shorter then. He never guessed he would live double those years. Since retirement was not forced upon him, he felt no depression for cutting himself off from his work. He moved his family from Market Street to a more spacious rented house. It was on the northwest corner of Race and Second, a quieter part of town, and nearer to the river. Although he did not live luxuriously, he acquired slaves to help with the household chores and errands.

Now he was ready to plunge headlong into his life as a scientist. Science as a way of exploring and explaining the world was a path he had entered long ago. Recall how his <u>inventiveness</u> was revealed in boyhood when he devised new ways to speed himself through water. At twenty, sailing back from England, he had crammed his notebook with observations of wind and weather and ocean currents and animal life. His scientific curiosity could be aroused by what others brushed off as trivial. Once he found that an open pot

You Need to Know...

When most people hear Benjamin Franklin's name, they think of a short, stocky fellow who "discovered" electricity by flying a kite in a thunderstorm. Actually, Ben Franklin's contributions to science soar far beyond this quaint image. At what we would now consider an early age, Franklin retired from his successful career as a printer to devote himself to his interests in science and practical inventions. It could even be said that among Franklin's many inventions was the invention of science itself. He developed a method of experimentation that many scientists depend upon today. He applied what he learned to inventions that were useful to everyone. He also organized the scientists of his time into a professional group so that knowledge could be more easily shared. Read on to learn more about this busy and creative period in Franklin's long life.

inventiveness (in·ven′tiv·nis): the quality of being able to make something that did not exist before.

▲ Benjamin Franklin performs his famous experiment with the kite.
❓ What was Franklin trying to prove?

of molasses in Debby's pantry was crawling with ants. He removed all of them but one, then tied the pot to a string suspended from the ceiling, led the string across the ceiling and down the wall, and sat by to observe. The one ant gorged itself in the pot, then clambered along the string and down the wall, and disappeared. About thirty minutes later, the pot was once again thick with ants that had crossed over to it on the string. How, Ben asked, had the first ant communicated to the others the feast awaiting them in the pot?

Again and again he saw in everyday aspects of nature questions that demanded answers. Where others before him had noticed nothing interesting or significant, his mind saw something wonderful. He was born to be a "natural philosopher," the term used then for scientists.

He was born to be a "natural philosopher," the term used then for scientists.

It was Sir Francis Bacon who began the turn toward modern science. In 1620—the same year the Puritan dissenters fled England to find refuge in New England—he published the first statement of a new attitude. It would change the way people lived in the world and the way they thought about it. Bacon believed the whole world was open for genius to explore. The object of knowledge was to increase man's power over nature and to make life better. Only by a true understanding of the physical world could we master our fate.

genius (jēn′yəs): the intellectual and creative powers of human beings.

Later, in 1662, Bacon's followers founded the Royal Society in London "to promote the welfare of the arts and sciences." The great Isaac Newton, one of the Society's original members, had shown that the universe moved by its own laws and that mathematics could chart those movements of the planets. Only a few Americans, Cotton Mather among them, were familiar with science. Mather, when Franklin was fifteen, had published America's first popular book on science. He wanted people to break from stale myths and go out and dig for the truth in the real world of nature. It was an appeal young Ben responded to.

Scientific research back then was vastly different from what it is now. In Ben's time it was an <u>amateur</u>'s game. No government, no corporation, no university, no foundation was on hand to pour funds into research. Scientists—the few there were—did not combine their specialized knowledge to work together in large laboratories under ideal conditions. Nor was there any kind of training for them in research. Like Ben, they taught themselves and worked alone, usually at home, funding their own expenses. It was a kind of game, but with an intellectual edge that gave it great excitement, especially when you could claim a discovery.

Several months after he retired, Ben wrote to his friend Cadwallader Colden that he was happy "to make experiments, and converse at large with such ingenious and worthy men as are pleased to honor me with their friendship on such points as may produce something for the common benefit of mankind, uninterrupted by the little cares and fatigues of business."

Years earlier Ben had suggested that people interested in science ought to form an organization "to promote useful knowledge" in the colonies. His notion was to expand the Junto on a continental scale. He had already corresponded with scientists throughout the colonies, as well as with some in England and Europe. He knew how rapidly interest in science was growing and saw that pooling information and ideas would greatly benefit everyone. He wrote out his proposal in 1743 and printed and circulated it.

Inquiring Minds Want to Know

"I love company, chat, a laugh, a glass, and even a song," Ben Franklin once said. Indeed, his love of spirited company led the young Franklin to form a club known as the Junto, which means "group." Among the members were men from all walks of life— printers, silversmiths, mathematicians, and even shoemakers. However, they all had one thing in common: their love of knowledge. At each meeting one member would read an essay he had written on a topic such as politics, travel, history, or science. After that the essay would be discussed and debated. Soon the group had become so popular that several similar groups formed across the city of Philadelphia.

amateur (am'ə•chər): a person who participates in an activity for enjoyment rather than money.

Out of it came the American Philosophical Society. It is the oldest American learned[1] society, and the first to be devoted to science. Ben's desire was to make it a center for exchanging information on all aspects of the natural world and on all experiments that "tend to increase the power of man over matter, and multiply the conveniences or pleasures of life." Franklin became its first president, to be followed later by Thomas Jefferson and other distinguished Americans. Today, as at its founding, it concerns itself with many diverse fields of knowledge—medicine, physics,[2] anthropology,[3] history, literature—and its publications and projects are important to the international world of science.

A look through the pages of Ben's *Gazette* shows how early it began to reflect the range of his scientific curiosity. Esmond Wright has traced his stories of "the weather and waterspouts; why salt dissolves in water; why the sea is sometimes luminous; cures for kidney stones and cancer; mortality rates in Philadelphia; the cause of earthquakes; 'on making rivers navigable'; how many people could stand in an area of 100 square yards."

---

1. **learned** (lur'nid): having learning in a special area of expertise.
2. **physics:** science that studies the interaction of matter and energy, including electricity, heat, and mechanics.
3. **anthropology:** study of humans.

Electrical Leaps and Bounds

Franklin used a popular device known as a Leyden Jar to determine how electricity was conducted. The jar was made of glass, and it had a cork stopper. Sometimes the jar had a metal coating. Water was placed in the jar, and a metal rod hung from the cork down into the water. When the water was charged and someone touched the jar, a strong shock was felt. This experiment was often used to entertain people—it once caused 180 French guardsmen, holding hands, to leap into the air at the same time. However, Franklin wanted to know *how* it worked. After many experiments he discovered that the glass itself—the insulator—held the electricity. This discovery laid the groundwork for later developments in radio, television, and telephone technologies.

The Granger Collection, New York

Ben's <u>voracious</u> appetite for learning made him ask the why and how of everything he came across. When he was still tied down by his business, he did his best to encourage others in the pursuit of science. For instance, he raised a fund to enable John Bartram, a botanist, to continue his research on the condition that he report his findings to contributors to the fund.

In Franklin's mind there was nothing that could not be improved. Take his invention of the Franklin stove. One of the questions he had posed for the Junto was, "How may smoky chimneys be cured?" How strange it was, he thought, that while chimneys have been so long in use, no workman would pretend he could make one that would carry off all the smoke. Then, too, fireplaces were often too hot to sit near, and when you did, while the heat toasted your front, the cold air nipped your back and legs. It was next to impossible to warm a room with such a fireplace. So in 1739 or 1740 he invented a stove that fitted into the fireplace and radiated the heat outward. It warmed rooms better, and at the same time saved fuel. The important feature was the flue, which doubled back and formed a sort of radiator around which warm air circulated. It cured most smoky chimneys, thus protecting both the eyes and the furniture. He turned over his model to a friend with an iron furnace, who cast the plates for the stoves. They were soon in great demand as people learned about them through a pamphlet Ben wrote and printed.

A profitable invention—but not for him. As with all his inventions, he refused to patent his stove, on the principle "that as we enjoy great advantages from the inventions of others, we should be glad of an opportunity to serve others by any invention of ours, and this we should do freely and generously."

He was as much interested in ventilating rooms as in warming them. He believed it healthier to keep windows open and let in fresh air, a practice that annoyed many of his friends. To keep rooms warmer in cold weather, he developed a damper, a metal plate that fits horizontally

voracious (vô•rā'shəs): having an enormous appetite for something.

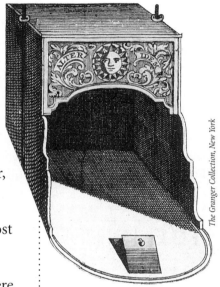

The Granger Collection, New York

▲ The Franklin stove. **❓ Why did Franklin refuse to apply for a patent for this invention?**

into the base of the chimney passage and can completely close it off, or when opened a small distance, creates a slight draft, allowing smoke to go up the chimney while keeping most of the warm air in the room.

To improve the lighting of rooms, he devised a new candle made from whale oil. It gave a clearer and whiter light, could be held in the hand without softening, and its drippings did not make grease spots. His candles lasted much longer and needed little or no snuffing. He also developed a four-sided lamp to light the city streets. The lamps stayed clean much longer and thus gave more light.

When Franklin's scientific fame comes up, most people think of the spectacular kite experiment. That was not his greatest contribution, and it was made well after his international reputation was established. Most important was his experimental approach: it was this that made all his contributions possible. His experiments in so many different fields were completely original and crucial. The way he went about his research displayed his analytic powers and his objectivity. He never rested with merely amplifying what someone else had done.

analytic (an'ə·lit'ik): able to study carefully to determine what something is or how it works.

His work on electricity is the best example. Before he began to think about it, electricity was a mass of uncoordinated observations and confusing theories worded in obscure and puzzling language. Franklin's mind was able to unify what was already known, then to add his own original findings so that he came out with a new and simple theory that would stand the test of time. The very vocabulary of modern electricity originated with him: as he went along he had to invent words like *condenser, conductor, charge, discharge, armature, battery, electrician, electric shock, positive* and *negative* electricity, and concepts of *plus* and *minus* charges.

Few of his contemporaries were equipped to perceive how different and advanced his approach was. Those who did understand his work thought it extraordinary. By the time Ben went abroad on his first diplomatic mission (1757), scientists in England and Europe greeted him as the Newton of electricity.

✓ Reading Check

1. What did Benjamin Franklin do after he retired at the age of forty-two?

2. How was scientific research during Ben Franklin's time different than it is today?

3. What organization for scientists did Ben Franklin help start?

4. Why did Ben Franklin refuse to patent his inventions?

5. According to the author, what was Ben Franklin's most important contribution to science?

MEET THE *Writer*

Historian and writer of documentary films **Milton Meltzer** (1915–   ) has authored dozens of books and films for both children and adults. His works often address complex topics such as slavery, crime, and religion. Meltzer believes that everyone has a role to play in history. "History is what we *make* happen. Each of us. All of us." Meltzer's books have earned many awards, including Best Children's Books of the Year from the Library of Congress and Outstanding Children's Books of the Year from *The New York Times*.

The men weren't the only ones who fought the British. Find out about the role colonial women played in securing their new nation's independence.

The Women of the American Revolution

from *Who Were the Founding Fathers? Two Hundred Years of Reinventing American History*

by STEVEN H. JAFFE

It would take over seventy years of struggle by feminists[1] for American women to win the right to vote through an amendment[2] to the Constitution in 1920. During those years, feminists tried to convince others that women had proven their equality throughout American history. The Revolution provided them with some of their most effective examples.

One piece of evidence they could use was a book, first published in 1848, by a writer named Elizabeth Ellet. Her work was entitled *The Women of the American Revolution*. As a little girl in upstate New York, Ellet had first become interested in history when she heard tales about her grandfather, who

You Need to Know...

Colonial women led demanding, industrious lives. Most worked in the home. Some ran farms and businesses, such as bakeries, clothing stores, and grocery stores. Yet, in spite of their contribution to society, colonial laws did not grant women any economic power of their own. A married woman could not hold a job outside the home unless she first gained her husband's permission. Whatever money she earned belonged legally to her husband. Some women found this system fundamentally unfair. In the mid-1700s, a group of women wrote to a New York newspaper that "We are House keepers, Pay our taxes, carry on Trade, . . . and as we . . . contribute to the Support of Government, we ought to be Intitled to some of the Sweets of it." At the time of the Revolution, the laws of the land continued to deny women legal rights and to keep them from playing active roles in the government. However, as you will see in this selection, many women found ways to participate—ways to make their power felt and their voices heard.

---

1. **feminists:** people who believe that women should have the same political and economic rights as men.
2. **amendment:** a change.

had fought as a captain in the Revolutionary War. Like William C. Nell, Ellet wanted to <u>revive</u> memories of a forgotten group of revolutionaries.

Ellet herself was not a feminist; her goal was not to win political or civil rights[3] for women. But she felt the need to do justice to those women who had played a part in the revolutionary struggle. The standard history books said little or nothing about the contribution of women to the cause of independence. Ellet was determined to tell their stories. She tracked down old diaries and letters hidden away in family scrapbooks, and she interviewed elderly people who still remembered the events of the Revolution. Ellet recovered the stories of so many female patriots that the first edition of her book had to be published in two volumes. *The Women of the American Revolution* went through several editions,[4] and was still being published in the twentieth century.

Ellet discovered that women had helped the revolutionary movement in a surprising variety of ways. Throughout the thirteen colonies, housewives boycotted British tea and other imports. Rather than buy English textiles, they wove their own cloth and made their own clothing. Once the war started, women also played <u>crucial</u> roles. They organized drives in their villages and towns to raise money for the Continental Army. Because British officers rarely took the political and military interests of women seriously, females made excellent spies and messengers behind enemy lines. While their men were off fighting the redcoats,[5] wives and daughters ran family farms and businesses. By doing so, they helped to keep the American economy going and fed the troops.

All ranks of women contributed, and a select few even influenced the men who ran the new nation. Mercy Warren, for example, was the sister of lawyer James Otis and the wife of James Warren, both

---

3. **civil rights:** a citizen's claims to power and privilege which are lawful and just.
4. **editions:** forms in which a book is published.
5. **redcoats:** British soldiers.

revive (ri•vīv′): to remember; to bring to mind.

Ellet discovered that women had helped the revolutionary movement in a surprising variety of ways.

---

crucial (krōō′sh•əl): extremely important.

Courtesy of the Free Library Of Philadelphia

▲ Woman spinning thread for weaving. ❓ **What other tasks did women perform that helped the revolutionary movement?**

▲ Portrait of Mercy Warren.

prominent Boston patriots. In a society that frowned on the idea of higher education for women, Warren managed to attain an impressive knowledge of history, literature, and politics by teaching herself. Because of her husband's involvement in the revolutionary cause, Warren knew Samuel Adams, John Adams, Thomas Jefferson, and other Founding Fathers, all of whom recognized her brilliance. As Ellet put it, "these men asked her opinion in political matters, and acknowledged the excellence of her judgment." After the war, Warren wrote a history of the Revolution, making her the first serious female historian in America.

Others became revolutionaries in more active ways. In order to be close to their husbands and fathers, the families of many revolutionary soldiers followed the troops in their movements through the thirteen states. The wives of soldiers performed traditional duties by cooking and cleaning for their men. But in the heat of battle, some proved their courage and skill as soldiers. When her husband, an artilleryman,[6] was killed during a British attack on Fort Washington in New York, Margaret Cochran took his place at the cannon and was wounded herself. After the war, Congress awarded her a military pension in thanks for her service. Mary McCauley, who became known as "Molly Pitcher" for similar coolness under fire at the Battle of Monmouth, also received a government reward in later years.

But the most dramatic and unusual case of wartime bravery was that of Deborah Sampson. Sampson's story had become legendary by the 1840s, but Ellet attempted to sort out the facts of her life. Sampson was born in 1760 in Massachusetts, where her father, who had trouble making a living out of his small farm and who drank too much, abandoned his family and disappeared. As a child, Deborah was "bound out"[7] as a servant to another family. She possessed a "mind naturally superior," and like Mercy Warren, she insisted on getting as much education as she could. At age eighteen, she enrolled herself as a pupil in

---

6. artilleryman: soldier who operates a heavy mounted gun.
7. bound out: legally required to work for another person for a specific length of time.

Abigail Adams was one of the most educated women of her time. She was married to John Adams, who would serve as President of the United States from 1797 to 1801. The frequent letters she wrote to her husband while he was away reveal that Abigail was a strong supporter of the rights of women and African Americans. In the following excerpt from a letter she wrote to her husband while he was a delegate to the Second Continental Congress, Abigail urges John to "remember the ladies" when he and the other delegates are drafting the rules of the new country.

Culver Pictures, Inc.

"I long to hear that you have declared an independancy—and, by the way, in the new Code of Laws which I suppose it will be necessary for you to make, I desire you would remember the ladies, and be more generous and favorable to them than your ancestors. Do not put such unlimited power into the hands of the husbands. Remember all men would be tyrants if they could. If particuliar care and attention is not paid to the ladies, we are determined to foment a rebellion, and will not hold ourselves bound by any laws in which we have no voice, or representation."

the local schoolhouse, and excelled as a student. The growing struggle over colonial rights aroused Sampson's patriotism. She "bitterly regretted . . . that she had not the privilege of a man, of shedding her blood for her country."

But in 1782 she found a way around this problem. Leaving her job as a village schoolteacher, she went into the woods carrying a bundle of men's clothing. She reemerged with a new identity. As "Robert Shirtliffe," she enlisted in the Fourth Massachusetts Regiment of the American army. Sampson was able to conceal her identity through an entire year of wartime service. During that time, "Shirtliffe" took part in several engagements[8] with the enemy, and was wounded during a skirmish with British troops near Tarrytown, New York. It was only after "he" was hospitalized for fever that a doctor discovered the soldier's secret. Following the discovery, General Henry Knox gave Sampson an honorable discharge from the army in October 1783.

skirmish (skur′mish): a minor fight or conflict.

---

8. **engagements:** battles.

exploits (eks'ploits'): acts of bravery

The Granger Collection, New York

▲ Deborah Sampson delivers a letter praising her military service to George Washington.

stereotypes (ster'ē·ə·tīps'): oversimplified ideas or beliefs about a group of people

After the war, Sampson returned to the Massachusetts countryside, married a farmer named Benjamin Gannett, and raised three children. But the stories of her wartime exploits circulated widely. In 1802 a writer named Herman Mann persuaded Sampson to tour New England and New York, delivering an "Address" written by Mann before audiences of paying theatergoers. Adults paid twenty-five cents, children half price to hear "Mrs. Gannet, the celebrated American Heroine." Many came expecting to see a hoax.[9] Sampson noted in her diary that she overheard some in the audience who "swore that I was a lad of not more than eighteen years of age." Dressed in full military uniform, Sampson took the stage and admitted that she had been "unnatural, unwise and indelicate"[10] in leaving the "paths of female delicacy" to play a man's part in the Revolution. But her patriotism and anger at redcoat cruelty, she claimed, got the better of her judgment. Recalling her skirmish, Sampson told her audience, "I was there! The recollection makes me shudder!—A dislocated limb draws fresh anguish from my heart!" After finishing a performance, Sampson noted that the audience had given her its "serious attention and peculiar[11] respect, especially the ladies."

Whether or not Sampson really agreed with the apology for her "unfeminine" behavior that Herman Mann wrote for her, the tour was a success. Sampson made money from it, and the address stirred up publicity that helped her to win a government pension in 1805 for her wartime service; another veteran of the Revolution, Paul Revere, helped her to get the money by writing to Congress.

Sampson actually broke two stereotypes of female behavior. Not only had she proved her ability as a soldier, but she was one of the first American women to become a public lecturer. Sampson's brief military career put her

---

9. hoax: a trick; a deception.
10. indelicate: offensive or improper.
11. peculiar: special; unique.

way ahead of her time. But her accomplishments, like those of Mercy Warren, also made assumptions[12] of female inferiority seem unjust and inaccurate.

Didn't Deborah Sampson's success as a soldier suggest that women possessed abilities that were wasted if they were confined to the kitchen and nursery? Forced to confront the life story of Mercy Warren, how could American men argue that women were intellectually inferior, and deny them equal access to higher education? Words written by a Bostonian named Hannah Winthrop in the revolutionary 1770s and published by Elizabeth Ellet in 1848 could only boost the morale of feminists as they fought to win the vote for American women: "Be it known unto Britain, even American daughters are politicians and patriots, and will aid the good work with their female efforts."

---

12. **assumptions:** beliefs which are taken for granted.

✓ Reading Check

1. How did Elizabeth Ellet find stories to include in her book?

2. Name two ways in which women contributed to the Revolution.

3. How did Deborah Sampson participate in the Revolution?

4. Describe what Sampson did during the year 1802.

5. How did Sampson's actions help the cause of women's rights?

MEET THE *Writer*

Stephen Jaffe earned his Ph.D. in American history from Harvard University. Today, he is senior historian at the South Street Seaport Museum in New York City. He lives in Brooklyn with his wife and son.

A group of archaeologists gain a rare glimpse into the lives of African Americans during the Revolutionary era, revealing one of the most amazing archaeological discoveries of our time.

from Ground Truth

from *Breaking Ground, Breaking Silence: The Story of New York's African Burial Ground*

by JOYCE HANSEN and GARY McGOWAN

phase (fāz): stage.

critical (krit′i·kəl): important.

organic (ôr·gan′ik): of or related to a living thing.

The following morning, the archaeologists returned to the burial for the next phase of their work. They had to clean away the moist alluvial[1] clay that was practically glued to the skeleton, now called Burial #6. Using dental picks, aspirators,[2] and small brushes, most of the dirt was removed from the surface of the bone.

Absorbing the soil's moisture, the bones had turned soft and spongy. If not cleaned and allowed to properly dry, they would crumble like pieces of rotted wood.

When cleaning skeletal remains, the thorax or chest cavity is a critical area, for often it contains vital organic material. Soils taken from around the thorax can be analyzed to help find out which diseases were present in the body when the person died, or what the person ate as a last meal.

Soils taken from the chest cavity usually yield seeds

You Need to Know...

In late September, 1991, a group of archaeologists dug their way deep below the city streets of New York—straight into the past. The scientists were on a routine assignment, analyzing a site on which a skyscraper would be built. They knew that the site had once been a burial ground for people of African descent, but they didn't expect to find much more than a few scraps of wood or fragments of bones. Then, in the cool, damp earth sixteen feet below the surface—far away from the noise and congestion of Manhattan—the archaeologists uncovered an old, twisted nail. The nail, in turn, led to a coffin lid, which, when carefully removed, revealed a complete human skeleton.

---

1. alluvial: made up of alluvium, or dirt and sand deposited by running water.
2. aspirators: tools that suction liquid out of a space.

and food <u>particles</u>. These materials are <u>extracted</u> by sifting the soils through screens <u>immersed</u> in water. This process is called floatation.

As the earth was cleared away from this important middle section of the burial's body, nine small objects were found in a line down the chest. Two larger objects were found in the tailbone area. Not only had the archaeologists discovered a well-preserved skeleton, but there were possible artifacts[3] as well.

That afternoon, as the skeleton dried, a team of osteologists, or bone scientists, arrived at the site. They began to analyze the skeleton in order to determine the age, sex, and race of the individual in Burial #6.

The osteologists concluded that Burial #6 was either an African or African-American man, thirty to forty years old and five feet eleven inches tall. The archaeological team could see that the objects lying in a line down his torso[4] were buttons. The two large objects near his tailbone area were buttons as well, suggesting that he may have been wearing a long coat.

Thin metal pins in and around his head area indicate that he had been wrapped in a winding-sheet, or shroud—a cloth substituted for clothing when burying the dead; however, as the buttons show, he may have been wearing clothing. (The archaeologists did not expect to recover cloth or material in the wet and marshy environment of the burial ground, where fabrics such as cotton, linen, and wool would rapidly decompose.[5])

An iron pellet, most likely an eighteenth-century bullet, was also found in the grave. The archaeological crew removed the buttons and other artifacts and took them to the Foley Square Laboratory, not far from the excavation

particles (pärt′i•kəlz): very small pieces.

extracted (ek•strakt′id): taken out.

immersed (i•mʉrst′): dipped completely into.

AP/Wide World Photos

▲ Excavation site in lower Manhattan. ❷ **What were archaeologists expecting to find?**

---

3. **artifacts:** objects made by humans that tell something about the past.
4. **torso:** trunk of a body.
5. **decompose:** break down.

Early Weapons of War

The pellet found in the burial was probably shot from a musket or a rifle, two important weapons of the Revolutionary War. A rifle was more accurate than a musket, but it took longer to reload. This made the musket preferable in battle. The musket shot large lead balls in rapid succession. Additionally, a bayonet, or blade, could be fastened onto the musket's front end. Because the musket was not very accurate at great distances, soldiers would usually advance as far as possible before shooting. Afterwards, the soldiers still standing would engage in hand-to-hand combat. In the early years of the war the Americans had few bayonets, though, which gave the British an advantage.

---

eroded (ē·rōd′id): worn away.

verify (ver′ə·fī′): to show the truth of.

deceased (dē·sēst′): dead.

site. The skeletal remains would be taken to another laboratory for further study.

Surrounded by microscopes, slides, file cabinets, and books, the archaeological team began the exciting work of investigating the artifacts from Burial #6. There could be a wealth of cultural information in the eroded, damaged items.

These artifacts might provide what archaeologists call "ground truth." When a people and their culture have been written about and distorted by those who oppress them, artifacts found in burials are often the only way for archaeologists to gain a true idea of the people's culture and to either verify or dispute what had already been written about them. In a sense, it is as though people who have been written out of history have found a way to tell us about themselves through the objects buried with them.

In the days that followed, the team would try to find out what the artifacts were made of, where and when they were manufactured, and, most importantly, what the objects would tell us about the deceased.

The team followed the usual steps for processing artifacts. The buttons and other articles had to be:

a. cleaned.

b. labeled, showing where the buttons, nails, etc., had been located in the burial site—their provenance. Location of an artifact can provide vital information about culture and lifestyle. For example, because the buttons in Burial #6 were found in a line down the deceased's chest, the archaeologists could safely assume that he had been wearing clothing when he was buried. When further analysis of the artifacts are carried out in the laboratory, it is important that the researchers know exactly where the objects were found.

c. stabilized[6] and conserved in order to stop deterioration (metals are soaked in baths of water and treated with acrylic resin and other chemical agents).

d. reconstructed—fragments are pieced together.

---

6. **stabilized:** to have been put in conditions that will not allow further change.

e. analyzed—using either chemical or microscopic analysis the archaeologist will draw conclusions based on the information he or she has gathered (hypothesis[7]). This data or information will be compared with historical documents and texts.

The archaeologists realized that of all of the artifacts discovered in Burial #6, the buttons would probably provide important cultural information. Using a dental pick, they cleaned the buttons under a microscope so that they did not inadvertently erase or smudge patterns and designs within the fragile object.

After the buttons were cleaned, the scientists realized that three of them were gilded (covered with gold). The other buttons were made out of pewter. Damaged by years of erosion, they looked small, hard, and leaflike. However, the anchor and rope insignia of the British Navy was clearly visible.

A large brass button, approximately the size of a fifty-cent piece, was so badly deteriorated that even after cleaning, they could not tell whether there was any decoration on the button. Patterns and designs are like messages providing possible information about when and where an artifact was made.

The button was placed under the probing eye of a microscope, where raking light (shining light on an object sideways) revealed that it, too, had an anchor and rope insignia. At times, the metal artifacts were so badly corroded that X-ray machines had to be used in order to determine what was disguised by the corrosion.

After the buttons were labeled and stabilized, the team needed to find out when similar buttons were used. Studying photographs and illustrations of colonial-style buttons helped the archaeologists determine that the buttons were the kind worn by British sailors during the American Revolution. A picture was emerging; the team began to form a hypothesis.

AP/Wide World Photos

▲ Visitors read about the burial ground. The New York City Council voted to declare the site a historic district in 1993.

corroded (kə•rōd′id): rusted; worn away.

---

7. **hypothesis:** a theory that is as yet unproved.

Perhaps the deceased had been a sailor buried in uniform and wrapped in a shroud,[8] according to military custom. He might have been one of the thousands of African Americans enlisted in the British Navy. This was an amazing discovery. A black man in British military uniform, dating back to the American Revolution, buried in the manner accorded a soldier. Yet, the body, when found, was facing east, a burial custom of many people of African descent in the eighteenth and nineteenth centuries.

Burial #6 was just the beginning. There would be more discoveries as the ground opened up like an ancient history book. Over the next ten months, the team would repeat many times the same careful process of excavation that they had used to exhume Burial #6.

---

8. shroud: material in which a corpse is wrapped for burial.

✓ Reading Check

1. Besides buttons, what objects were found near the burial?

2. What does "ground truth" mean to archaeologists?

3. Briefly list the five steps for processing artifacts.

4. What pattern could be clearly seen on some of the buttons?

5. What hypothesis did the archaeologists form about their discovery?

MEET THE *Writers*

Joyce Hansen used to teach school in New York City. Now a full-time writer, Hansen is a two-time winner of the Coretta Scott King Honor Award. She lives in Columbia, South Carolina, with her husband.
Gary McGowan is the head conservator—or protector of specimens—of the burial ground team. He lives in New Jersey with his wife.

The idea that all men are created equal was radical when the Declaration of Independence was first written. How has this dream of access for everyone to "certain unalienable rights" stood up to the passing years?

Your Rights and Mine

from *Give Me Liberty! The Story of the Declaration of Independence*

by RUSSELL FREEDMAN

Although many changes were made to it by Congress, the Declaration of Independence remained essentially Thomas Jefferson's creation. Jefferson began by stating the purpose of the document: to explain why the colonies had voted to free themselves from British rule. "All men are created equal," Jefferson wrote. They have certain God-given rights, including the rights to "Life, Liberty and the pursuit of Happiness." And governments are created to secure those rights.

Jefferson then charged that King George III had repeatedly violated the colonists' rights, his purpose being "the establishment of an absolute Tyranny[1] over these States." He gave a long list of examples, including "imposing Taxes on us

You Need to Know...

When the Second Continental Congress met in May of 1775, most colonists did not want to declare the colonies' independence from British rule. The delegates that had gathered together still held some hope that the British king would revoke the Intolerable Acts, but the Revolutionary War had already begun, and by June the delegates' hopes were fading. So when Richard Henry Lee of Virginia insisted that "these United Colonies are, and of right ought to be, free and independent States," the others decided that he was right—it was time to make a formal move. Delegate Thomas Jefferson, also of Virginia, was given the task of drafting a declaration of independence. Two weeks later, Jefferson presented the Congress with his draft. After making a few revisions—such as taking out a passage condemning the slavery trade—the Congress adopted the Declaration on July 4, 1776. This historic event continues to shape the American dream.

---

1. **tyranny:** the government of an oppressive ruler.

without our Consent," "depriving us in many cases, of the benefits of Trial by Jury," "suspending our own Legislatures," and "waging War against us."

indictment (in·dīt′mənt): accusation.

Today, Jefferson's indictment of King George as a tyrant[2] may seem like ancient history. But the preamble to the Declaration, the opening statement, is recognized as a timeless affirmation of human rights and representative government.

affirmation (af′ər·mā′shən): a statement or declaration that something is true or right.

Governments must have "the consent of the governed," Jefferson wrote. Whenever any government fails to protect the rights of its citizens, the citizens have the right to change it or abolish it and to create a new government. That powerful idea has inspired popular resistance to tyranny in countries all over the world.

abolish (ə·bäl′ish): to do away with.

The preamble to the Declaration . . . is recognized as a timeless affirmation of human rights and representative government.

One measure of the Declaration's lasting influence is that the values it expresses have taken on expanded meanings with the passage of time. More than two centuries ago, when Jefferson wrote that "all men are created equal," few people gave much thought to women's rights. Women were shut out of public life. They did not vote, hold office, or even attend town meetings. Jefferson did not mention women in any of his drafts. Later he wrote that American women were "too wise to wrinkle their foreheads with politics."

Did Jefferson, a slave owner, mean to include black men when he wrote "all men are created equal" and endowed with "certain unalienable[3] Rights"? In colonial America, enslaved Africans had no rights at all. Yet Jefferson knew

---

2. tyrant: a person who rules in an oppressive and cruel way.
3. unalienable: cannot be taken away (less common spelling of inalienable).

that slavery was wrong, and he said so in the long passage of his declaration that <u>denounced</u> the slave trade. That passage was <u>eliminated</u>, but the idea of *equality* remained embedded in the Declaration of Independence; and as American history unfolded, that was the idea that prevailed.

During the 1780s, 1790s, and early 1800s, the lofty ideas expressed in the Declaration of Independence led northern states to free slaves within their borders. And in 1848, women's rights advocates meeting at Seneca Falls, New York, drafted a Declaration of Sentiments based on the Declaration of Independence; they proclaimed that "all men and women are created equal."

Abraham Lincoln believed that the Declaration of Independence expressed the highest political truths in history. He said that blacks and whites alike were entitled to the rights it spelled out. Lincoln regarded equal rights as an *ideal*, a set of goals to be "constantly looked to, and constantly labored for, even though never perfectly attained . . . augmenting[4] the happiness and value of life to all people of all colors everywhere."

The signers of the Declaration of Independence did not mean that all men are "equal in all respects," said Lincoln. People differ greatly in intelligence, strength, talent, character, and many other attributes. What the signers stated in "plain, unmistakable language," Lincoln insisted, was that all men are equal in having "'certain inalienable rights.' . . . This they said, and this they meant."

▲ (left to right) Benjamin Franklin, Thomas Jefferson, John Adams, Robert Livingston, and Roger Sherman drafting the Declaration of Independence.

Bettmann/CORBIS

denounced (dē·nounsd′): condemned as wicked or wrong.

eliminated (ē·lim′ə·nāt·id): gotten rid of.

---

4. **augmenting:** making greater or larger.

The Promised Land?

It's no accident that the American Revolution and the Great Awakening occurred during the same century. The Great Awakening, a religious movement that spread throughout the colonies in the mid-1700s, was in many ways a revolution within the Christian church. It emphasized a person's ability to experience God directly, without the help of traditional church doctrines (creeds or principles), priests, or sacraments (rites, such as baptism, confirmation, or marriage). In the same way, the Revolution insisted that each individual should experience certain rights and freedoms—even when traditional governments tried to stand in their way.

"They had no intention of affirming the obvious untruth, that all were then enjoying that equality," Lincoln continued. The signers meant "simply to declare the *right* so that the *enforcement* of it might follow as fast as the circumstances should permit."

Lincoln pointed out that Americans could have declared independence from England without ever mentioning equality and unalienable rights. But they chose "to introduce into a merely revolutionary document, an abstract truth, applicable to all men and all times."

In 1963, a century after Lincoln signed the Emancipation Proclamation, Martin Luther King, Jr., stood on the steps of the Lincoln Memorial in Washington, D.C., and proclaimed his dream that Americans of all races would one day live in harmony: "It is a dream deeply rooted in the American dream, that one day this nation will rise up and live out the true meaning of its creed—we hold these truths to be self-evident, that all men are created equal."

Like Lincoln, King regarded the Declaration of Independence as a living document that speaks anew to each generation. Here is the passage that most people remember and that is inscribed, in part, on the Jefferson Memorial in Washington, D.C.:

We hold these truths to be self-evident, that all men are created equal, that they are endowed by their Creator with certain unalienable Rights, that among these are Life, Liberty and the pursuit of Happiness.—That to secure these rights, Governments are instituted among Men, deriving their just powers from the consent of the governed,—That whenever any Form of Government becomes destructive of these ends, it is the Right of the People to alter or to abolish it, and to institute new Government, laying its foundation on such principles and organizing its powers in such form, as to them shall seem most likely to effect their Safety and Happiness.

1. According to Thomas Jefferson, what was the purpose of the Declaration of Independence?

2. What did Jefferson mean when he wrote that governments must have the "consent of the governed"?

3. What did a group of women's rights advocates declare in 1848?

4. Did Abraham Lincoln believe that equality in America was a reality or an ideal? Explain.

5. In 1963, who echoed Jefferson's belief that "all men are created equal"?

MEET THE *Writer*

Russell Freedman (1929–   ) grew up in a household where stories were constantly being told. Because his father worked for a publisher, their house was always brimming with literary figures such as John Steinbeck and William Saroyan. Today, Freedman himself is the widely known author of more than three dozen nonfiction books for children and young adults. In 1988, he was given the Newbery Medal for *Lincoln: A Photobiography*—the first Newbery awarded to a nonfiction book in over 30 years. In addition to the historical subjects Freedman loves to explore, he has also written many books about animals in the wild.

▲ Benjamin Banneker.

Archive Photos

How do you build a clock if you don't know how it works? Young Benjamin Banneker solved this problem, as well as many other mechanical and scientific problems.

Benjamin Banneker

from *Pioneers of Discovery*
(Profiles of Great Black Americans)

edited by RICHARD RENNERT

Astronomer[1] and mathematician Benjamin Banneker was born on November 9, 1731, in what was then the British colony of Maryland. His father was a former slave, born in Africa, who had bought his freedom. Benjamin's mother was the daughter of a white Englishwoman, Molly Welsh, and a freed African slave.

In 1682 Molly Welsh had been falsely accused of stealing milk on the farm in England where she worked as a dairy maid. She was put on trial and convicted, and as her punishment she was deported to the English colonies in North America. In 1683 Welsh settled on a farm in Maryland as an indentured[2] servant, a person who was legally bound to work for an employer for a certain number of years.

You Need to Know...

Even while slavery was still a fact of life, African Americans found ways to contribute to and improve society. Here the focus is on Benjamin Banneker, also known as the "Sable Astronomer." Banneker is important not only as an early African American scientist—some say the first—but also for the work he did in this role. Astronomy was an important science in the colonies for several reasons. First, since many colonies were located on the Atlantic coast, knowledge of the stars helped sailors navigate their ships. Also, as the colonies expanded westward, calculations based on astronomy were used to define boundaries. Finally, colonial scientists had a reputation to establish. Most European scientists considered American science to be second-rate. As the colonies grew wealthier and more powerful, though, more people were able to buy telescopes and other stargazing equipment. Gradually, with the help of men like Benjamin Banneker, colonial science could begin to command a new respect.

---

1. **astronomer:** a person who studies the stars and planets.
2. **indentured:** contracted to work for another person for a specified length of time. Originally the written contract and a copy had matching notched edges, or indentations, which identified them.

Welsh's term of servitude was seven years. When she received her freedom in 1690, she rented a small plot of land and grew tobacco. After several years she had made enough money from the sale of her crop to buy a small patch of land near the Patapsco River. A few years later Welsh bought two slaves to help her farm the land. One of the slaves, named Bannaka, told Welsh that he had been a prince in Africa. This may have been true, because during this time, rival African states at war often captured the opposing tribe's royal family and sold them to European slave traders.

Bannaka was said to be "a man of bright intelligence, fine temper, with a very agreeable presence, dignified manners, and contemplative habits." He held pride in his African heritage, maintaining his faith while other slaves converted to Christianity. He also kept his African name, although it was changed slightly.

By 1696 Welsh had freed both of her slaves. About this time she married Bannaka, and the couple took the surname of Banneky. They operated a prosperous tobacco farm and eventually had four children, all of whom worked on the farm. The oldest, Mary, married a freed slave named Robert from a neighboring farm in 1730. Their first child, Benjamin, was born a year later. The couple took Mary's surname, which was later changed to Banneker.

Throughout his childhood Benjamin and his three younger sisters worked on the family farm. They helped with the household chores and sowed the tobacco seeds. Although tobacco farming took up most of Benjamin's time, he did not like it very much. Whenever he was able to take a break from farm work, he read. His grandmother Molly Welsh taught him how to read and write and to perform simple arithmetic. She also arranged for him to attend classes for several years at a local Quaker school, and his interest in mathematics and science grew. He enjoyed calculating mathematical problems and figuring out statistics.

At the age of 21, Banneker decided to build a clock, even though he did not know how one worked. Mechanical

servitude (sûr′və·to͞od′): labor or service.

contemplative (kən·tem′plə·tiv′): thoughtful.

statistics (stə·tis′tiks): facts or data collected as numbers and arranged so as to give information.

> He took the watch apart and made drawings of its interior to teach himself how it worked.

timepieces were rare in colonial America, but Banneker managed to borrow a pocket watch to use as a model. He took the watch apart and made drawings of its interior to teach himself how it worked. He then reproduced the watch parts by carving them from wood, making them considerably bigger, and assembled them into a large clock. He even added a bell, so that the clock chimed on the hour. Neighbors often came to see it, and Banneker himself became celebrated locally for his mathematical ability.

In 1759, following the death of his father, Banneker became responsible for running the family tobacco farm. During the next 20 years he spent most of his time doing farm work; for relaxation he bought a flute and violin and learned to play both instruments. He like to sit on the porch and play music in the evening. Being a free black, Banneker led a lonely life. He did not have many friends, and he never married. However, neighbors did visit to have him help make mathematical computations on deeds[3] and other things.

In the 1780s Banneker became acquainted with the Ellicotts, a white Quaker family who lived nearby. One of the family's sons, George Ellicott, was a surveyor, and when he learned of Banneker's interest in mathematics and mechanics, he lent Banneker a telescope, drafting instruments,[4] and several books on surveying and astronomy. Using all these materials, Banneker proceeded to teach himself both surveying and astronomy.

Soon Banneker was able to predict when eclipses[5] of the sun and moon would occur. . . . Banneker also calculated a table showing the locations of celestial bodies—the sun, moon, stars, and planets—at different times of the year. Such a table is called an ephemeris; the plural is *ephemerides*.

In 1791 a cousin of George Ellicott's, Andrew Ellicott, became the chief surveyor of the nearby federal territory. A new national capital was being created on this land that

---

3. deeds: documents relating to the transfer of property from one owner to another.
4. drafting instruments: equipment used to make a plan or drawing of a piece of work.
5. eclipses: blocking out of one object by another; overshadowing or cutting off of light.

later became Washington, D.C. Andrew Ellicott, hearing of Banneker's skills, invited him to help with the survey.

Several months later, after finishing this work, Banneker returned to his farm and calculated an ephemeris for the following year. In August of 1791 Banneker sent a copy of his ephemeris to Thomas Jefferson, who was then Secretary of State. Along with the calculations he enclosed a letter that complained about the "abuse and censure" of African Americans by whites, and he criticized Jefferson for not opposing slavery. In his letter, Banneker compared the enslavement of blacks to the way in which England had treated the American colonies before the colonies declared their independence.

censure (sen'shər) blame or disapproval.

Jefferson wrote back to Banneker, acknowledging the receipt of his letter and calculations. The future president, who was also an amateur scientist, then sent Banneker's calculations to an acquaintance, the head of the French Academy of Sciences in Paris. Jefferson's and Banneker's letters were later published in pamphlet form and received wide publicity.

In December 1791 Banneker published his ephemeris as part of an almanac[6] entitled *Benjamin Banneker's Pennsylvania, Delaware, Maryland and Virginia Almanack and Ephemeris, for the Year of Our Lord, 1792; Being Bissextile, or Leap-Year, and the Sixteenth Year of American Independence, Which Commenced July 4, 1776.* In addition to the ephemeris, the almanac included several essays on scientific topics.

"... Sir, how pitiable is it to reflect, that although you were so fully convinced of the benevolence of the Father of Mankind, and of his equal and impartial distribution of these rights and privileges, which he hath conferred upon them, that you should at the same time counteract his mercies, in detaining by fraud and violence so numerous a part of my brethren, under groaning captivity and cruel oppression, that you should at the same time be found guilty of that most criminal act, which you professedly detested in others, with respect to yourselves."

▲ An excerpt from the letter from Benjamin Banneker to the secretary of state, Thomas Jefferson, dated August 19, 1791, in which he discusses the subject of slavery.

The publication of Banneker's almanac was sponsored by several abolitionist societies—groups of men and women who worked for the abolition of slavery. At that

---

6. **almanac:** calendar for the whole year that gives weather forecasts, astronomical data, and other useful information.

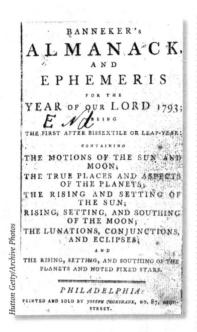

▲ Banneker's almanac. **?** **What information did it contain?**

time many people who supported slavery believed that Africans were not as intelligent as people of European ancestry. Abolitionists used Banneker's work to show that blacks had abilities equal to those of whites.

The first edition of the almanac sold out quickly, and a second edition was printed. The book's widespread popularity freed Banneker from heavy farm work. Instead of raising cash crops, he kept only a small home garden and raised bees. This gave him more time to continue his calculations and to chat with the many visitors who flocked to his cabin, for Banneker had become a celebrity.

Abolitionists used Banneker's work to show that blacks had abilities equal to those of whites.

Banneker published a new *Almanack and Ephemeris* each year for several years. The *Almanack* for 1793 included copies of Banneker's letter to Jefferson and Jefferson's response. The last known issue of Banneker's *Almanack and Ephemeris* appeared in 1797, probably because support for the antislavery movement was then declining. However, Banneker continued to prepare an ephemeris for each year until 1804. He also published a book about bees and calculated the life cycle of the seventeen-year locust.

One of Banneker's closest friends in his later years was Susanna Mason, a cousin of the Ellicotts. Mason was the founder of an association for the relief of the poor in Baltimore. She met Banneker in 1796, and the two wrote letters to one another. Mason wrote a poem in one of these letters:

> But thou, a man exalted high,
> Conspicuous in the world's keen eye
> On record now thy name's enrolled
> And future ages will be told,
> There lived a man called Banneker,
> An African Astronomer.

Banneker died at his cabin on October 9, 1806, one month before his 75th birthday. He had left many of his personal effects, including his journals and scientific instruments, to George Ellicott, and these were quickly carted away. Banneker's funeral service was held on his farm two days after his death. As the body was being buried, his cabin nearby burst into flames and burned to the ground. Everything remaining in the structure was destroyed—including the famous clock that he had built many years before.

✓ Reading Check

1. How did Benjamin Banneker's mother and father meet?

2. What did Banneker build at the age of twenty-one?

3. What important piece of land did Banneker help to survey?

4. In a letter to Thomas Jefferson, what did Banneker compare the enslavement of blacks to?

5. How was Banneker's almanac used by abolitionists?

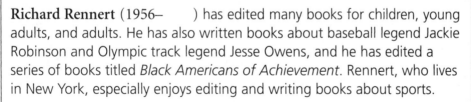

MEET THE *Writer*

Richard Rennert (1956–   ) has edited many books for children, young adults, and adults. He has also written books about baseball legend Jackie Robinson and Olympic track legend Jesse Owens, and he has edited a series of books titled *Black Americans of Achievement*. Rennert, who lives in New York, especially enjoys editing and writing books about sports.

Were the "terrible roarings" of the woolly mammoths still thundering through the unexplored regions of colonial America? Jefferson thought so and set out to find remains of these prehistoric creatures. Read this excerpt to discover what he found.

Independence National Historical Park, Philadelphia, Pennsylvania

▲ Thomas Jefferson.

from **Thomas Jefferson**

from *Science in Colonial America*

by BRENDAN JANUARY

Thomas Jefferson was born in 1743 and raised in central Virginia. As a young boy, he enjoyed roaming through the mountains and forests around his home. A multitalented genius, Jefferson achieved brilliance in several different fields. Today, we also remember Jefferson as the author of the Declaration of Independence.

As a young man, Jefferson developed a passionate interest in science. At his home, Monticello, in Virginia, he pursued new techniques in farming and raising animals. Like other philosophers of his time, Jefferson believed that the study of science would greatly benefit humanity. He also believed that science should be practical. "Science never appears so beautiful," he once wrote, "as when applied to the uses of human life."

In 1780, Jefferson received a request from a French statesman. He wanted Jefferson to answer several questions about the people, climate, plants and animals,

You Need to Know...

Among Europeans, the discovery of North America created a new interest in natural history—the study of natural objects, such as plants and animals, and their history. What kinds of plants and animals lived in this strange new world? What other mysteries lay deep within the vast, unexplored forests beyond the colonies? At first, Europeans themselves would travel to the New World to collect samples of its wildlife. They would then return to Europe, study the samples, and write books describing what they had found. Soon, though, they began to ask American colonists to collect and ship the samples to them— and the first American scientists entered the wilderness. As you will see in this selection, Thomas Jefferson knew quite a bit about the terrain he loved so well. He was also eager to prove to uncertain Europeans that America was a strong, vital land— a land to be reckoned with.

and landscape of Virginia. Jefferson answered these questions in the form of a book called *Notes on the State of Virginia*. It was printed in France in 1781.

Jefferson's book discussed such topics as religion, slavery, Native Americans, <u>geology</u>, wildlife, farming, and education. In clear and precise language, Jefferson presented a vivid portrait of his beloved state. He noted the size of the animals and the most common types of trees. He discussed the various landscapes, such as the rolling mountains in the west and the tidewater regions along Chesapeake Bay. Jefferson also rejected widely accepted European theories that North America was a crippled continent of stunted trees, small animals, and simple people.

Despite the popularity of Jefferson's *Notes*, the leading French natural historian, Georges du Buffon, continued to describe North America as <u>inferior</u>. Stung[1] by Buffon's remarks, Jefferson decided to prove the Frenchman wrong. From Paris, he sent letters to friends in the United States, requesting that they send him "the skin, the skeleton, and the horns" of several large North American animals. Jefferson confidently predicted that one North American moose would quickly prove Buffon wrong.

The animals arrived, but Jefferson was disappointed. He had anticipated larger and more <u>impressive</u> samples. Again he wrote to the United States, requesting larger <u>specimens</u>. Jefferson's friends shipped another moose to France. This time, Jefferson was pleased, and he displayed the 7-foot (2.1-m)-tall animal in the lobby of his hotel. Buffon inspected the specimen but remained unconvinced.

Jefferson Studies Ancient Bones

As he looked for evidence that North America was not inferior to Europe, Jefferson made several discoveries. While still in France, he <u>sponsored</u> a North American expedition to locate fossilized[2] bones of extinct animals. Jefferson was convinced that woolly mammoths, huge

geology (jē·äl′ə·jē): study of the nature and history of the earth.

inferior (in·fir′ē·ər): lower in rank or class.

impressive (im·pres′iv): producing a strong effect.

specimens (spes′ə·mənz): examples; representatives of a larger group.

sponsored (spän′sərd): organized; supported.

---

1. **stung:** upset; made unhappy.
2. **fossilized:** hardened; rock-like, as the fossilized bones of animals from a previous time.

▲ *Disinterment of the Mastodon* by Charles Willson Peale. Peale, a painter and naturalist, directed the digging up of a mastodon skeleton near Newburgh, New York, in 1801.

elephant-like animals, had once lived in North America. To his great delight, mammoth bones were discovered and sent to France. Jefferson even claimed that the woolly mammoth still existed in unexplored regions of North America. He listened with great interest to Indian and pioneer stories about "terrible roarings" and "eyes like two balls of fire."

Jefferson continued to be fascinated by ancient bones after his return to the United States. In 1796, he received a collection of unusual bones that had been discovered in western Virginia. He called the animal *Megalonyx*, which is a Latin word meaning "giant claw." Jefferson was confident that this animal, a giant ground sloth,[3] had not yet been identified by science.

In 1797, Jefferson brought the bones with him to Philadelphia, where he was being sworn in as vice president of the United States. He planned to announce his discovery of the *Megalonyx* to the American Philosophical

---

3. sloth: slow-moving animal that lives in trees in tropical Central and South America.

Society. Before he could, though, Jefferson read a London magazine. In its pages, he discovered an illustration of an animal that appeared similar to his *Megalonyx*. The author of the article had identified the animal from bones discovered in South America almost 10 years earlier. That scientist called the animal *Megatherium*.

Jefferson changed some details of his paper and read it to the American Philosophical Society. Years later, Jefferson was honored for the discovery of *Megalonyx*. A French scientist used the Linnaean system to name Jefferson's skeleton *Megalonyx jeffersonii*. After Jefferson's death, he was honored in France for his tremendous contributions to their collection of ancient fossils.

Jefferson remained passionately interested in natural history when he became president of the United States in 1801. He was convinced that the western half of North America contained new species of animal life waiting to be discovered. In 1803, Jefferson made a historic purchase of land from Napoleon I, who ruled France. The Louisiana Purchase doubled the size of the United States. In 1804, Jefferson launched one of the most famous exploratory journeys of all time—the Lewis and Clark Expedition of the northwestern United States.

Natural history was the first true science practiced in America. It promoted scientific ties between Europe and North America. The first Americans to win general praise in Europe studied natural science.

Mammoth Matters

In 1997, a frozen woolly mammoth was discovered in the icy terrain of Siberia, in Russia. Although the specimen has been dead for about 20,000 years, scientists believe that some of its genetic material may have been preserved. If so, it may be possible to create a clone of the animal or to crossbreed it with an Asian elephant. Some day, the eight-ton, twelve-foot-tall woolly wonder may walk the earth again! Regardless of whether this happens, though, the frozen creature will help scientists answer some important questions, such as how the species became extinct and who the mammoth's modern-day descendants are.

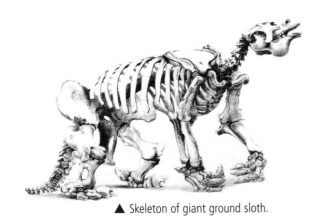

▲ Skeleton of giant ground sloth.

Class, Come to Order

In 1753 and 1758, a Swedish scientist named Carolus Linnaeus (Li·nē′əs) published books in which he proposed a system for classifying and naming plants and animals. According to this system, now known as *taxonomy*, living things are grouped according to their similarities. Each living thing is then given two names. The first name refers to the organism's *genus*, or group. The second refers to its *species*, or kind. Linnaeus's system immediately created a kind of classifying craze in Europe. Natural scientists began to classify and catalog species from all over the world, and indeed, the system was a wonderful tool. It is still in use today.

✔ Reading Check

1. In 1780, what request did Jefferson receive from a French statesman?

2. At this time, what did most Europeans believe about North America?

3. When he was in Paris, what did Jefferson ask his friends to send him from America? Why?

4. Name two extinct animals whose bones were discovered in North America and examined by Jefferson.

5. According to the selection, what two major events in our country's history were related to Jefferson's interest in natural science?

MEET THE *Writer*

Brendan January has written several books for young people about American history. After growing up in Pleasantville, New York, January earned a degree in history and English from Haverford College.

Cross-Curricular ACTIVITIES

■ SCIENCE/ART

How Does This Work? Often we use objects and machines without truly understanding how they work. Benjamin Banneker's curiosity prompted him to take apart a watch, make sketches of the different parts, and then use the drawings to build a clock of his own. You don't have to take things apart, though. Select a common object and use your resource center to find out how it works. Make a drawing of your object, using as much detail as possible. Present your findings to the class.

■ MUSIC/LANGUAGE ARTS

Keeping Time You've always known the tune of "Yankee Doodle," whose lyrics tell the story of the colonies' growing restlessness. Did you know that the song was originally written from the point of view of the British? Now, think of an event in recent history that created conflict between two groups of people. This could be a world event, a national event, or an event in your community or school. Then, write at least two verses that tell the story of this conflict from your own point of view and that can be sung to the tune of "Yankee Doodle." Recruit a group of three or four classmates to rehearse the song with you and then sing it for the class. Afterwards, discuss the message you were trying to convey. Does your audience think you've succeeded?

■ DRAMA/HISTORY

"I Was There!" After her one-of-a-kind experience as a soldier in disguise, Deborah Sampson took her story on the road. Dressed in costume, she delivered an address, or monologue, to dozens of spellbound audiences, describing her adventures in vivid detail. Choose one of the historical figures you've read about in this chapter. Then, write a monologue that tells about a particular experience that character has had. Your monologue should be as entertaining as possible, and it should be written in first person (using "I"). Finally, memorize your address and perform it, in costume, for an audience of classmates. Use gestures, facial expressions, and movement to help communicate your character's ideas.

■ DRAMA/DANCE

Show, Not Tell Choose a selection from this chapter and create a pageant, a pantomime, or a dance. For example, you might choreograph Benjamin Franklin's experiment with the kite, or the Boston Tea Party as a dance. The writing of the Declaration of Independence could be presented as a pageant, with visuals that express the important points of that document. Working in a group, write your script, design and create your costumes and props, and present your final product to the class.

■ LANGUAGE ARTS/HISTORY

Who Said That? Benjamin Franklin's greatest publishing success was his *Poor Richard's Almanac*, which contained the sayings of the fictitious Poor Richard and his critical wife, Bridget. Create a class almanac or card game of sayings of famous Americans. Be sure to list the origin of the saying in the almanac or put it on the back of the card for the game. Present your finished product to the class.

READ ON: FOR INDEPENDENT READING

■ NONFICTION

Abigail Adams: Witness to a Revolution
by Natalie S. Bober (Atheneum Books for Young
Readers, 1995). Abigail Adams was free with her
advice. While her husband was away serving in the
Continental Congress, she wrote a letter reminding
him that attention must be paid to "the ladies,"
who also wanted a voice in the new government.
Excerpts from Abigail Adams' letters give a firsthand
account of Colonial America from an extraordinary
woman's point of view.

***The American Revolutionaries: A History
in Their Own Words 1750–1800*** edited by
Milton Meltzer (HarperTrophy, 1993) is a prize-
winning collection of excerpts from letters, diaries,
journals, speeches, and ballads that give eyewitness
accounts of the American Revolution.

Fireworks, Picnics and Flags by James Cross
Giblin, illustrated by Ursula Arndt (Clarion Books, division of Houghton Mifflin, 1983). The turkey as the
national bird of the United States? Benjamin Franklin
thought the bald eagle's bad habits made it an
unsuitable choice, but, fortunately, the wild turkey
lost out. This book explores the symbols and history
of America's Independence Day.

***Thomas Jefferson: The Revolutionary
Aristocrat*** by Milton Meltzer (Franklin Watts,
1991) is the biography of a man whose brilliance
and complexity had a powerful influence on the
future of the American colonies. Meltzer's text
dramatizes the contradictions between Jefferson as
humane philosopher, political realist, and aristocrat.
The text is illustrated with maps, portraits, and
original documents from the period.

■ FICTION

The Fighting Ground by Avi (HarperTrophy,
1987) takes place during one day in the life of thirteen-year-old Jonathan—a day in which he learns
the horrible truth about war. Jonathan learns that
war is not about uniforms, about shooting a gun, or
about the glory of fighting for an ideal. For him it is
about being huddled together with other frightened
men, blinded by fog, and disoriented by the unintelli-
gible German language of the Hessians. The
detailed, minute-by-minute account reveals the true
nature of war and death.

***Hang a Thousand Trees with Ribbons:
The Story of Phillis Wheatley*** by Ann Rinaldi
(Harcourt Brace, 1996) is a fictionalized biography of
a woman who lived one of the most remarkable
lives in American history. Kidnapped from her
Senegal home as a child, Wheatley was educated
and nurtured by the prominent Wheatley family in
Boston. She was America's first African American
poet, and the story of her life shows the dilemma
that some African Americans faced—that of belong-
ing neither to the white nor to the slave society.

Johnny Tremain by Esther Forbes, illustrated by
Lynn Ward (Yearling Books, 1987). Winner of the
Newbery Award in 1944, this classic tells the story of
a young silversmith who loses his trade when an
accident cripples one of his hands. Johnny Tremain
goes on to claim his birthright of freedom and
become involved in the revolutionary Sons of Liberty.

CHAPTER 3

Separate Roads
The United States from 1800 to 1850

A Perpetual Picnic?

"Thoughts rule the world," said Ralph Waldo Emerson. Other members of Boston's Transcendental Club agreed. Writer Nathaniel Hawthorne, feminist Margaret Fuller, writer Henry David Thoreau—all had radical ideas about how to live life. People should live simply and believe in sharing and hard work. They should love philosophy and art, not money and power.

One member of the club wanted to do more than talk. In 1841, Unitarian minister George Ripley moved to the country with sixteen others to create a community at Brook Farm in Massachusetts. This community was to be a utopia (yoo·tō´pē·ə)— a perfect society. Hawthorne quit his job and went with Ripley, but few of his famous friends joined him. Emerson visited several times but made fun of the community, calling it a "perpetual picnic."

Hawthorne could have told him it was no picnic. The group was determined to run the farm themselves, but most of the Boston writers and thinkers who joined had never done farm work before, or any other kind of manual labor. After a long day in the fields, Hawthorne was often too exhausted to write.

Breaking the Prison Bars

Dorothea Dix loved to learn as much as she loved to teach. So when the retired schoolteacher came to teach Sunday school to female prisoners in 1841, she insisted on touring the jailhouse first.

She was horrified by what she saw. Two mentally ill women—not criminals at all—shivered in bare, filthy cages made out of rough boards. Why weren't they given any heat? she asked the jailer. He laughed and said, "Lunatics don't feel the cold."

The Granger Collection, New York

INVESTIGATE: Who are some other reformers who worked to improve society in the nineteenth century?

Memorable Quote

"There was some talk between us of your coming to this country. For God's sake think not of it. Stay at home. Tell all whom you know that are thinking of coming that they have to sacrifice everything and face danger in all its forms, for George, thousands have laid and will lay their bones along the routes to and in this country."

—William Swain, writing to his brother George Swain after going to California in search of gold, January 6, 1850

▲ Sequoyah and his written version of the Cherokee language.

The Granger Collection, New York

For the next twenty years Dix crusaded for better treatment of the mentally ill. Thanks to her efforts, state hospitals where people suffering from mental illness could be decently cared for and housed were built across the country.

The Facts in the Case of Mr. Poe

When Edgar Allan Poe wrote the first modern detective story, "The Murders in the Rue Morgue," he could never have guessed that his own death would leave behind a mystery that would remain unsolved for nearly one hundred fifty years.

Library of Congress

On October 3, 1849, Poe collapsed in front of Ryan's Saloon in Baltimore. He was taken to the hospital, where his delirium and tremors (combined with his reputation as a drunkard) persuaded everyone that alcohol was finally taking its toll. He recovered briefly, but a few days later, he died.

In 1996, a Baltimore doctor reviewing Poe's case said the facts didn't fit. Poe refused alcohol in the hospital, and some said he hadn't had a drink in six months. Nor did some of his symptoms—difficulty swallowing, a short recovery and then relapse—match those of alcohol withdrawal. However, they perfectly matched a different disease: rabies.

Talking Leaves

The Cherokee people were amazed. It had to be a trick. They had told Sequoyah some words, then he had made marks on a leaf of paper. Now Sequoyah's daughter Ah-yo-kah, who had not heard the words, stood before them holding the paper and repeating the same words. Could this leaf of paper really speak to her in the Cherokee tongue?

It had taken him years of work, but Sequoyah had invented a Cherokee alphabet. Each letter of his alphabet stood for a sound which was always the same—a syllable such as *nee* or *quah*. (If English worked that way, NME would spell *enemy* and MT would spell *empty*.) With eighty-six letters representing eighty-six syllables, Sequoyah could write any word in the Cherokee language.

Imagine planning to cross an unexplored wilderness. How would you prepare? What dangers would you expect? The following article describes how Lewis and Clark and their team faced these and other challenges.

Into the Unknown: The Incredible Adventures of Lewis and Clark

from *National Geographic World*

by MARGARET MCKELWAY

Expedition leaders Captains Meriwether Lewis and William Clark were restless. They had spent the summer and early fall of 1804 transporting supplies 1,600 miles up the Missouri River from St. Louis, Missouri, northwest to present-day North Dakota. Traveling by boat, they had hauled 200 pounds of gunpowder, 150 pounds of soap, and hundreds of pounds of other food and supplies. Unable to travel in winter, the men stayed at Fort Mandan. They talked to the Indians, French-Canadian trappers, British traders—anyone with even a shred of information about the mysterious lands ahead. By early April 1805, the ice in the river was breaking up, making travel by boat possible again.

You Need to Know...

In 1800, about two thirds of the people in the United States lived within fifty miles of the Atlantic Coast. Only ten percent lived west of the Appalachian Mountains! For most Americans, the West was a vast, unknown region. Anxious to learn more about what lay beyond the Mississippi River, President Thomas Jefferson asked his friend and personal secretary, Captain Meriwether Lewis, to lead an expedition into the wild West. Lewis, in turn, asked Captain William Clark to be his cocommander. Both were experienced military men, but each brought his own unique qualities to the team. Clark, like Jefferson, respected the Indians. He was outgoing and cheerful, and his skills as a surveyor and engineer came in handy. Lewis, on the other hand, was wary of Indians. He was more reserved and enjoyed studying the plants and animals encountered by the group. In this selection, you'll learn how this exceptional team forged their way westward—and into the pages of history.

▲ Meriwether Lewis.

▲ William Clark.

The Granger Collection, New York

acquired (ə•kwīrd′): gained possession of something by one's own efforts.

commissioned (kə•mish′ənd): gave an assignment or an order.

Lewis, 30, and Clark, 34, were eager to continue their journey.

President Thomas Jefferson himself had sent out this expedition. He had just closed the biggest land deal in the history of the United States. From the French he had acquired the Louisiana Territory, an area so huge that it doubled the size of the country. It extended far west of the Mississippi River, where no American citizen had ever stepped foot. Jefferson had long been fascinated by the territory's unknowns. He dreamed of finding a river route large enough to carry trade vessels from the Mississippi River to the Pacific Ocean. He imagined finding minerals and new species of plants and animals. He also wanted to learn about the Indians who lived there. He commissioned army officers Lewis and Clark to explore and map the land. Their mission: Find the source of the Missouri River, cross the Rockies, then follow the largest river west to the Pacific Ocean. They would also establish trade with the Indians, assuring them the United States government wanted only friendship.

Finally, on April 7, 1805, the expedition left its winter quarters to push into unfamiliar lands. Thirty-four people set out that day: Captains Lewis and Clark; York, Clark's slave; 26 army volunteers; a Mandan Indian; and two French-Canadian interpreters, one with his Indian wife, Sacagawea, and their infant son. Jefferson called the group of explorers the Corps of Discovery.

The territory was uncharted. The captains would have to make maps as they went, getting directions from the Indians they met along the way. The explorers would have to carry their supplies in canoes, camp in tents, hunt animals for food, and trade for other supplies. From what they understood, Lewis and Clark planned to canoe to the Missouri's source; portage, or carry, the canoes across a narrow range of low mountains; then paddle the rivers all the way to the ocean. In the planning, such a journey seemed relatively easy. The actual journey was not.

Danger Ahead

The expedition had heard rumors of warlike Indians ahead. They saw no such Indians during the summer of 1805. They did see a great variety of animals roaming the treeless prairies in what is now Montana. In his journal one explorer wrote that he spotted "buffalo, elk, and antelopes, with some deer and wolves."

The Mandans had told of the strong, fierce grizzly bear. Lewis found tales of the bear difficult to believe until May 14. That evening six hunters shot a grizzly, but the bear chased them, even when shot again. Two men fled to a cliff above the river, with the bear close behind. Now they had nowhere to go but into the water 20 feet below. The bear followed! Finally a man on land killed the animal with a shot to the head.

The bear chased them, even when shot again. Two men fled to a cliff above the river, with the bear close behind.

As the explorers paddled farther up the Missouri River, the landscape began to change. Now there were rolling hills. And by late May they saw huge mountains in the distance. To survey the area Lewis climbed a bluff overlooking the river. To the west he saw a few peaks. "From this point," he wrote on May 26, 1805, "I beheld the Rocky Mountains for the first time."

Lewis led the group upstream but soon reached a fork in the river. Which stream was the Missouri? The Hidatsa Indians had said there would be a great waterfall on the Missouri. Ten days later he heard the "tremendous" roaring of the falls and knew the explorers had chosen the right course. Lewis wrote that the beauty of the falls filled

Secret Mission?

Lewis wrote Clark a letter asking him to help lead the expedition. In the letter, he asked Clark to keep the mission confidential, since the team was planning to illegally cross land owned by France. By the time Lewis accepted the offer a month later, however, there was no need for secrecy: The United States had purchased the Louisiana Territory from France.

him with "pleasure and astonishment." As the men continued, they discovered a second set of falls, then a third, fourth, and fifth. For 18 difficult miles they had to portage their boats and all the supplies past the falls.

On August 12 Lewis and several explorers hiked up a slope and at last came to the source of the mighty Missouri. Then Lewis scrambled to the top of a pass and looked out over the great Northwest. He was among the first American citizens to see this part of the world. The view thrilled him—but it also must have chilled him: As far as he could see were ridge after ridge of jagged, snow-capped peaks. He gave up hope of making an easy journey.

Soon, he realized, travel by water would be impossible. The group would need horses to travel over the mountains. Their only hope lay in obtaining horses from the Shoshone Indians who lived somewhere in this vast wilderness.

Sacagawea, a Shoshone herself, had already recognized some landmarks. On August 13 the explorers found the Shoshone. A few days later Sacagawea recognized the chief, Cameahwait: He was her brother! She hadn't seen him since the Hidatsa Indians had kidnapped her five years earlier. Clark wrote in his journal that the brother and sister had an emotional reunion. Later Cameahwait agreed to sell horses to the explorers and provide them with a guide for the next leg of their journey.

On September 1 the Corps of Discovery continued its journey into the Bitterroots, one of the most rugged ranges of the Rocky Mountains. The group crawled up and down steep, rocky hills, and hacked through thick growth and fallen trees. Horses slipped, stumbled, and fell; one died. In mid-September even their guide got lost.

reunion (rē•yōōn′yən): a meeting of people who have been separated from one another.

North Wind Picture Archives

▲ William Clark's diary. **?** **Why was it necessary for Lewis and Clark to keep detailed records of the team's experiences?**

It hailed and snowed. With no game to hunt and no grass for the horses to eat, all faced starvation. Exhausted and desperate, the explorers ate some of their horses. After days of bitter cold and miles of rocky ridges, the explorers finally got past the mountains and reached a plain in what is now Idaho.

The Nez Perce Indians who lived there fed the grateful explorers berries, roots, and dried fish. But the new diet sickened most of them. Slowly they recovered and built canoes to continue the journey. The rivers flowing west carried them into the Columbia, the powerful river of the Northwest. Now there was another obstacle: a series of roaring, boiling rapids. To the surprise of Indians watching from a rock, the men steered their canoes safely through treacherous rapids, thanks to their skill and determination.

By mid-October the explorers met Indians using items made from European materials they must have obtained from trading ships. That meant the Pacific Ocean couldn't be far away! Flocks of waterbirds flew overhead. Fog rolled in. On November 7, 1805, Clark wrote, "Great joy . . . in view of the ocean." They were still on the Columbia but close enough to hear waves crashing on the shore. They had done it! They were the first American citizens to have crossed the continent.

Journey's End

After spending an uncomfortable, rain-soaked winter at Fort Clatsop near the mouth of the Columbia River in what is now Oregon, the explorers in the Corps of Discovery headed back, reaching St. Louis, Missouri, on September 23, 1806. They had traveled more than 8,000 miles in 28 months. Throughout the expedition Lewis, Clark, and others carefully made maps and drawings and recorded in their journals information about plants and animals and Indians. They discovered hundreds of species of plants and animals—including the prairie dog and coyote—that were unknown to American scientists. Thanks to the expedition, the U.S. would eventually claim

She Moved in Mysterious Ways

Sacagawea has puzzled historians for years. For one thing, the spelling of her name is uncertain. When spelled with a *j*—*Sacajawea*—the name translates as "Boat Launcher." When spelled with a *g* it means "Bird Woman." We do know that, as a young Shoshone girl, Sacagawea was kidnapped and later sold to a French-Canadian fur trader. Lewis and Clark met the trader and his Indian wife in North Dakota and invited them on their journey. During the expedition, Sacagawea translated the words and customs of the Indians they met.

Afterwards, some believe that Sacagawea died of a fever. According to Native American accounts, though, she went on to live, speak, and teach among the Shoshone people until the age of 96.

obstacle (äb'stə•kəl): something that stands in the way.

treacherous (trech'ər•əs): dangerous.

▲ Sacagawea acted as a guide and interpreter for Lewis and Clark.

the Oregon region, making it possible for pioneers in the 1840s and '50s to settle the West. The expedition also strengthened the fur trade. And Sacagawea? She is believed to have died of fever in 1812. The fate of some of the other explorers is unknown. But not forgotten is the important role they all played in the expedition of Lewis and Clark.

✓ Reading Check

1. Who sent Captains Lewis and Clark on their famous expedition?

2. What was the expedition's mission?

3. At what point did Lewis decide that travel by water would be impossible? How did the group solve this problem?

4. Name two difficulties faced by the expedition in September or October of 1805.

5. The members of the Lewis and Clark expedition were the first American citizens to cross the continent. Name another of their accomplishments.

For Americans who were poor or simply bored, the West meant a fresh start. First, though, they had to get there. The following selection describes what everyday life was like for the many who traveled the Oregon Trail.

from *The Oregon Trail*

by LEONARD EVERETT FISHER

During Marcus Whitman's mission years the United States government sent young Lieutenant John Charles Frémont on expeditions to the West. In 1842, 1843, and again in 1844, Frémont explored much of the Oregon Trail. He sent back detailed reports on its condition, weather, and general environment. He also suggested where the government might build army posts. Frémont's explorations and enthusiasm caused additional waves of excitement among thousands of restless Americans.

"Oregon societies" sprang up everywhere. Contracts were signed between the organizers and those who wanted to go to Oregon. Wagon trains were organized. Leaders or "captains" were elected by the emigrants themselves. Later the "wagon master" took charge of the wagon train. His word was the law. Rules of conduct were spelled out. Lectures were given on how to create a campsite of wagons and

You Need to Know...

Inspired by Lewis and Clark, a fur trader by the name of John Jacob Astor sent his own expeditions out west. In 1812, a group of Astor's men made a monumental discovery—a wide, flat passage through the Rocky Mountains. The sloping land formed a pass that horses and wagons could easily cross. At first supply wagons used the "South Pass" to connect with traders on the eastern slopes. Indeed, there was little reason for regular folks to undertake such a journey—until the Panic of 1837, that is. When this crisis struck the nation, money became scarce, and jobs were few. People grew restless. They began looking for new lives and new opportunities. The West, it seemed, was the answer to their prayers. Although many thought the Rockies impassable, others remembered the discovery, years before, of the South Pass. Thousands of farming families loaded their wagons and took to the trail, with "Oregon or Bust!" as their motto.

emigrants (em′i·grants): people who move out of one country or region into another.

▲ Emigrant family.

multitude (mul′ti•tōōd′): a great many.

how to draw the wagons in a circle or square for protection against attack. Experienced "pilots" or scouts who knew the Oregon Trail were hired by the <u>multitude</u> gathering along the Missouri River to guide the wagon trains safely to Oregon.

"It is estimated that the company . . . will consist of . . . one thousand persons, one hundred wagons, and about two thousand cattle . . ." reported the *St. Joseph* [Missouri] *Gazette* on May 2, 1845, ". . . and the whole wealth of the company is near one hundred thirty thousand dollars . . ."

Hundreds of pounds of food were stored in the supply wagons—flour, grain, bacon, salt, coffee, sugar, dried fruits, pickles, and so on. There had to be enough horses, rifles, pistols, and ammunition "for every male over 18 years of age." Spare parts, tools, medicines and tonics, cooking ware, plates and eating utensils were packed in a family's wagon.

"There is space in the middle of the wagon, the bottom is carpeted, two chairs and a mirror make it appear like a home," wrote one immigrant in 1845.

As noted, one wagon train could consist of a thousand men, women, and children, as many as three thousand to four thousand head of cattle, pet dogs and cats, and more than a hundred wagons. At times, these trains formed a line five miles long. They were the largest outdoor camping caravans[1] ever seen in America!

While the courage of the emigrants was the heartbeat of the wagon trains, the white-canvassed, bright blue, red-wheeled prairie schooners[2] were their symbol. They were not the tough, canvas-covered Conestoga wagons that nudged the eastern frontier westward before 1850. These earlier wagons were first built in Conestoga, Pennsylvania, around 1725. Dubbed "camels of the prairies," they were drawn by teams of four to six horses or mules. They were too clumsy to take across the sharp and steep mountainous areas. Also, they were too heavy to be lowered by ropes from high cliffs to lower ground, a <u>maneuver</u> that many found necessary in the mountains.

Experience quickly taught the emigrants that a smaller, lighter wagon would be better. These newer wagons, some fourteen or fifteen feet long, were straighter, narrower, and just as <u>durable</u> as the Conestogas. One emigrant described his wagon as "narrow . . . the hoops over which the cover

1. **caravans:** groups of people traveling together, usually with equipment or belongings.
2. **schooners:** large sailing ships.

Denver Public Library, Western History and Genealogy Department

▲ Fording a river on the Oregon Trail. ❷ **In addition to this kind of problem, what other difficulties might a wagon train face?**

Too Much, Too Little, Too Late

The Oregon Trail was not the best place to go grocery shopping. Because of the law of supply and demand, the things that everyone needed—and that were often scarce—were sold for outrageous prices. Pioneers paid as much as $1.00 for a pint of flour and $1.50 for a pint of sugar, expensive even by today's standards. On the other hand, bacon was downright cheap—sometimes as little as a penny a pound! In fact, bacon was so abundant that heaps of the unused meat were often left by the side of the road.

maneuver (mə·nōō′vər): a planned move.

durable (dōōr′ə·bəl): long lasting despite hard use.

Footloose

Most people traveled west in wagons, but a few adventurous folks tried other, less typical methods. For example, several dozen people tried to make the journey by pushing their belongings in wheelbarrows. Others pulled handcarts that looked like small covered wagons. These foot-faring individuals believed they could move faster than full-sized wagons did. They were also spared the burden of feeding and caring for livestock. It is uncertain, however, whether any of these travelers completed the entire 2,000-mile marathon.

brackish (brak'ish): having a disagreeable taste; sickening.

is laid, is bent so as to make the top almost flat. The cover is cotton drilling, two thicknesses, the outside oiled. The outside cloth comes down below the bottom on the end boards, so as to admit no rain . . ."

They were made sturdy by the same hardwoods used in the Conestogas. They boasted the same huge, reliable iron-tired wheels, but were usually drawn by teams of four oxen. The oxen were not only better suited for pulling heavily loaded wagons, they were more manageable than mules or horses. Mules and horses were used chiefly as pack and riding animals. If the oxen gave out, then the mules were hitched to the wagons.

Usually, the day began at sunup. The cows were milked. Breakfast was cooked and eaten. Dishes were washed and stored. The oxen were yoked to the wagon and the wagon train was ready to move by eight o'clock. Noon was lunchtime and the wagon train came to a halt. After a couple of hours of eating and resting, the wagon train continued its journey until the early evening—about five o'clock—when a suitable campsite was found. Eight wagons called a "mess" were arranged in a circle. There could be a dozen such circular encampments in one wagon train. The oxen were unhitched. Supper was cooked and eaten. Afterward, people either read their Bibles, prayed, listened to a sermon, if a minister happened to be along, played cards, or sang songs around a campfire. Guards were posted throughout the night. By dawn of the next day they were ready to move on.

Water, fodder,[3] cattle feed, and campfire fuels—wood or buffalo dung called "chips"—were picked up along the way. Too often good drinking water could not be found. Driven by heat and unbearable thirst to drinking brackish, often poisonous water, many became sick and died. "Passed five graves this morning," wrote a pioneer woman in 1852, ". . . passed two graves today . . . one young lady died last night . . . the other could live but a few hours longer . . . both sisters . . . their father had buried his wife, one brother, one sister, two sons in law. . . ."

---

3. fodder: dry food for animals.

Those who got an early spring start in April had little trouble feeding their animals on the new grasses along the way. But those who left later in May found no grass left for their animals. If they did not wander far off the trail to graze their cattle, the cattle died. As the emigrants wandered from side to side looking for grazing opportunities for the thousands of head of cattle that they were moving westward, the course of the Oregon Trail changed from time to time. A late spring or early summer start also put a slow-moving wagon train at the mercy of the snows that came early to the Rocky Mountains.

✓ Reading Check

1. What were "Oregon societies"?

2. How many people, animals, and wagons might a wagon train consist of?

3. How were the red, white, and blue "prairie schooners" different from the Conestoga wagons of earlier years? How were they the same?

4. Briefly summarize a typical day on the Oregon Trail.

5. Name two difficulties the people in a wagon train might face if they left in May rather than April.

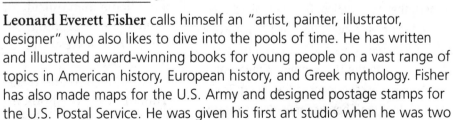

MEET THE *Writer*

Leonard Everett Fisher calls himself an "artist, painter, illustrator, designer" who also likes to dive into the pools of time. He has written and illustrated award-winning books for young people on a vast range of topics in American history, European history, and Greek mythology. Fisher has also made maps for the U.S. Army and designed postage stamps for the U.S. Postal Service. He was given his first art studio when he was two years old—a hall closet stocked with a table, crayons, pencils, and paper. "I was cozily in business," he recalls. He has been ever since.

In 1838–1839, U.S. soldiers drove thousands of Cherokee from their homes. The westward journey these American Indians took is today remembered as the Trail of Tears.

from The Trail of Tears
from *Cowboys & Indians*

by JOHN WADSWORTH

A very long time ago, Cherokee Elders climbed today's Clingman's Dome in North Carolina to receive counsel from the Creator. They shared these visions with their people who gathered in Kituwah, the spiritual center of the Cherokee Nation.

The Elders foretold the approach of their white brothers who would desire the Cherokee homeland. The Elders taught that no man could claim exclusive right to any place on earth. The Creator had prepared their new home in distant lands toward the setting sun.

I heard this account from a medicine man outside of Tahlequah, Oklahoma, the capital of the Western Band of Cherokee.

When I asked about the Trail of Tears, he shook his head with an expression of disgust.

"I wish people would just drop the whole thing," he

You Need to Know...

As white settlers moved into the western frontier, American Indians grew unwilling to surrender their lands. When colonists arrived in the Appalachian region in the 1760s, the Cherokee resisted. They even fought on the side of the British during the American Revolution. By the early 1800s, however, the Cherokee had begun to live more like the white colonists. Many Cherokee in Georgia were educated and owned their own farms or businesses. Soon, white Georgians began to resent the Indians. They asked the federal government to help move the Cherokee elsewhere. When the Cherokee realized that their time was running short, they took action. They organized their own nation and wrote their own constitution. In 1828, however, Georgia declared that Cherokee rights and laws did not exist. The Cherokee took their case to the U.S. Supreme Court—and won—but President Andrew Jackson ignored the ruling. The U.S. government decided that the Cherokee must leave Georgia and move west of the Mississippi. If they did not, they would be removed by force. Some Cherokee left. At least thirteen thousand stayed—and faced the consequences.

said. "The Trail of Tears is an embarrassment to everyone, both the Indians and the white man."

His family listened to the Elders and migrated west without incident. He is a full-blooded Cherokee, a prominent member of the Kituwah Society, whose membership preserves the oldest Cherokee traditions.

"If the Elders were obeyed, there would have been no Trail of Tears. It was never our tradition that we were given land for eternity. No man owns the earth. The people refused the protection of the old way. And the harder they struggled against the truth they were told, the warning they were given, the worse became their fate.

"The true decline of the Cherokee began when people took pride in their possessions. We once practiced communal ownership. If someone needed anything, there was always another willing to share. When the Cherokee caught the white man's sickness of private ownership, we stopped living as a united people."

A visit to Cherokee, North Carolina, offers a multi-dimensional[1] explanation for why the Elders' counsel was ignored. The land is majestic. When the prophecy was received, the Cherokee nation encompassed 40,000 square miles of paradise—surely, it seemed to them, enough land for all.

Today's Eastern Band of Cherokee, 11,000 in number, live on a verdant 56,000-acre fragment of their original home. Together with the Western Band's population of 200,000 centered in Oklahoma, the Cherokee comprise the second largest tribe in the United States.

The historical Trail of Tears officially begins in the Museum of the Cherokee Indian in Cherokee, North Carolina. Recently refurbished, the Museum introduces

John Elk III Photography

▲ Clingman's Dome, North Carolina.
❓ **What significant event occurred at this site?**

communal (kə•myōōn′əl): shared; related to a community.

prophecy (präf′ə•sē): a prediction about a future event believed to be given to a person by God.

encompassed (en•kum′pəsd): surrounded on all sides.

verdant (vʉr′dənt): green.

refurbished (ri•fʉr′bishd): fixed up; made new again.

---

1. **multidimensional** (mul′tē•də•men′shə•nəl): made up of many dimensions, parts, or aspects.

visitors to Cherokee culture through sophisticated multimedia presentations and establishes a strong foundation from which to <u>embark</u>.

To drive the 900-mile auto route of the Trail of Tears is a slow journey, guided by <u>random</u> brown signs bearing the blue <u>silhouette</u> of a wind-swept, fate-swept warrior. Most of the original routes of the Trail pass through private land, but many important sites are still accessible.

I met Freeman Owle, a Cherokee storyteller, in the New Echota historical site near Rome, Georgia. He taught me that Indians refer to the Trail of Tears as "The Trail Where They Cried," with the "They" referring to those who witnessed the Indians' passage.

"The Cherokee internalized[2] their emotions. We're told of mothers carrying their dead children for days, in

---

2. **internalized:** hid inside; did not show.

WOOLAROC MUSEUM, BARTLESVILLE, OKLAHOMA

▲ *The Trail of Tears*, by Robert Lindneux.

tearless, silent mourning. No, it was the people who observed us who cried. They cried for everyone."

Red Clay, Tennessee, where the Cherokee held council in 1832 after tribal gatherings were outlawed in Georgia, is today an <u>immaculately</u> maintained state park. The Western and Eastern Bands of Cherokee reunited here in 1984 for the first time since the removal and dedicated a memorial, "The Eternal Flame of the Cherokee Nation."

immaculately (i·mak′yə·lit·lē′): perfectly.

Champion of the Cherokee

John Ross was elected Principal Chief of the Cherokee Nation in 1828. Ross, who was one-eighth Cherokee, grew up in Georgia. A military man, Ross fought with General Andrew Jackson in the War of 1812. Ross understood white Americans as well as Native Americans, and he worked to prevent the removal of the Cherokee through legal action, petitions, and the press. In the end, Ross was unable to save his beloved nation. Although some Cherokee agreed to leave Georgia in exchange for a sum of money, Ross refused. In 1838, he unwillingly led his people to the Indian Territory. Ross's wife, Quatie, died on this mournful journey, along with thousands of others.

In Dayton, Tennessee, I met descendants of the Trail—Big Bear, Sweetie Bird, and Running Moon, the Claude Jenkins family of Triple J Ranch. Big Bear is a big man, with long reddish hair, of Scots-Irish complexion and, like his wife Sweetie Bird, of Indian heritage.

Big Bear <u>embodies</u> one of the most intriguing aspects of Cherokee culture. The Cherokee never associated tribal membership with bloodlines.[3] If anyone of another tribe, or another race, decided to live as a Cherokee, they were accepted as Cherokee. This explains how John Ross, one-eighth Cherokee by blood, could serve as Chief for over 30 years. This also explains Sam Houston's[4] Cherokee identity as The Raven and why Houston, adopted by a Cherokee family as a child, returned to Oklahoma to live and die as a Cherokee after retiring from public life.

embodies (em·bäd′ēz): represents; gives form to.

3. **bloodlines:** lines of connection through one's family; lineage.
4. **Sam Houston:** president of the Republic of Texas. Houston later served as a United States senator.

Big Bear's mother revealed his Indian heritage from her deathbed and explained her parents' warning to keep her Indian identity a secret "because life is never safe for Indians." During the Cherokee roundup, sympathetic white friends protected her grandparents by identifying them as relatives on an extended visit. Many mixed-bloods were saved this way, relying on their white skin to mask their Indian identity.

"I can understand why my mother kept her secret. Now that we have assumed our Indian identities, we feel what it's like to be outcasts. Most of our friends and even our families have turned away. We've raised Running Moon to be proud of being Indian. Being Indian is the foundation of our world."

Big Bear's family reminded me of something Freeman Owle said in New Echota. Owle, who also bears Scots-Irish features, stated that the American Indian is the only race on earth measured by blood content, "like Thoroughbred horses." Officially, if someone's blood isn't at least one-sixteenth Indian, they aren't allowed to be Indian.

✓ Reading Check

1. Long ago, what did the Cherokee Elders predict about the Cherokee homeland?

2. According to one Cherokee member of the Kituwah Society, why did the Trail of Tears occur?

3. According to a Cherokee storyteller, what do many Indians call the Trail of Tears? What does this name mean?

4. In the past, how did the Cherokee choose or identify their members?

5. Today, how does the U.S. government define an Indian?

To gain equal rights with men, women had to do more than just change the law: first they had to change people's minds. The following article describes how two courageous women took the first step toward women's rights.

The Birthplace of Women's Rights

from *Cobblestone*

by HOWARD MANSFIELD

Here's a page from history: a row of young women's pictures and under each one a plan for a lifetime of work—nurse, teacher, nurse, teacher, librarian, teacher, teacher. The world was just that limited for women. Only a handful of jobs were open to them. What year was this? 1890? 1920? 1945? No, it was more recent than that. The page of photos is from a high school yearbook for the graduating class of 1966.

A high school yearbook today would, of course, show women planning to be doctors, astronauts, architects, and many other things. But in the background of these individual dreams is almost one hundred fifty years of women protesting, petitioning, and organizing to win the vote and equality in the workplace. Much has changed since 1966, but much remains to be done.

You Need to Know...

The year 1848 marked a time of change and restlessness in the United States. The Mexican War had recently ended, adding a vast new territory to the United States map. Gold had been discovered in California. In France, slavery had been abolished, and debates over slavery in America were heating up. It was a good time for women to make a move. Without the vote, without the right to own property after marriage, without the right to hold office—or in many cases a job—many women began to feel resentful. Two of these women, Elizabeth Cady Stanton and Lucretia Mott, decided to do something about it. Both had been active abolitionists (people who want to do away with slavery) for years. In 1840, the women had attended the World Anti-Slavery Convention in London, but the male delegates of the convention had voted to exclude women. From this moment on, the two had pledged to work for women's rights. In this selection, you'll see how they did just that.

▲ Portrait of Elizabeth Cady Stanton.

inadvertently (in′ad•vʉrt′′nt•lē): accidentally; thoughtlessly.

On a summer morning in 1848, Elizabeth Cady Stanton pushed her nephew through a window so that he could unlock the church that would be the site of the first Women's Rights Convention. It was a slow start for what would become a national movement, but one that aptly symbolized the condition of women in America: locked out of jobs, locked out of education, locked out of the vote.

The setting was Seneca Falls, a small town in upstate New York. During the next three days, more than three hundred women and men discussed "the social, civil, and religious condition and rights of women."

Stanton and four other women had organized the convention. Sitting around a parlor table, trying to figure out what they could do, the women "felt as helpless and hopeless as if they had been suddenly asked to construct a steam engine," Stanton wrote in *The History of Woman Suffrage*. They took their cue from the antislavery and temperance movements that had made upstate New York a center of reform. Those movements used conventions, declarations, and petitions to dramatize their cause, and the women thought they could do the same.

The women placed a small notice in the *Seneca County Courier* and persuaded a minister to open his church to them. With that simple preparation, on the morning of July 19, the roads to the church were jammed with carriages and carts. A crowd was milling around outside when Stanton arrived to find the church inadvertently locked and the key missing.

The first day of the meeting was to be for women only, but Stanton and the others did not know how to ask the men who were present to leave. The convention had strong support from some men. In fact, the women asked a man to preside at the convention.

For Stanton, then thirty-two, it was only her second public appearance, and when she spoke, some spectators had trouble hearing her. In the convention's first order of business, she read the Declaration of Sentiments. The organizers had modeled it after the Declaration of

Independence. Males took the place of the <u>tyrannical</u> King George and were charged with denying women their rights and their pursuit of happiness. The document detailed the ways in which women were denied property rights, rights in marriage and divorce, and the vote. The Declaration of Sentiments was reread, amended, and signed by sixty-eight women and thirty-two men.

The next day, the convention met to debate a set of twelve resolutions. The third clearly stated that "woman is man's equal—was intended to be so by the Creator, and the highest good of the race demands that she be recognized as such."

That resolution passed unanimously, as did all the others, with the exception of the ninth resolution. It was extensively debated and only narrowly approved. The ninth resolution called for women to have the vote. Most of the convention's organizers had argued against including a call for woman suffrage. Lucretia Mott, then fifty-two and a noted abolitionist, feared that asking for the vote would make the meeting "look ridiculous." But Stanton argued that the vote was essential if women were to take their place in the world.

When the convention <u>adjourned</u> on the third day, members of the historic meeting had sat through eighteen hours of debate packed into three days.

The reaction from the nation was immediate. A Philadelphia newspaper said that outside of the role of wife and mother, women had no rights. "A woman is a nobody. A wife is everything. A pretty girl is equal to ten thousand men, and a mother is, next to God, all powerful."

tyrannical (tə·ran'i·kəl): cruel and unjust.

adjourned (ə·jʉrnd'): closed until a later time.

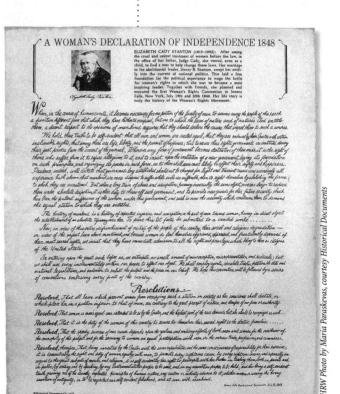

HRW Photo by Maria Paraskevas, courtesy Historical Documents

❓ **Why do you think the Declaration of Sentiments (above) was modeled after the Declaration of Independence?**

A newspaper in Albany, New York, claimed that giving women their rights was "all wrong" and that "the order of things established at the creation of mankind, and continued *six thousand years*, would be completely broken up."

A few papers were sympathetic. Frederick Douglass's *North Star* and Horace Greeley's *New York Tribune* offered some support. Douglass, a freed slave and leading abolitionist, had spoken at the convention and remained a supporter of women's rights.

The negative response surprised the convention's organizers. They "were neither sour old maids, childless women, nor divorced wives, as the newspapers declared," Stanton said. But rather they had "souls large enough to feel the wrongs of others."

strategy (strat′ə•jē): plan of action.

After Seneca Falls, the young movement was left without a specific strategy or direction. A convention followed two weeks later in Rochester, New York, and as newspaper attacks spread the word, conventions were held in small towns in Ohio, Indiana, Pennsylvania, and Massachusetts. Still, it would be twenty years before a national organization was created and seventy-two years before the Nineteenth Amendment granted women the right to vote.

In 1979, the town of Seneca Falls again made history when the National Women's Hall of Fame opened. It is the only national institution dedicated to honoring the

The Right Man

Bettmann/CORBIS

Frederick Douglass was a leading black abolitionist and orator. He was born into slavery in Maryland in about 1818. With the help of his master's wife, Douglass educated himself, and in 1838 fled to Massachusetts. There he began speaking out against slavery. He protested segregated seating on trains. He protested segregated churches, workplaces, and schools. In 1845, he published his autobiography, and he later founded an antislavery paper in New York. Having suffered injustice himself, Douglass was an avid supporter of women's rights. "I would give woman a vote," Douglass writes, ". . . precisely as I insisted upon giving the colored man the right to vote; in order that she shall have the same motives for making herself a useful citizen. . . ."

achievements of American women. Currently, one hundred seven women are honored there. Two new women are inducted each July to <u>commemorate</u> the anniversary of the first Women's Rights Convention.

commemorate (kə·mem′ə·rāt): to remember with honor.

Some of the more famous women featured are Susan B. Anthony, Helen Keller, Eleanor Roosevelt, and Amelia Earhart. Other women who are not as well-known also are honored. These include Juliette Low, founder of the Girl Scouts; artist Mary Cassatt; and Belva Lockwood, the first woman to run for president (1884).

✓ Reading Check

1. What event took place on July 19, 1848, in Seneca Falls, New York?

2. What issues did the Declaration of Sentiments deal with?

3. What did the ninth resolution call for? Why was it debated?

4. How did most newspapers respond to the convention? Give an example.

5. What happened in 1979 in Seneca Falls?

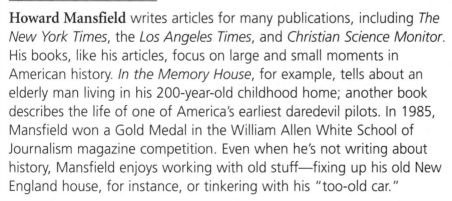

MEET THE *Writer*

Howard Mansfield writes articles for many publications, including *The New York Times*, the *Los Angeles Times*, and *Christian Science Monitor*. His books, like his articles, focus on large and small moments in American history. *In the Memory House*, for example, tells about an elderly man living in his 200-year-old childhood home; another book describes the life of one of America's earliest daredevil pilots. In 1985, Mansfield won a Gold Medal in the William Allen White School of Journalism magazine competition. Even when he's not writing about history, Mansfield enjoys working with old stuff—fixing up his old New England house, for instance, or tinkering with his "too-old car."

For African Americans in the nineteenth century, trying to get an education was a difficult undertaking. Even free blacks in the north encountered persecution and limited opportunities. The following article describes how Quakers helped create educational opportunities for African Americans.

A Quaker Commitment to Education

from *Cobblestone*

by JUDITH FOSTER GEARY

abolition (ab'ə•lish'ən): the doing away with something.

Members of the Religious Society of Friends (Quakers) believe that there is something of God in everyone. Because of this belief, Quakers have long worked for equal opportunity for all people. They have led and supported movements for the abolition of slavery and the establishment of education for everyone.

In the early 1700s, Quaker schools in Pennsylvania were often dame schools, with one person (usually a woman) teaching several children in her home. These schools accepted all children regardless of their race or gender. In 1750, Anthony Benezet began teaching several African American students in his Philadelphia home. By 1764, Quakers were supporting a school for

You Need to Know...

The Religious Society of Friends was formed in 1647 by an Englishman named George Fox. The Quakers, as they came to be known, believed that all people carried a divine spark within them. They also believed that people could communicate directly with God, without the help of priests or organized churches. This made many English people uncomfortable. According to the Church of England, only priests could interpret and preach the Word of God. In 1681, though, after years of persecution in England, the Quakers were given a second chance. William Penn, an outspoken Quaker who had been imprisoned several times, was granted a piece of land in the colonies as repayment for a debt. Penn used the land to establish a Quaker colony. Since that time, the Quakers have worked to bring peace and equality to American society. They have opposed war, racism, and the poor treatment of prisoners. They have helped improve conditions in mental hospitals. As you will read in this selection, they have been an important force for the education of all Americans.

African American students in Alexandria, Virginia. That same year, at Benezet's urging, Philadelphia opened its first free African American school, one of seven such schools by 1797.

Quakers in other states also supported education for African Americans. In North Carolina, they opened schools as early as the 1770s. In 1821, Levi Coffin, later known as the "President of the Underground Railroad," and his brother Vestal operated a Sabbath school in Guilford County, North Carolina. It met weekly on the Sabbath (Sunday) and taught slaves to read from the Bible.

In 1831, a slave named Nat Turner plotted a revolt in Virginia. After killing the family that owned him, Turner and his rebellious band went on to kill more than fifty white people. After their quick capture, laws in the South became much more restrictive. This ended for a time the Quakers' open support of education for southern African Americans. However, education for freedmen, free African Americans, and escaped slaves continued wherever the opportunity was found.

The South was not the only place where some people violently opposed the education of African Americans. In 1831, Prudence Crandall, the twenty-eight-year-old daughter of a local Quaker family, opened a boarding school for girls in Canterbury, Connecticut. The leading families of the town welcomed her into their homes and sent their daughters to her school. When Sarah Harris, a seventeen-year-old girl of mixed white, Native American, and African American descent, asked to attend day classes at the school, Crandall agreed.

The parents of the other students threatened to withdraw their daughters if Harris was not removed from the school. Crandall contacted other Quakers and abolitionists of other faiths and gathered financial and moral support for an African American school. In 1833, she sent the white girls home and opened a school for "young ladies and little misses of color."

Crandall's troubles did not end with the establishment of the new school. She and her sixteen students were

The Granger Collection, New York

▲ Prudence Crandall.

restrictive (ri·strik′tiv): limiting.

financial (fī·nan′shəl): relating to money.

Walk the Walk, Talk the Talk

In 1758, a Quaker named John Woolman protested slavery at the yearly Quaker meeting in Philadelphia. This topic was not new to Quaker meetings. Nearly 20 years earlier, Woolman had listened to Benjamin Lay, a spirited elderly man, speak out against slavery. Inspired, Woolman had begun traveling on foot throughout the colonies, preaching against slavery. Finally, at the 1758 meeting, his efforts bore fruit. There, the Quakers resolved to stop owning or selling slaves—the first such resolution in the colonies. Woolman continued to work for African American rights until his death in 1772. For the last ten years of his life, Woolman wore only white—a protest against the slave labor that produced the dye used in clothing.

petitions (pə•tish'ənz): formal requests.

legacy (leg'ə•sē): something passed down from one person or group to the next.

openly harassed. They were sometimes attacked by boys throwing manure chips. Crandall's well was filled with manure and dirty hay from a stable, and her neighbors refused to give her drinking water. A law was passed in response to the petitions of Crandall's "neighbors" who hoped to get rid of her school using the fact that some of her students came from other states. She was arrested three times for willfully and knowingly helping African Americans who were not inhabitants of the state of Connecticut.

Then, in September 1834, the school was attacked in the middle of the night by people carrying clubs and iron bars. Rather than put her students in further danger, Crandall closed the school. But her legacy was not lost. Sarah Harris raised two daughters who became schoolteachers, and Crandall's example changed many minds about education for African Americans.

African Americans themselves became educators, too. In 1837, Orthodox Quakers in Philadelphia founded the Institute for Colored Youth, which evolved into today's Cheyney University of Pennsylvania. It was first intended as a trade school but became an important center for classical education and teacher training. Fanny Jackson Coppin, a principal of the school, was one of the first African American women to obtain a full college degree (from Oberlin College in Ohio), as was her assistant, Mary Jane Patterson. In fact, the faculty of the school were all African Americans.

Throughout the Civil War and Reconstruction, Quakers continued to help displaced African Americans prepare for their new lives. The Penn School, part of the Port Royal Experiment, was founded in 1862 as a refuge and school for escaped slaves on an island off the South Carolina coast. It continues today as an African American cultural center.

Many of the Quaker-founded schools became part of state educational systems. Others operated for only a brief time but met important short-term needs. By the 1920s, the leadership and formal support of most of these schools passed into the hands of African Americans.

Library of Congress, Historic American Buildings Survey

▲ The building which housed Prudence Crandall's school for African American girls still stands today.

✓ Reading Check

1. What do Quakers believe? How does this belief affect Quakers' work in society?

2. How did Quakers provide educational opportunities for African Americans in the 1700s?

3. Nat Turner's rebellion resulted in two changes that were harmful to African Americans. What were these two changes?

4. Name two events that led to the closing of Prudence Crandall's school.

5. What was the Penn School?

MEET THE *Writer*

Judith Foster Geary writes literature for young adults and teaches at Appalachian State University in North Carolina. She is also a member of the Society of Friends and attends Quaker meetings near her home.

In the early 1840s, Texas had recently gained its independence. While Mexico refused to acknowledge the new Republic of Texas, the United States anxiously desired to add Texas (and California) to the Union. The following selection tells what happened next in this story of conflict.

from The Birth of Modern Mexico

from *The Mexican Americans*

by JULIE CATALANO

assimilated (ə•sim′ə•lāt′id): brought into; absorbed.

lured (lo͞ord): attracted; tempted.

collage (kə•läzh′): a grouping of apparently unrelated parts.

During Mexico's fight for independence, the Anglo presence in Mexican territory had grown considerably. For example, Kentucky mountain men had traveled west to take advantage of the rich trapping trade. They also played a primary role in the development of the major trade routes. Many Anglo trailblazers set their sights on California. They became Mexican citizens, married into California's prominent families, and assimilated into Mexican society. In the 1840s, news of California's wealth and magnificence lured increasing numbers of Americans from the East Coast. California soon became the focus of the United States's belief in its Manifest Destiny—that it was meant to possess the continent from shore to shore. This penetration of Mexican territory created a collage of diverse cultures. For the most part the

You Need to Know...

By the early 1800s, the United States was growing stronger and larger, but tensions ran high between the eager young nation and its southern neighbor, Mexico. Mexico had spent the years between 1810 and 1821 fighting for its own independence from Spain. During this time, it had paid little attention to its northern territories—those that bordered the United States. Meanwhile, Anglo American settlers had begun to move into these areas. Many cultural differences separated these settlers from the Mexican citizens who lived there. Still, the white population continued to grow. By 1830 in Texas, Anglo Americans outnumbered Mexicans 6 to 1. Soon Texas began to demand its independence from Mexico. The Mexican leaders, however, ignored these demands. In 1835, Texas revolted against Mexican rule, and by spring 1836 had declared victory. It was now an independent republic.

blending process was peaceful until a new area of conflict arose.

By the early 19th century, hostility between abolitionists and slave owners divided the United States. The South and the North were both eager to bring like-minded new states into the Union, thereby tipping the scale in their favor. The pro-slavery South looked to the independent Republic of Texas, where, two decades earlier, slavery had been instituted in defiance of Mexican law. When the U.S. House of Representatives offered the Republic of Texas statehood in 1845, Texas accepted. The Mexicans who stayed in the republic when it joined the Union became the first sizable group of Mexicans living in the United States.

▲ *On the Way to a Ball*, by Theodore Gentilz. **❓ What cultural traditions did the new Mexican Americans contribute to the United States?**

The Spoils of War

Mexico refused to acknowledge Texas's U.S. statehood; it had never even <u>ratified</u> the treaty that recognized Texas's independence. Still, the Mexican government did not think that losing the territory was reason enough to go to war. But then American settlers in Mexican-controlled California staged an armed bid for independence—the Bear Flag Revolt of 1846. This new territorial skirmish <u>aggravated</u> the tensions between the neighboring countries. Tension between the two nations was worsened by the fact that the United States wanted to acquire California and the Southwest. The U.S. government tried several times to buy this territory from Mexico, but Mexico refused to sell. In 1846, U.S. president James Polk used a minor border skirmish as an excuse to declare war upon Mexico, knowing that what Mexico had refused to sell could be seized by force of arms.

The Mexican War was bitter but short. It ended in 1848 with the Treaty of Guadalupe Hidalgo, under which Mexico surrendered the present-day states of California, Nevada, New Mexico, Arizona, and parts of Utah and

ratified (rat′ə·fīd): approved.

aggravated (ag′rə·vāt′id): made worse.

Bettmann/CORBIS

▲ The frontiersmen of the 1800s learned how to herd cattle from the Mexican cowboys, or *vaqueros* (vä•ker′ōs), who had lived and ranched in the region for years.

Colorado to the United States. The treaty was followed in 1853 by the Gadsden Purchase, which gave the United States the southern strips of Arizona and New Mexico, drawing the border between the United States and Mexico where it remains today. The United States government assumed responsibility for the 75,000 or so Mexicans living in its new territory, giving them the choice of becoming U.S. citizens or returning to Mexico. The 80 percent who stayed became the first Mexican Americans.

✓ Reading Check

1. What was "Manifest Destiny"?

2. Why did the South want to bring Texas into the Union?

3. List three events that led to the Mexican War.

4. When did the Mexican War end? What was the result of the war?

5. What became of the Mexicans who lived in the new U.S. territories?

MEET THE *Writer*

Julie Catalano lives in San Antonio, Texas. She has written a variety of newspaper and magazine articles on culture, politics, and the arts.

According to the newspapers back East, the discovery of gold in California meant opportunity for anyone with a pick or a pan—or did it? Find out in the following selection about Chinese immigrants during the gold rush.

Gold Mountain

from *The Gold Rush*

by LIZA KETCHUM

The Chinese left few written records of their life in California, so we don't know for certain how news of the gold rush traveled across the Pacific. It may have been spread by a Cantonese miner named Chum Ming, who struck it rich at Sutter's mill and wrote home to tell his relatives about his good fortune.

In 1848, census figures listed only three nameless Chinese as California residents. Two years after Chum Ming's success, more than four hundred Chinese had made the long journey to the land the Cantonese called Gum San, or Gold Mountain. By 1852, about twenty thousand Chinese men were living in the state, including two thousand who had arrived in San Francisco in a single day.

Most Chinese immigrants were young men fleeing terrible poverty. They did not intend to stay in California, and most had promised their families they would return as soon as they had made their fortune.

census (sen′səs): an official count of people.

You Need to Know...

In 1848—the year after California became an American territory—a man named James Marshall found gold near the mill of his business partner, John Sutter. Although Sutter tried to keep the discovery a secret, word leaked out. Soon, prospectors from all over California turned up near Sutter's land bearing baskets and frying pans. Suddenly, the gold rush was on. Thousands traveled west by way of the Oregon-California Trail. Others chose to sail around the tip of South America. Indeed, people from all over the world went racing to California—Germans, English, Irish, and French; Mexicans and Chileans; Chinese, Australians, Italians, and Swedes. In many mining camps, half or more of the residents were foreign-born. Sometimes this mix of cultures was joyful and positive, marked by celebrations open to all. Yet often this "melting pot" rose to a boil, and some ethnic groups suffered violence and discrimination.

famines (fam′inz): widespread shortages of food.

One young dreamer was a sixteen-year-old named Lee Chew. Chew grew up in the province of Canton, China, in a house made of blue brick. Although <u>famines</u> and wars had torn his country apart, the Lee family lived comfortably on their small farm. By the time he was ten, Lee Chew was working in his father's fields. Each day, he visited his grandfather, who told him stories about the terrible red-haired *fan qui*, or foreign devils, in America.

When Lee Chew turned sixteen, a neighbor who had emigrated to America as a poor young man suddenly returned home with full pockets. He took "ground as large as four city blocks and made a paradise of it." The neighbor invited the whole town to a banquet at his new palace, where he served a hundred roasted pigs and "such an abundance of dainties that our villagers even now lick their fingers when they think of it."

Lee Chew made up his mind. In spite of his grandfather's warnings, he would take a ship to Gum San. At first, his parents protested, but finally Chew's father gave his son his blessing and sent him off with one hundred dollars—a small fortune in those days—which paid for his passage on a steamer and left him fifty dollars to spend when he reached San Francisco.

San Francisco Public Library

▲ Unknown Chinese immigrant working in San Francisco, 1850s. **⁇ Why did many Chinese immigrants come to California?**

Most Chinese crossed the Pacific in small boats, crammed below deck in dark cabins smelling of sweat and vomit, their bunks piled up "like stacks of coffins in a death house." The food was so bad and the seas so rough that one immigrant carved these words on the wall of Angel Island when he arrived: "I ate wind and tasted waves for more than twenty days." Others, like Lee Chew, were "afraid to eat the provisions[1] of the barbarians." Epidemics swept through the holds of the ships. Some men, who had been tricked into emigrating, were

---

1. **provisions:** supplies for a journey.

chained to the boats and beaten when they tried to escape. A few threw themselves into the sea in despair.

Those who survived staggered off the ships four to eight weeks later, carrying their few belongings in double-ended baskets slung across their shoulders, their long black queues (pronounced kyo͞oz), or single braids, hanging to their waists, their faces hidden under broad-brimmed hats.

Americans and Europeans were fascinated by the men they called the Celestials. They welcomed the early Chinese ships, eager to trade gold dust for precious goods on board: dried fruit, candied ginger, lumber, brocaded[2] silks—even houses, shipped in pieces.

Some Chinese found "Gold Mountain" right in San Francisco and never went to the mines. They took jobs in small restaurants with the Chinese characters ENTER AND DEPART IN PEACE written on flags over the doors. They sold vegetables or worked in gambling dens. Many, like Lee Chew, opened laundries.

In China, washing clothes was considered women's work, but a man in America could start a laundry without too much money, even if he didn't speak English. Young Lee Chew's first job was working for an American

---

2. **brocaded:** stitched with an elaborate, raised design.

Courtesy of the Bancroft Library

▲ Chinese grocery store in San Francisco.

More Dungarees, Please

People from all over the world discovered new ways to make money during the gold rush. A man named Levi Strauss, for example, had recently come to America from Germany. After helping his brothers run their dry goods business in New York for several years, Strauss headed for California. There, he planned to make tents for miners out of heavy canvas. When he met a miner who needed some sturdy pants, Strauss crafted him a pair using the thick material, and presto—Strauss had "struck gold." His jeans are still in demand all over the world.

---

diverted (də•vʉrt'id): turned in a different direction.

prosperous (präs'pər•əs): yielding wealth.

woman and her family. She taught him how to wash and iron the family's clothes, sent him to school to learn English, and paid him $3.50 a week. Even though Lee Chew sent money home to his parents, he saved most of his earnings. In two years, he was able to open his own hand laundry.

Most Chinese arrivals, though, headed straight for the diggings, where they were an instant curiosity. Many Americans and Europeans had never encountered Asian people. The artist J.D. Borthwick was particularly interested in the Chinese he met in the mines. Coming on one group at supper time, he sketched the men as they cooked dinner and braided each other's queues. "They squatted on the rocks in groups of eight or ten round a number of curious little black pots and dishes, from which they helped themselves with their chopsticks," Borthwick wrote. The Chinese welcomed him warmly, offering to share their meal, but he was too nervous about their unusual food to accept.

Chinese miners were usually organized into companies of fifty or more men. They used a device known as a Chinese waterwheel, a series of buckets operated by pulleys. They diverted the water in the streams with wing dams, which cut the stream in half, leaving the rocky bottom exposed and dry for digging. Working long hours, seven days a week, they often extracted gold from places where less determined prospectors had given up. Their first prosperous claim, on Wood's Creek, became known as the Chinese Diggings.

Many Chinese miners took their shares of gold to jewelers, where it was made into ornaments and belts. These could be stitched into clothing and hidden from American customs agents, so they wouldn't have to pay a duty on their earnings when they returned to China.

Before long, Chinese success in the diggings made other miners angry. Whenever they heard about a new Chinese strike, jealous American and European miners drove the Chinese out. They stoned them, burned their houses, broke up their equipment, hacked off their queues, and

▲ California gold miners.

sometimes murdered them, knowing they wouldn't be punished. "White men are not usually hanged for killing Chinamen," the *San Francisco Bulletin* stated casually.

Violence against the Chinese also broke out in San Francisco. Children stoned Chinese workers, broke their bamboo baskets, and <u>taunted</u> them while their parents looked the other way. Restaurant owners fired their Chinese cooks or kept their identity a secret. People made fun of the Chinese for their loose clothing, their wooden shoes, and their habit of drinking tea. (If Americans had boiled their water as the Chinese did, they could have avoided dysentery.[3]) Even some Native Americans, who were treated as badly as the Chinese, looked down on the arrivals from Asia. When someone was told he "didn't have a Chinaman's chance," it meant his situation was hopeless.

Lee Chew's experience was similar to that of many other immigrants to Gum San. His laundry customers cheated him and stole bundles of clothing. When he became a merchant, he decided that Americans "treat you as a friend while you are prosperous, but if you have a misfor-

taunted (tônt′id): ridiculed, made fun of.

---

3. dysentery (dis′ən•ter′ē): an illness in the intestines.

tune, they don't know you." Every day, he put up with insults. Even though he realized that not all Americans were "foreign devils," he insisted, until the end of his life, that "their treatment of us is outrageous."

Unfortunately the Chinese were not the only people being hounded by Americans. By the early 1850s, an undeclared, ugly war against most foreigners was breaking out all over California.

✓ Reading Check

1. What persuaded Lee Chew to set out for "Gold Mountain"?

2. Briefly describe what the journey to America was like for most Chinese.

3. Name four ways many Chinese made money in California.

4. Give two examples of violence or injustice suffered by the Chinese in California.

5. What did Lee Chew conclude from his experience in America?

MEET THE *Writer*

When she was in second grade, **Liza Ketchum** began writing "tiny, palm-sized books about a girl who escaped all her troubles by riding . . . a fleet-footed white stallion." Since then she has earned two college degrees, founded a school in Vermont, taught college courses and writing workshops, and published over a dozen books for children and young adults. Several of her books have won awards. *West Against the Wind*, the story of a young pioneer girl's cross-country journey, was honored by the Virginia Library Association in 1988. *Fire in the Heart*, a companion book, was named best young adult novel for 1990 by the American Library Association.

Cross-Curricular ACTIVITIES

■ ART/LANGUAGE ARTS

A Game of Chance Reread "Into the Unknown: The Incredible Adventures of Lewis and Clark" (page 81) making notes about where Lewis and Clark's expedition began and ended and what course it followed. Then, alone or with a partner, create a board game based on the expedition. In the game, use details from the selection that describe the journey, such as obstacles the travelers encountered, supplies they needed, the weather and landscape they passed through, and forms of transportation they used. Write a set of rules for the game and give it a name. Then invite another student or pair of students to play the game with you.

■ SCIENCE/GEOGRAPHY

Weather Watchers Use a U.S. map, the selection "from *The Oregon Trail*" (page 87) and history books to chart the course of the Oregon Trail. Where did it begin? What regions of the United States did it pass through? Where did it end? How long did it take most pioneers to make the journey? Then, in an almanac or on the Internet, look for information that tells about the climate of each region covered by the trail. What are the average temperatures for each month of the year? What kinds of weather are common during each month? Finally, create a weather guide for the Oregon Trail. Your guide should be designed for pioneers who begin their journey in April. The guide can take any form you wish, but it should include information that will help the pioneers predict the kinds of weather they are likely to encounter.

■ HISTORY/ART

Landscapes of Lament Locate a map that shows where the Trail of Tears began and ended. Then look in books and magazines to find photographs of the landscape in these parts of the country. Next, use watercolors or colored pencils to create a series of four to five artworks. Your pictures should show some of the different types of landscape the Native Americans saw as they made their way from the southeastern United States toward the Indian Territory. Finally, imagine that you are an American Indian on the Trail. Write a short poem or series of statements to accompany the artworks. Tell how each landscape makes you feel as you pass through it. Does it deepen your anger and sorrow, or does it provide a sense of hope?

■ LANGUAGE ARTS

Talk of the Town You are a citizen of Canterbury, Connecticut, in the year 1831. Soon after Prudence Crandall opens her boarding school for girls, you buy a newspaper at the town store. On the back page of the paper, you read a letter to the editor that expresses an opinion about the school. Write this letter. Then, compose a response in which you express a different opinion. With a group of classmates, create two editorial pages, one containing the first set of letters and the other containing the responses. If possible, use a computer to help make your newspaper pages look real and old-fashioned. Include dates and the title of the newspaper at the top of each page.

READ ON: FOR INDEPENDENT READING

■ NONFICTION

Anthony Burns: The Defeat and Triumph of a Fugitive Slave by Virginia Hamilton (Laureleaf, 1993). In 1854, in Boston, a young man was arrested for stealing. He knew he'd never stolen anything in his life—except himself. The trial of Anthony Burns caused a storm of controversy, as Boston's radical abolitionists clashed with those determined to enforce the federal fugitive slave laws.

The Great American Gold Rush by Rhoda Blumberg (Bradbury Press, 1989). *Want to buy a jar of gold digger's grease, guaranteed? Just rub it all over yourself, roll down a hill, and you'll be covered in gold—and nothing else!* In 1849, gold fever could make folks believe just about anything. This Orbis Pictus Honor book brings back all the amazing characters who wanted to get rich quick, from Rufus Porter and his "arrowproof aerial locomotive" to a poor peddler who sewed trousers out of tent canvas and made Levi Strauss a household name.

An Indian Winter by Russell Freedman (Holiday House, 1992). In 1833, the German prince Maximilian and a young Swiss artist named Karl Bodmer set out across the northern plains to spend the winter with the native Mandans and Hidatsas. The words of Maximilian's journals combine with Bodmer's drawings and paintings to make an unforgettable picture of a people whom, just four years later, smallpox would nearly destroy.

Sojourner Truth: Ain't I a Woman? by Patricia C. McKissack and Fredrick McKissack (Scholastic, 1992). She was a mother, a preacher, an abolitionist, and an activist for women's rights. Enslaved for the first twenty-eight years of her life,

Sojourner Truth never learned to read and write. When she spoke, though, *everyone* listened, from Frederick Douglass to Harriet Beecher Stowe to Susan B. Anthony.

■ FICTION

The Birchbark House by Louise Erdrich (Hyperion Books, 1999). In this best-selling writer's first book for young people, Erdrich delves into her own Ojibwa roots. Learn what it was like to live on an island in Lake Superior in 1847, as seen through the eyes of a girl named Omakayas, or Little Frog.

A Gathering of Days: A New England Girl's Journal, 1830-1832 by Joan W. Blos (Charles Scribner's Sons, 1979). Blos won the Newbery Medal for this novel of early American farm life, written in the form of the diary of a fourteen-year-old girl. Join Catherine in her adventures, from sugaring and "breaking out" to a startling encounter with a runaway slave.

Lyddie by Katherine Paterson (Lodestar Books, 1991). Lyddie is grateful to have a job, even though she is working long hours for little pay in the noisy, dust-filled cloth factories of Lowell, Massachusetts. Lyddie makes friends with a dangerous radical named Diana. Dare she sign Diana's petition and risk all she's struggled for?

The Slave Dancer by Paula Fox (Bradbury Press, 1973). One moment, Jessie is strolling along the docks of New Orleans, earning pennies as usual by playing his fife. The next thing he knows, he's been kidnapped onto a slave ship, where the captain commands him to make music amidst the horror. What is Jessie to do? Another Newbery Medal winner.

CHAPTER 4
A Nation Divided
The Civil War and Reconstruction   1860–1876

The War Begins

Everyone was in the mood for a party the day the Union army marched into Virginia to face the Confederates. Hundreds of civilians loaded up their carriages with picnic hampers and drove from Washington to Manassas Junction to watch the battle. Some brought bottles of champagne.

By 4 P.M. the horrified civilians had fled, leaving the meadow littered with parasols and shawls. A thousand men lay dead, and the Union army was in full retreat. Over 600,000 more men would die before the Civil War was to end.

© Bettmann/CORBIS

▲ These soldiers are but a few of the thousands who died during the Civil War.

Master of Disguise

Union spy Frank Thompson was a master of disguise. Dressed as "Ned," a slave, or "Bridget," an Irish cake-and-pie peddler, he would slip behind enemy lines and gather information. Once, he darkened his face with silver nitrate and dressed as an African American cook so that he could spy on Confederate officers at supper and steal some of their papers. Those papers turned out to be a plan to capture Washington, D.C.

In 1863, Thompson came down with malaria, but instead of seeing the doctor, he deserted. He was afraid a medical exam would reveal who he *really* was—a young woman from Flint, Michigan, named Sara Emma E. Edmonds!

VOCABULARY MATTERS

Although the nation was tragically divided by the Civil War, it was united by words. *Confederate* and *Union* both mean much the same thing: "a group joined together in a league or alliance; a coming together to form a whole." The idea of joining together for a common goal is an old one—*confederate* and *union* have been in our language for over five hundred years.

"Whenever I hear anyone arguing for slavery, I feel a strong impulse to see it tried on him personally."

—Abraham Lincoln

"Is this the little woman who made this great war?"

—Abraham Lincoln to Harriet Beecher Stowe, author of *Uncle Tom's Cabin,* the powerful novel that brought attention to the evils of slavery, from Annie Fields, *Life and Letters of Harriet Beecher Stowe* (1898)

The Granger Collection, New York

▲ The 100,000th copy of *Uncle Tom's Cabin.*

When Edmonds recovered, she returned to help the Union army under her own name, as a nurse. No one ever saw Frank Thompson again. But twenty years later, Edmonds shared her secret with Union officers who had known her as a spy. Just like the Confederates, they'd never suspected a thing.

This Land Is Your Land; This Land Is My Land

In the first months of the Civil War, U.S. gunboats sailed into the Georgia and South Carolina Sea Islands and opened fire on Confederate forts. The island's plantation owners fled to the mainland, leaving behind acres of cotton fields—and the 15,000 slaves who had worked those fields.

Southern Historical Collection, Wilson Library, of the Manuscripts Department, University of North Carolina, Chapel Hill. From the Penn School Collection.

▲ Children of newly freed slaves on St. Helena Island attended Sea Island School.

The Union army told the newly freed slaves that the abandoned land was now theirs, so they divided it up and set to work. The freed slaves built houses, planted food, and sent their children to school.

After the war the plantation owners sent lawyers to Washington, D.C., demanding that their land be returned to them. They got it—all of it. The former slaves who had worked the land were given nothing. When they tried to defend their homes, the U.S. Army came to force them out. They had nowhere to go. Most had to go back to work in the white landowners' fields as barely paid sharecroppers—enslaved again, on the land that for a few short years had been their own.

Who feeds and clothes the army? Today, the army itself, but during the Civil War, volunteers—many of whom were women—supplied the armies. Who were they, and what did they do? Read on to find out about the many contributions made by women during the Civil War.

Supplying the Armies

from *A Separate Battle: Women and the Civil War*

by INA CHANG

As troops in both the North and South drilled[1] endlessly, waiting for the action to begin, thousands of women were busy outfitting volunteers for the army. Each soldier would need a uniform, as well as bedding, socks, and whatever few comforts of home he could carry on his back. Women went to work at a <u>frenzied</u> rate weaving, cutting, and sewing. Whole companies were completely outfitted by local women, with everything from clothing to tents to battle flags.

Neither the troops nor those at home realized what camp life would be like. Women were sending soldiers off with such <u>impractical</u> items as down pillows and fancy quilts with lines of poetry lovingly embroidered on them. Encouraged by men who wanted to look dashing as they departed for war, the

frenzied (fren′zēd): frantic; in a hurried manner.

impractical (im·prak′ti·kəl): not suitable or useful.

You Need to Know...

Much of the work of the Civil War went on behind the scenes. Both sides, North and South, depended on volunteers to serve as soldiers. They also relied on volunteers to work as nurses, suppliers, cooks, trainers, and even doctors. Many of these volunteers were women.

Even with the help of so many volunteers, the war effort was beset with problems. In the mid-1800s, people's knowledge of medicine and machines was still quite limited. In battlefield hospitals, medical equipment was rarely cleaned properly, and thousands of soldiers perished from infection and contagious illnesses. Transportation—of food, supplies, and troops—was slow and unreliable. Communication was poor, too, which made getting needed supplies difficult. Still, the women of America carried on, giving all they had to help turn the wheels of war.

---

1. **drilled** (drild): trained as a group.

ornate (ôr•nāt′): excessively showy or decorated.

array (ə•rā′): display; collection.

efficiency (e•fish′ən•sē): capability to do something with the least amount of effort and waste.

pooled (pōŏld): brought together for a common goal.

women created a hodgepodge[2] of ornate "uniforms." In New Orleans, brightly colored fabrics and loud patterns were preferred. One woman described the outfits as "the most bewildering combination of brilliant, intense reds, greens, yellows, and blues in big flowers." A Louisiana company was fitted out in baggy scarlet trousers with wide blue sashes, blue shirts, and jackets trimmed with lace. Northern soldiers were sent off in equally showy costumes, some featuring broad-brimmed hats with feathers and baggy pantaloons.[3]

Among the items that women made in a wide array of colors was a cotton headdress called a havelock. Invented by a British general stationed in India, the havelock was a cap with a piece of cloth that hung down in back and shaded the neck. A northern newspaper had suggested that havelocks were just the thing to protect Union soldiers from the unfamiliar, glaring heat of the southern sun.

"Havelocks were turned out by the thousands," one woman recalled, "of all patterns and sizes, and of every conceivable material." But when a group of northern women visited the Nineteenth Illinois Regiment in camp, they found the havelocks being used as bandages, nightcaps, and everything but what they were intended for. The word went out, and havelock production stopped just as suddenly as it had begun.

Women learned from their errors, and in time they were producing supplies with factory-like efficiency. "The amount of *work* we have accomplished is a wonder to ourselves, to say nothing of the world," a South Carolina woman remarked in 1861. Church groups and casual sewing circles were transformed into soldiers' aid societies. Foot-treadle[4] sewing machines, invented in 1849, were in great demand, and women pooled their money to buy them. Production increased dramatically: A shirt that took two days to sew by hand took only about an hour by machine.

Women brought their knitting everywhere. "I do not know when I have seen a woman without knitting in her

---

2. **hodgepodge** (häj′päj′): mixed-up collection.
3. **pantaloons** (pan′tə•lōōnz′): trousers.
4. **treadle** (tred″l): pedal.

hand," said Mary Chesnut of South Carolina, whose husband was a Confederate officer. " 'Socks for the soldiers' is the cry. . . . It gives a quaint[5] look, the twinkling of needles, and the everlasting sock dangling."

As the shirts and blankets piled up, it was not always clear where they should be sent. Neither army had an organized supply system, so packages were often delivered to the wrong place, or arrived after the troops had moved on.

Dr. Elizabeth Blackwell of New York, the first woman in the United States to earn a medical degree, realized early on that the Union Army needed a system for distributing its supplies. She organized thousands of women in New York City in April 1861 into a volunteer organization called the Women's Central Association of Relief, or WCAR. They planned to collect and distribute donations of all kinds from citizens, including medical supplies, and they set up a training course for nurses, taught by Dr. Blackwell.

But the WCAR had no official status, and people soon began pressuring Union leaders to create an official organization to handle supplies and manage army hospitals. The U.S. Army Medical Bureau certainly wasn't up to the job; at the start of the war, the bureau employed only

status (stat′əs): rank; position.

5. **quaint** (kwānt): old-fashioned.

A Stitch Without a Hitch

Isaac Singer is often given credit for inventing the sewing machine. In fact, Singer was only one of many inventors who helped turn a popular idea into a practical reality. Englishman Thomas Saint, for example, created a machine for sewing leather in 1790, and in 1846, Elias Howe patented the first American version of the machine. However, these early machines were awkward, often proving more trouble than they were worth. Singer's machine, patented in 1851, was the first that really worked. Unlike the others, it fed cloth through continuously. Singer, known for his self-centeredness and disregard for others, died a wealthy man. Strangely enough, though, his machine went on to improve the lives of many people who were poor.

▲ Daguerreotype portrait of a woman working at a sewing machine. ❓ **In what other ways did women assist the war effort?**

The Granger Collection, New York

▲ Nurses and officers of the U.S. Sanitary Commission at Fredericksburg, Virginia. ❓ **Why was the Sanitary Commission created?**

twenty-eight surgeons, had no general hospital, and lacked a system for collecting or transporting supplies.

In July 1861, the Union government established the U.S. Sanitary Commission. The WCAR became a major branch of the commission, and soon seven thousand local soldiers' aid societies joined the network. Headed by men but staffed mainly by women volunteers, the commission took charge of setting up supply stations and hospitals, hiring nurses, and collecting donations. It sent inspectors to Union hospitals and taught troops in camp how to cook their food properly and prevent the spread of disease.

Commission volunteers sorted and mailed donations and made sure people knew what supplies were needed. They also educated citizens about what not to send. At the outset of the war, women had sent butter, pies, crates of fresh eggs, and even fried chicken to the commission

> **[The U.S. Sanitary Commission] sent inspectors to Union hospitals and taught troops in camp how to cook their food properly and prevent the spread of disease.**

offices. After traveling hundreds or sometimes thousands of miles, much of the food rotted. "Baggage cars were soon flooded with fermenting[6] sweetmeats, and broken pots of jelly, that ought never to have been sent," said one Sanitary Commission volunteer. "Decaying fruit and vegetables, pastry and cake in a demoralized condition, badly canned[7] meats and soups . . . were necessarily thrown away *en route*."[8]

demoralized (dē·môr′ə·līzd′): corrupted; changed for the worse.

---

6. **fermenting** (fər·ment′iŋ): undergoing a chemical change in which sugars are broken down.
7. **canned** (kand): preserved in sealed jars.
8. **en route** (än rōot′): as they traveled.

Death the Cure

"I believe the Doctors kill more than they cure," an Alabama private wrote home from the war. He may have been right. During the Civil War, nearly twice as many men died from disease or infection as died from battle wounds. Contaminated water, bugs and pests, unclean rags,  spoiled food, crowded quarters, and limited medical knowledge helped infections such as malaria and typhoid spread quickly. Epidemics were a constant threat, delaying many major battles. According to one historian, epidemics added about two years to the length of the war. The Civil War, though, was the last great war fought without the knowledge of how germs worked. Shortly afterward, scientist Louis Pasteur would show that diseases are spread through bacteria and that these bacteria can be controlled.

▲ Wounded soldiers in a field hospital.

Library of Congress

By the second year of the war, aid societies had a better idea of what the soldiers needed. Women who had put their money and effort into making havelocks now concentrated on such items as mosquito netting. When army doctors asked for supplies for dressing wounds, women quickly formed "lint and bandage associations." The bandages were simple strips of cloth, rolled and fastened. Lint, used to dress wounds, was gathered by turning a plate bottom-side-up, laying a piece of cloth over it, and scraping the cloth with a knife. Old tablecloths, sheets, and even rags were turned into piles of lint. At the time, doctors believed that keeping the lint wet helped wounds heal faster, and many nurses spent long hours going from bed to bed, moistening wounds with a sponge dipped in a basin of water.

The Chicago office of the Sanitary Commission was one of the largest branches, and it received mountains of donations from several states. Curious to see what was coming in, a volunteer named Mary Livermore went into the packing room one day to poke through the newly arrived boxes. She found a neat assortment of handmade socks, shirts, trousers, and edible treats. One package held a dressing gown with one pocket filled with hickory nuts and another stuffed with ginger snaps. Nearly every parcel contained a personal note, wishing the soldiers well or asking them to write. One woman enclosed a note that read, "These cookies are expressly for the sick soldiers, and if anybody else eats them, *I hope they will choke him!*"

By 1863, the Chicago branch had sent thirty thousand boxes of supplies to army camps and hospitals. But the cost of transporting the supplies had nearly depleted its treasury. Somehow, the volunteers needed to raise more money. Mary Livermore and her friend Jane Hoge devised an ambitious plan: They would collect donations of goods from citizens throughout the region and sell the items at a huge fair.

When the women said that the fair could raise $25,000, commission officials laughed at them. They went ahead with the project anyway. With the help of other women volunteers, they placed notices in newspapers in several states, asking for goods and money. The women wrote to governors, ministers, and teachers, telling them to spread the word. They mailed out twenty thousand <u>flyers</u> with instructions on how to send contributions. Within a few months, major cities were holding "fair meetings" to collect pledges and donations for the Chicago fair. Throughout the North people rifled through attics and closets for long-forgotten treasures to donate. Everything from silverware to pianos, horses, and even barrels of cologne arrived at the fair offices. A fifty-year-old free black woman who had nine children still enslaved in the South sent a handmade sheet. Another ex-slave gave a pair of socks that she had made for her teenage son, who died fighting for the Union Army. Michigan farmers donated crates of fruit, and the women of Dubuque, Iowa, sent hundreds of cooked ducks, chickens, and turkeys.

The fair opened on the morning of October 27, 1863, with a spectacular parade. After two and a half years of war, the people of Chicago needed a celebration to lift their spirits. By the time the procession began at ten o'clock, eager spectators lined the streets. A military band

flyers (flī'ərz): usually spelled *fliers*; copies of a single printed sheet circulated over a wide area.

kicked off the parade with a long drum roll, and soon patriotic music was blaring all along the three-mile route. Flags flew from rooftops and church steeples. When a line of carriages rolled by filled with wounded soldiers from nearby army hospitals, the crowd gave a great roar and showered the men with flowers. A wagon displaying captured Confederate flags drew thundering cheers all along the parade route.

At noon, the six huge fair buildings were opened. Flags were draped everywhere, and band music echoed from building to building. The halls became so crowded that ticket sales had to be stopped repeatedly. The dining hall, which fed three hundred people at a time, was packed all day long, and dozens of performers entertained the fairgoers. Outside, thoroughbred colts and oxen were auctioned off.

The fair was a stunning success. The Chicago Sanitary Commission had raised close to $100,000. Before long, "sanitary fairs" were being organized in New York, Cleveland, Boston, Pittsburgh, St. Louis, and dozens of other cities, each fair more elaborate than the last.

The 1864 Philadelphia fair was perhaps the most ambitious. The organizers formed dozens of committees, each responsible for collecting a certain kind of donation to sell. There was a committee on Umbrellas, Parasols, and Canes, and a Committee on Trimmings, Ribbons, Laces, and Embroideries. Even artificial teeth and dental instruments had their own committee. The Miscellaneous Committee was a huge success, collecting hoop skirts and corsets, soap and candles, billiard tables, and artificial arms and legs.

The South had no Sanitary Commission, and women of the Confederacy organized on a much smaller scale. They took turns meeting troops at train stations with hot meals, even as their own pantries dwindled, and they delivered hospital supplies in their own wagons. Women donated their brass goods to the army to be melted down and made into weapons.

In Charleston, in the spring of 1862, the Ladies Gunboat Fair sold four thousand raffle tickets for a chance to win

Dover Publications, Inc.

▲ Items gathered by the committees included parasols and umbrellas, ribbons and laces, and hoop skirts.

dwindled (dwin′dəld): became less full.

silverware, watches, and a diamond ring. In Columbia, a group of young women set up a refreshment area at the train station for sick and wounded soldiers waiting for connecting trains. Before long, the women were also providing each soldier with a bath, a change of clothes, and a cot to sleep on. They served as many as three hundred men in one day.

The Confederate government depended even more than the North on contributions from its plantations, farms, and homes. "The supply of money, clothing, and hospital stores[9] derived from this generous source is not only of immense value in itself," said one government official, "but the most cheering indication of the spirit of our people."

---

9. **stores** (stôrz): supplies of items for future use.

✓ Reading Check

1. What were soldiers' uniforms like early in the war? Why?

2. What invention had a great impact on the production of supplies?

3. Who organized the Women's Central Association of Relief? What was unique about this person?

4. Name two functions of the U.S. Sanitary Commission.

5. What services did women at a Columbia train station provide for wounded soldiers?

MEET THE *Writer*

A Separate Battle: Women and the Civil War is **Ina Chang**'s first book. In 1992, the book won a Governor's Writers Award for being one of ten outstanding books published by Washington authors. Chang, who lives in Seattle, Washington, has also worked as a freelance writer, an editor, and a reporter.

They joined the army with bravery and idealism in their hearts. In the end, though, many young boys' time in the army during the Civil War ended in fear, loneliness, home-sickness—even death.

from What a Foolish Boy
from *The Boys' War*

by JIM MURPHY

"Day after day and night after night did we tramp along the rough and dusty roads," writes sixteen-year-old Confederate soldier John Delhaney, " 'neath the most broiling sun with which the month of August ever <u>afflicted</u> a soldier; thro' rivers and their rocky valleys, over mountains—on, on, scarcely stopping to gather the green corn from the fields to serve us for rations. . . .[1] During these marches the men are sometimes unrecognizable on account of the thick coverings of dust which settle upon the hair, eye-brows and beard, filling likewise the mouth, nose, eyes, and ears."

Boys on both sides soon learned a boring fact about life in the army. Soldiers spend more time marching from one place to another than fighting.

At each town, new units[2] would join the troops until

afflicted (ə•flikt′id): caused to suffer.

You Need to Know...

At the beginning of the Civil War, neither side had an organized way to recruit soldiers. Both sides relied mainly on volunteers. Young men and boys liked the glamorous idea of becoming war heroes, and many thought the war would not last long, so the volunteer response was strong at first. Later, when the novelty of the war had worn off, both sides began drafting soldiers—choosing young men to fight in the war, whether they wanted to or not. Although boys under seventeen were never drafted, their offers of service were not usually turned down; the weary troops needed all the help they could get. Boys sixteen years old and under made up anywhere from 10 to 20 percent of all the soldiers who fought in the Civil War. Several hundred of these boys were as young as thirteen. Such boys were usually drummers, but not always. Some of them fought, just as adult soldiers did. As you will see in this selection, the long, tedious war was no picnic for these lonely teenagers looking for adventure and a sense of purpose.

---

1. **rations** (rash′ənz): supply of food.
2. **units** (yōō′nits): single groups of soldiers that fight together.

The Museum of the Confederacy, Richmond, Virginia,
Photography by Katherine Wetzel

▲ A Confederate soldier.

the column[3] stretched for miles with no beginning or end in sight. A messenger might fly past on horseback carrying orders for the officer in charge. The column would halt for a half hour or an hour with no explanation of what was happening up ahead. Then suddenly the order would be shouted up and down the line, the drumbeat would sound, and the troops would be on their way again.

Not that they understood what all of this maneuvering[4] was about. It did not take Elisha Stockwell very long to comment on this with his dry wit: "We didn't know where we were going, as a soldier isn't supposed to know any more than a mule, but has to obey orders."

What the common soldiers did not realize was that the commanders for both sides were engaged in a large-scale chess match in which they were the pieces.

What the common soldiers did not realize was that the commanders for both sides were engaged in a large-scale chess match[5] in which they were the pieces. The first two commanders of the Union army, Lieutenant General Winfield Scott and then Major General George McClellan, had decided on a defensive[6] war, at least until they could amass, outfit, and train a vast army. Both feared that if Confederate troops were able to capture Washington, D.C., civilians and politicians in the North would become demoralized[7] and abandon the fight. They also hoped that the South would lose energy and give up its quest for independence.

amass (ə•mas'): gather together.

---

3. **column** (käl'əm): arrangement of troops in which one soldier follows directly behind another.
4. **maneuvering** (mə•nōō'vər•iŋ): acting according to a plan.
5. **match** (mach): game; contest.
6. **defensive** (dē•fen'siv): guarding against attack.
7. **demoralized** (dē•môr'ə•līzd): frustrated and beaten down in spirit.

The Confederate commander, General Robert E. Lee, adopted a cautiously offensive[8] plan. He knew the Union army outnumbered his by almost two to one and that it had more supplies. He could never hope to win any head-to-head battle. Instead, he decided to use smaller, fast-moving groups of soldiers and cavalry[9] to strike at Union forces in many places, then wheel[10] around and strike again. By poking at the enemy, he hoped to hold his losses down while buying time to build up his forces. And he, like Scott and McClellan, hoped the other side would abandon the fight.

When boys enlisted in the army, they expected to fight the enemy and settle the dispute very quickly. After all, Lincoln's <u>initial</u> call for enlistments asked for only ninety days of service. But after what seemed like an endless amount of marching and a few hard fought battles, it became clear that neither side was going to surrender easily or quickly. And once they realized the war would last a long, long time, these boys began to miss the things they had left behind—namely their family and friends.

Homesickness was a common problem and found expression in many forms. Singing was one way to express such feelings. One of the most popular war songs for both sides, called "Tenting Tonight," was written even before the first year of fighting was completed. A few of its lines go:

We're tenting tonight on the old camp ground,
Give us a song to cheer our weary hearts,
A song of home, and the friends we love so dear.

We've been tenting tonight on the old camp ground,
Thinking of days gone by, of the loved ones at home
That gave us the hand, and the tear that said
"good-bye!"

initial (i·nish′əl): first.

Library of Congress

▲ Cover of piano version of "Tenting on the Old Camp Ground" (also known as "Tenting Tonight"). ❓ **Why do you think this song was so popular?**

---

8. **offensive** (ə·fen′siv): initiating an attack; aggressive.
9. **cavalry** (kav′əl·rē): group of soldiers on horseback.
10. **wheel** (hwēl): turning action of a line of soldiers with one end acting as the pivot or anchor.

Many boys simply put down what they felt in their own words. One Southerner, J. B. Lance of Buncombe County, North Carolina, was already tired of life away from home in October 1861. His message was simple and direct, and yet poignant: "Father I have Saw a rite Smart of the world Sence I left home But I have not Saw any place like Buncomb and hendersn yet."

It's easy to see why these boys developed such feelings. They were so young they had little real sense of who they were and how they fit into the world. The one solid and reliable thing they knew—their families—had been left behind. Their futures were uncertain. And they had not had time to develop real friendships with the others in their units. John Delhaney managed to capture in his journal this feeling of being apart and alone: "I felt strange enough, lying down this my first night in camp. The strange faces and forms, the near and distant sounds of an army of men talking, shouting, singing, and all upon different subjects; the croaking frogs, cries of the Whip-poor-Will, the glare of the camp fires and the neighing of

reliable (ri·lī'ə·bəl): sure; stable.

The Great Adventure

Imagine living during the time of the Civil War. Are you bored or tired of doing chores? Why not run off and join the army?

If you're too young-looking to pass for eighteen, you can get in anyway—as a drummer, fifer, or bugler. Don't know how to play? No problem: You'll pick it up soon enough. All day, every day, you play the same tunes over and over: wake-up call, call to drill, call to meals, on and on until lights out. As tired as you get of playing those tunes, you can be sure the soldiers are even more tired of hearing them.

In the heat of battle, though, when the roar of gunfire drowns out the officers' shouts, the soldiers will be glad you're there to bang out commands on your drum or blast them on your bugle. Will you be glad though? You may be too young to carry a gun, but unfortunately, you're not too young to get hit by an enemy bullet.

Library of Congress

▲ Portrait of Pvt. Joph White, drummer boy, Virginia Regiment, C.S.A. **?** **Why was the drummer boy important? What was his job?**

horses and the deep shadows of a dark night overhanging all; all these were not calculated[11] to <u>allay</u> my uneasiness of mind or lighten my heart of its cares."

---

11. calculated (kal′kyo͞o•lāt′ed): intended; designed.

Library of Congress/PRC Archive

▲ Young boys in a Union drum corps.

allay (a•lā′): to reduce; give relief.

✔ Reading Check

1. What "boring fact" about life as a soldier did boys on both sides quickly learn?

2. Who were the first two commanders of the Union army? What kind of war had they decided to fight?

3. Who was the Confederate commander? What was his strategy?

4. Name two ways in which the soldiers expressed their homesickness.

5. Why did young soldiers become homesick so easily? Give two reasons.

MEET THE *Writer*

Jim Murphy (1947–   ) began his career as an editor of children's books. However, after helping a number of writers focus their own ideas, he realized he had some of his own. Many of his award-winning books are about historical events such as the Civil War and the Great Fire of Chicago. He has also written books about dinosaurs, trains, and tractors. *The Boys' War: Confederate and Union Soldiers Talk About the Civil War* was named an ALA Best Book for Young Adults in 1992, a *School Library Journal* Best Book of the Year, and a Junior Literary Guild Selection.

"This is my seat and I will stay here!" the African American woman told the streetcar driver. Those words were not from the civil rights movement of the 1960s—Sojourner Truth spoke them during the Civil War. Who was Sojourner? How did her actions assist African Americans in their fight for freedom and equality?

from Freedom Rider

from *Sojourner Truth and the Struggle for Freedom*

by EDWARD BEECHER CLAFLIN

contraband (kän′trə•band′): goods or people moved illegally from one state or country to another.

segregated (seg′rə•gāt′id): divided from the main area or group.

adrift (ə•drift′): moving or floating in no single direction.

emancipation (ē•man′sə•pā′shən): freedom from slavery.

D uring the Civil War, slaves who fled to the Union side were called "contraband of war." In Washington, D.C. and many other cities, "contraband" could not ride streetcars with whites. They were barred from living in all white neighborhoods. Even if they could have afforded it, they would not have been allowed to attend many schools. Most churches, as well, were segregated.

By 1864 when Sojourner arrived in the nation's capital, it was flooded with former slaves cast adrift when emancipation cut the ties of bondage. To many of them, Washington, D.C. was the city of hope. Wasn't this where the Great Emancipator, Abraham Lincoln, lived?

Along the Washington Canal, a hundred families crowded into an area half the size of today's football field. Shacks had no windows or plumbing. They

You Need to Know...

Isabella Baumfree was born into slavery around 1797. Her home state, New York, passed a law banning slavery in 1828. Years later, in 1843, Baumfree claimed that God had commanded her to preach. It was then that she took the name Sojourner Truth as a symbol of her spiritual mission. She began traveling throughout New England and the Midwest on speaking tours. At first, Sojourner spoke about general topics, such as loving God and caring for others. Gradually, though, she began to focus her speeches on the evils of slavery. In 1864, Sojourner visited President Abraham Lincoln. She stayed on in Washington, D.C., and worked to improve the living conditions of African Americans who had come there to begin their lives free from slavery. In this selection, you'll meet the first African American woman to take a public stand against slavery.

were filthy. Among the white citizens of Washington the area was called "Murder Bay."

Even Mr. Lincoln could not think of a way to meet the crisis that was overwhelming his city. He could not make enough room for all the blacks who had come north, nor could he feed all the hungry children who roamed the streets.

Freedman's Village, where Sojourner took up residence,[1] was located across the Potomac River. Conditions in the temporary Village were certainly better than in Murder Bay. But many of the ex-slaves who lived in the long, wood-frame rowhouses were in desperate need of help.

Slavery left permanent scars. Up to the time the slaves were freed, all the organization and economy of their lives had been in the master's hands. Food, shelter, clothing—all the basic necessities had been provided by someone else. The master was even responsible for their children.

Emancipated slaves had the look of people stunned[2] by misfortune, as indeed they were. One observer of the time described them this way:

> *They had a dreamy look, taking no note of time; it seemed as if a pause had come in their lives—an abyss,[3] over whose brink they dared not look. With so few resources, with no education from books or contact with the world aside from plantation life— strangers in a strange land, hungry, thirsty, ragged, homeless—they were the very image of despair.*

Living among the contraband of war, Sojourner realized how much had yet to be done. The emancipated slaves had to learn everything—*everything*! Managing house-holds, looking for jobs, educating children, even asking for assistance—all the things that white people took for granted were new to the people who had just been born again in a different life.

crisis (krī′sis): a period of great difficulty.

economy (i·kän′ə·mē): use or management of money.

---

1. **residence** (rez′i·dəns): place where a person lives.
2. **stunned** (stund): overwhelmed; dazed.
3. **abyss** (ə·bis′): a space with no obvious end or bottom.

The challenge was enormous. Yet the people Sojourner met were eager to learn. And when she spoke, they came to listen.

After some months in Freedman's Village, Sojourner approached Captain Carse, who was the chief administrator. Could she and Sammy[4] stay on in the village and assist her people? "They have to learn to be free," she insisted.

On December 1, 1864 a letter arrived from New York:

> *This certifies that The National Freedman's Relief Association has appointed Sojourner Truth to be a counselor to the freed people at Arlington Heights, Virginia, and hereby commends her to the favor and confidence of the offices of government.*

But Sojourner Truth had not been idle while waiting for the letter to arrive. She had discovered that terrible crimes against black people were being committed every day. She wasn't going to stand by and do nothing!

Slave traders were preying on the residents of Freedman's Village!

In the Confederate states, slaves were free. But not in Maryland. There, the state courts were still debating[5] a law abolishing slavery.

To feed the Maryland slave trade, bands of cutthroat traders lurked on the outskirts of Freedman's Village. They struck suddenly, seized wailing children, and dragged them away to sell in Maryland. The slave traders were defying the laws of Virginia. But Captain Carse, administrator of Freedman's Village, did nothing to stop them.

It was Sojourner Truth who put an end to the kidnapping.

She rallied soldiers who were strong antislavery men. The next time kidnappers descended on the village, Sojourner's soldiers were waiting for them with fixed bayonets. The soldiers pounced on the slave traders, surrounded them, and demanded that they release the children.

While soldiers held the kidnappers at bay, the frightened children rushed off to the arms of their mothers.

---

4. **Sammy [Banks]:** her grandson and traveling companion.
5. **debating** (dē·bāt′iŋ): arguing; discussing.

Library of Congress

▲ Sojourner Truth.

The slavers cursed the tall, white-bonneted black woman who shook her cane at them. "We'll have you thrown in the guard-house, old lady," they threatened her.

"If you attempt it, children, I will make the United States rock like a cradle!" she retorted.

Sojourner's act of defiance lifted the cloud of dread from Freedman's Village. Antislavery soldiers remained on the alert, but the kidnappers had been sufficiently warned. They did not return. Now Sojourner could concentrate on the real task at hand. She had to teach these women the basics of cooking, cleaning, and caring for children.

It was Sojourner Truth who put an end to the kidnapping.

They were eager to learn. But their needs were almost overwhelming. Each day, more ex-slaves arrived, until they almost burst from the boundaries of the small compound. The Freedman's Bureau was furnishing seven hundred loaves of bread a day, but even that was not enough to feed those already in the Village. And now babies were being born—more mouths to feed!

After nearly a year's work at Freedman's Village, Sojourner was appointed to work in Freedman's Hospital. In the letter of recommendation, the assistant

Sojourner Truth

"I sell the shadow to support the substance."
—Sojourner Truth

This quotation provides the caption on a photographic portrait of Sojourner Truth, published around 1864. Sojourner presents an imposing figure, standing nearly six feet tall, in her spectacles, shawl, and peaked cap. Her cane seems to be more of an ornament than a necessity—such a strong woman does not need a cane. In a speech in 1867, Sojourner claimed to be over eighty years old and *The History of Woman Suffrage* reported that she died at the age of 110. The number of her years is not important—in all respects, Sojourner Truth was larger than life.

defiance (dē•fī′əns): daring rebellion.

industry (in'dəs•trē): hard work.

"I will make the
United States rock
like a cradle!"

commissioner noted her "energetic and faithful efforts." Her future responsibilities, as he described them, were to "aid in promoting order, cleanliness, <u>industry</u>, and virtue among the patients."

In her work for the hospital, Sojourner had to travel to many areas of D.C. and Georgetown. Horsedrawn streetcars clacked along rails through the city streets. Sojourner was told that she could only ride the "Jim Crow"[6] car set aside for blacks. She refused. In protest, she walked where she wanted to go, often carrying large bundles in her arms.

Not for long!

After a few days of this, Sojourner Truth went directly to the president of the street railroad to register an official complaint. When the deep-voiced, six-foot-tall, grandmotherly black woman strode into his office, the president paid attention. Sojourner set down her pipe, put aside her cane, and began lecturing him on the principles[7] of equality.

This was the woman who had met with Abraham Lincoln. What could he do but listen?

Sojourner had her way. The Jim Crow car was immediately taken out of service. Soon after, a law was passed giving black people the right to ride the streetcars with whites.

However, as Sojourner had discovered many times before, there was a huge gap between the law in theory[8] and the law in practice. Streetcar conductors and drivers were not easily changed in their ways. They ignored the new rules. Just as before, black people were passed by when they tried to hail streetcars.

But they couldn't ignore Sojourner.

The next time a streetcar driver tried to ignore her, she dashed after the car.

"I want to ride!" she shouted.

When the car did not slow down, she raised her voice even louder and waved her cane.

"*I want to ride!!* I WANT TO RIDE!!!"

6. **Jim Crow:** referring to laws that enforced segregation of African Americans, named after a song popular in black minstrel shows.
7. **principles** (prin'sə•pəlz): basic rules.
8. **theory** (thē'ə•rē): idea; plan.

All traffic on the street came to a halt. People crowded around to see what was happening. The car was forced to stop. Before it could move on, Sojourner made a flying leap, grabbed the handrail, and flung herself, breathless, among the startled white passengers.

By now, the crowd was cheering her on. "She has beaten him!" they laughed.

The streetcar conductor approached her <u>menacingly</u>. "Go forward where the horses are, or I will throw you out," he commanded.

menacingly (menʹəs·iŋ·lē): in a threatening manner.

"I know the laws as well as you do," she replied. "This is my seat and I will stay here."

And she did, riding the car farther than she needed to go. In fact, she rode all the way to the end of the line.

"Bless God! I have had a ride!" she said as she got off.

✓ Reading Check

1. Why did many freed slaves from the South head north to Washington, D.C.?

2. Why were many freed slaves unable to deal with the demands of daily life?

3. Name two ways in which emancipated slaves needed to be educated.

4. How did Sojourner Truth put an end to the kidnapping in Freedman's Village?

5. When Sojourner was not allowed to ride the city streetcars, what did she do? What was the result of this action?

MEET THE *Writer*

Edward Beecher Claflin has written another biography for young readers, *Jack London: Wilderness Writer*, as well as a play, *Scullers*, about Jack Kelly, Sr., who won an Olympic medal in 1920.

Although it was written more than 130 years ago, the novel *Little Women* is still read and loved by people today. Read on to learn about the author of this famous book.

When I Was a Kid

from *National Geographic World*

by SANDRA FENICHEL ASHER

"**N**o boy could be my friend till I had beaten him in a race," wrote Louisa May Alcott. "And no girl if she refused to climb trees [and] leap fences. . . ."

You Need to Know...

Louisa May Alcott showed early promise as a writer of poetry, short stories, and plays. However, her father's lack of success meant that while still young, Alcott had to work as a seamstress, a servant, and a teacher to help support her family. A number of her short stories and a book of fables were published but it was not until after the Civil War, during which she served as a nurse for the Union Army, that she achieved success and financial security with *Little Women*. Louisa May Alcott continued to write and several more of her novels were published successfully. She died in 1888 at the age of fifty-five.

Louisa May Alcott. ▶

Bettmann/CORBIS

Born November 29, 1832, Louisa grew up in Massachusetts. Her family was poor and moved often because her father had difficulty finding work as a teacher. Unlike many parents of the day, hers believed it was important for children to spend time outdoors, especially to learn about nature. Louisa wrote of days when she ran "twenty miles in five hours and went to a party in the evening."

Louisa was educated at home with her sisters Anna, Elizabeth, and May. Her parents also believed students should think for themselves, rather than memorize facts. They encouraged their daughters to record their activities and feelings in journals.

When Louisa was 11, her father tried to establish a community called Fruitlands, where people lived and worked together.

establish (ə·stab′lish): to set up.

community (kə·myōō′nə·tē): people living in a group apart from general society.

▲ At Fruitlands, Bronson Alcott and his family lived at Orchard House. **?** **Why do you think the community of Fruitlands failed?**

Living in such a community demanded lots of hard work. Louisa preferred writing poetry to working. The work took so much of her time and energy that it kept her from writing, so Louisa <u>rebelled</u> against the work. Her family <u>criticized</u> her. Full of sorrow, Louisa expressed herself in a poem:

> *How can I learn to rule myself,*
> *To be the child I should,*
> *Honest and brave, nor ever tire*
> *Of trying to be good?*

The Fruitlands community failed, and the Alcotts moved to Concord, Massachusetts. They lived there for almost four years, longer than they stayed anywhere else.

"Now that I have a room of my own to scribble in," wrote Louisa in Concord, "I'll be happy." At 13 she wrote plays to perform with her sisters in the barn. She created and played Duke Roderigo, a heroic character who stomped about in brown leather boots (made by Louisa). This successful presentation <u>inspired</u> her to write hundreds of poems, plays, and stories.

rebelled (ri·beld′): went against authority.

criticized (krit′ə·sīzd′): made a disapproving judgment.

inspired (in·spīrd′): caused a desire.

The Transcendentalists

Louisa May Alcott's financial success rescued her father, Bronson Alcott, from a life of poverty after Fruitlands. Utopian communities such as Fruitlands grew out of a movement known as Transcendentalism. Transcendentalists believed that the physical world was only a reflection of the spiritual world and that people could discover the truths of the spiritual world by looking within themselves. Only in this way, they thought, could society be changed for the better. Many Transcendentalists supported women's rights and the abolition of slavery, among other social reforms.

Louisa made a promise to herself: "I *will* do something by and by. Don't care what . . . teach, sew, act, write, anything to help the family; and I'll be rich and famous and happy before I die, see if I won't."

✔ **Reading Check**

1. Why did the Alcott family move from place to place when Louisa was a child?

2. Name two things Louisa's parents encouraged their children to do.

3. How did Louisa feel about life in the Fruitlands community? Why?

4. What inspired Louisa to begin writing hundreds of poems and stories?

5. What promise did Louisa make to herself at the age of thirteen?

Who are the Buffalo Soldiers? Read on to find out about this honored group that has served the United States well.

A Proud Tradition

from *Cobblestone*

by JOHN P. LANGELLIER

A letter dated June 1872 said, "The Indians called the black troops [they encountered in the West] 'buffalo soldiers,' because their woolly heads are so much like the matted cushion that is between the horns of the buffalo." It is believed that the Indians used the nickname out of respect for the fighting spirit of the African American soldiers, which reminded the Indians of the courage of the buffalo. The buffalo, a source of food, shelter, and clothing, was <u>sacred</u> to the Plains Indians.

African Americans had proven their patriotism and ability as soldiers since the Revolutionary War, but they had been unable to join the U.S. Army. This <u>policy</u> began to change during the Civil War. By the end of the war in 1865, more than 180,000 African Americans had served in the Union army as members of "colored volunteer" regiments.[1]

In 1866, the U.S. Congress passed a law allowing African Americans to join the peacetime Army in special units: the Ninth and Tenth Cavalry regiments and the Thirty-eighth,

sacred (sā′krid): believed to be holy.

policy (päl′ə·sē): course of action by a government.

You Need to Know...

Between the 1860s and the 1890s, the American frontier—once marked by the Mississippi River—expanded farther and farther westward. During this period the United States fought a number of wars with American Indians. The U.S. government had angered them by forcing them to move to reservations and by creating trails that ran through their hunting grounds.

The Buffalo Soldiers were sent west mainly to protect settlers from the Indians. Once there, they performed other jobs, quickly building reputations as brave, dedicated men. Between about 1870 and the mid-1890s, Buffalo Soldiers in the West won over a dozen Medals of Honor. Buffalo Soldier units fought in the Spanish-American War of 1898 and in World War II.

---

1. **regiments** (rej′ə·mənts): military units, term not used since 1963.

Thirty-ninth, Fortieth, and Forty-first Infantry[2] regiments. Three years later, the four infantry regiments were merged into the Twenty-fourth and Twenty-fifth Infantry regiments.

What made African American men want to join the military after the Civil War? Some of them, like Jacob Wilks, had served in the Union army and found that they liked being soldiers. Others, such as Horace Wayman Bevins, had never been in the Army. After Bevins finished school, he decided to become a soldier, "having a great desire for adventure and to see the wild West." Charles Creek turned to the Army as a chance to escape farming. "I got tired of looking at mules in the face from sunrise to sunset," he said. At twenty-six, George Bentley stated that he "joined the army simply to get away from his mother and a brother, neither of whom he liked."

Some African Americans thought that serving in the Army would be a good way for them to earn money (they were paid thirteen dollars a month). The desire to receive an education (the Army provided an opportunity for soldiers to learn how to read and write) was another reason they enlisted.[3] Other African Americans looked to the West for a better life, hoping to leave behind their past and the places where they had been forced to work against their will.

After a period of training at midwestern forts such as Fort Leavenworth, Kansas, African American soldiers were sent to the Great Plains, the western mountains, and the southwestern deserts. They were expected to maintain order between the Indians and the settlers, help build

Bettmann/CORBIS

▲ Several regiments of buffalo soldiers served in the western United States. **❓ How did they get their nickname?**

---

2. **infantry** (in'fən·trē): group of soldiers who fight mainly on foot.
3. **enlisted** (en·lis'tid): joined the army.

forts and roads, patrol borders, and protect mail coaches and railroad construction crews.

The buffalo soldiers were often given poor equipment and difficult assignments, and they regularly encountered prejudice. Yet despite the hardships they faced, their record of service is impressive. The cavalry boasted the lowest desertion[4] rate in the entire Army. As Rayford Logan, a famous African American professor, wrote, "Negroes had little at the turn of the century to help sustain faith in ourselves except the pride that we took in the Ninth and Tenth Cavalry, the Twenty-fourth and Twenty-fifth Infantry."

---

4. **desertion** (di·zʉr'shən): leaving without approval.

Reading Check

1. How did American Indians feel about the buffalo? Why did they feel this way?

2. Why did American Indians call black soldiers "Buffalo Soldiers"?

3. Name two reasons an African American might have wanted to serve in the U.S. Army in the late 1800s.

4. After training, where were African American soldiers sent? What did they do there?

5. Name three difficulties African American soldiers often encountered.

MEET THE *Writer*

John P. Langellier serves as Director of Publications and Productions at the Gene Autry Western Heritage Museum. He has written books on the Civil War, the Spanish-American War, and World War II, as well as on other topics in American history.

prejudice (prej'ə·dis): intolerance; discrimination.

sustain (sə·stān): to keep up or maintain.

▲ Stamp commemorating Buffalo Soldiers, 1994.

The Gettysburg Address took only about two minutes to deliver and is a mere 271 words long. What makes it one of history's greatest speeches?

"A Few Appropriate Remarks"

from *Highlights for Children*

by NANCY NORTON MATTILA

dedication (ded′i·kā′shən): setting apart for a special reason.

proclaimed (prō·klāmd′): stated or declared publicly.

appropriate (ə·prō′prē·it): suitable for a particular purpose.

Probably only a few of the fifteen thousand people who heard President Abraham Lincoln's speech at Gettysburg were impressed. He spoke so briefly that the photographer didn't even have time to take his picture.

President Lincoln was not the featured speaker for the dedication of the Soldiers' National Cemetery on November 19, 1863, a little more than four months after the Battle of Gettysburg. Yet history has proclaimed his Gettysburg Address one of the greatest speeches ever made.

Two weeks before the ceremonies, Lincoln received a letter from Gettysburg attorney David Wills. ". . . I am authorized by the Governors of the different States to invite you to be present. . . . It is the desire that after the Oration, you . . . formally set apart these grounds to their sacred use by a few appropriate remarks."

You Need to Know...

Abraham Lincoln's Gettysburg Address was given several months after the famous Battle of Gettysburg. This battle, fought from July 1 through July 3, 1863, marked the turning point in the war. Before Gettysburg, the Union had seemed to be losing and the death toll had been steadily mounting. In addition, the president had had a difficult time finding good generals to lead the Union troops. Even so, when the Union and Confederate armies met accidentally in Gettysburg, Pennsylvania, Union general George G. Meade managed to lead his troops to victory, pushing Robert E. Lee's Southern army back into Virginia. The cost was high for both sides. Over 7,000 lives were lost, and the total number of casualties—those killed, wounded, or captured—was over 50,000.

At the time, Lincoln's address hardly measured up to the spectacle of the battle. Today, however, the speech continues to remind Americans of the ideals for which the Civil War was fought—freedom, equality, and democracy.

Lincoln almost didn't attend the ceremonies. He had refused other invitations because of wartime business in Washington, D.C. Also, doctors were worried about the health of his son Tad, and Mrs. Lincoln did not want her husband to go.

But President Lincoln saw this as a chance to say something important about the meaning of the Civil War. Could he convince people to continue to fight in hopes of a Union victory that would bring national unity and freedom? In his mind and on paper Lincoln practiced ways to express his reverence for the sacrifices of all who had suffered at the Battle of Gettysburg.

Lincoln did not scribble his Gettysburg Address on the back of an envelope during the trip north to Pennsylvania, as many say. The Address was partly finished when Lincoln climbed aboard the special train full of Washington dignitaries[1] on Wednesday, November 18. He had hoped to do more work on the speech, but the train was too full of excitement and conversation to do so.

▲ Lincoln's funeral procession.

reverence (rev′ə·rəns): high regard; respect.

> ## President Lincoln saw this as a chance to say something important about the meaning of the Civil War.

The presidential party arrived just after dark and made its way to the Wills house through crowded streets noisy with band music. An elegant dinner was given for the honored guests. There Lincoln met the featured speaker, Edward Everett, a widely known statesman[2] and orator. After

orator (ôr′ət·ər): public speaker.

---

1. **dignitaries** (dig′nə·ter′ēz): high-ranking people.
2. **statesman** (stāts′mən): person skilled in carrying out government affairs.

The Final Act

President Lincoln died about a year and a half after his Gettysburg Address and only five days after the Civil War had ended. On April 14, 1865, John Wilkes Booth, an actor, shot Lincoln in the head during a play in Washington, D.C. Booth was a supporter of slavery and considered Lincoln responsible for causing the war. His first plan was to kidnap Lincoln, but after the Confederate army surrendered he decided on assassination instead. After shooting the president, Booth reportedly leaped down from Lincoln's private box onto the stage, breaking his leg in the process. Although he managed to escape to Virginia on horseback, he was soon found and shot.

▲ Wanted poster for Lincoln's assassins.

dinner, Lincoln spoke briefly to a crowd outside the house, but protested that he had nothing of importance to say.

Later the President retired to his room to put the finishing touches on his speech. Lincoln's lifelong love of poetry, the Bible, and Shakespeare shaped his final choice of words.

Rain fell early the next day, but the sun came out and shone on the people—some of them families of dead soldiers—gathered for the dedication. A band played and a prayer was offered before Everett spoke. Everett's two-hour oration contained exactly what people expected to hear, and it was greeted with much applause. It took two newspaper pages to reprint the entire speech.

At 2 P.M., President Lincoln put on his steel-rimmed glasses. (It is a matter of debate whether he wore his glasses and read, or recited his speech from memory.) Wearing white gloves, Lincoln pulled his two-page manuscript from the pocket of his black coat. He still wasn't sure if he had gotten it right as he unfolded his long legs, stepped forward, and paused before the crowd. When he started to speak, his high voice shrilled forth like the sound of a bugle.

"Four score[3] and seven years ago our fathers brought forth on this continent, a new nation," he began, with a reference to 1776, the year the United States declared its independence. The President's prayer-like speech lasted only about two minutes.

Lincoln had not expected people to clap much, but he was disappointed with the lukewarm[4] response to his "few appropriate remarks." He shook hundreds of hands before boarding the train back to Washington. During the trip,

---

3. **score** (skôr): twenty.
4. **lukewarm** (loōk′wôrm′): not excited.

he lay back with cold towels covering his eyes. Lincoln was coming down with a light case of smallpox and would be quarantined[5] in the White House for the next two weeks.

The President's spirits started to rise the next day when a letter from Everett was delivered to him. "I should be glad," wrote Everett, "if I could flatter myself that I came as near to the central idea of the occasion in two hours as you did in two minutes." Some American and European newspapers also liked the speech.

The official version of Lincoln's Gettysburg Address contains only 271 words. Though mostly short and simple, Lincoln's words hold deep meaning.

▲ Abraham Lincoln.

Library of Congress

---

5. **quarantined** (kwôr′ən•tēnd): isolated from other people.

✓ Reading Check

1. On what occasion did Abraham Lincoln deliver his Gettysburg Address?

2. Why did Lincoln decide to go to Gettysburg to give the speech?

3. How were Edward Everett's and Abraham Lincoln's speeches different?

4. What are three of the influences on Lincoln's choice of words in his address?

5. What was the audience's response to Lincoln's address?

This article challenges you to form your own opinion of a popular pastime—reenactments, or playlike performances, of historical events.

Reenactment of War Is Far Too Civil

from the *Los Angeles Times*

by JON LOVE

You Need to Know...

Officially, it ended on April 9, 1865, but if you happened to visit Gettysburg, Pennsylvania, on July 2, 1998, you might have believed that the Civil War was still being fought. On the 135th anniversary of the war's largest battle, 15,000 people donned Union and Confederate uniforms. Weapons in hand, they took to the field, while another 100,000 folks gathered to watch the drama. A one-time event? Not by a long shot. According to the National Park Service, there are war "reenactment units" in many states. As often as four times a year, some 20,000 to 25,000 people travel to major battle sites across the country. There they act out the historic battles, blow by blow. Actually, the guns aren't loaded, but that doesn't matter. "You smell the smoke, . . . you feel the adrenaline," says Preston Ware, a Civil War reenactor. "[Y]ou're charging up a hill with all these soldiers around you and you lose a sense of time. Boom, you're in 1861." Like Ware, most participants believe that reenactments are a wonderful way to honor our ancestors and to learn history hands-on. To others, such as the author of this article, this "hobby" has gone too far.

Something was wrong, and it took me awhile to figure out what.

Civil War buffs recently re-created the 1863 battle of Chickamauga at Fresno's Kearney Park. The participants all wore clothing <u>authentic</u> to the period, and camps had been set up so visitors could see how troops lived in the field. The highlight of the day was a battle in which opposing soldiers fired blank charges at each other.

I spent some time walking through the camps. The soldiers' uniforms looked good, the weapons were right. Men in the artillery unit had artillery sabers,[1] and cavalry troops carried

authentic (ô•then′tik): real.

1. **sabers** (sā′bərz): swords with curved blades used in battle.

a Sharps carbine[2] under their arms hooked to a leather shoulder sling. There was one man in a Confederate officer's uniform who had what looked like a LeMat revolver in his holster. Good stuff, all of it. Still, something was off, and it was hard to put a finger on just what it was.

Actors playing historic figures stood under a large tent and fielded[3] questions from an audience made up mostly of teens.

"Why did the North win?" a boy asked "President Lincoln."

"We won because we had a strong industrial base and the South didn't," Lincoln said. "Also, we had a much larger population. All those immigrants from Ireland and Germany settled in the North."

In the Union Army camp, a group of children questioned a soldier as part of a school assignment.

"Do you believe in slavery?" a girl asked.

"No," the soldier answered, then asked if the children would be at the battle. "I'll try to be brave for you," he said, and the girl giggled.

Warfare isn't a game, and I don't think it should be glorified.

I looked again at this young Union soldier, and I suddenly understood what was wrong. The problem wasn't with wardrobe or props;[4] it was with the soldiers. This soldier, this young man, wasn't the warrior he was dressed up to be. For one thing, he was too happy. There was no hardness in his eyes, no sense of impending battle, no fear, no terror. Like the replica carbine he carried, where the lines of the stock[5] didn't quite match the original, the soldier's stance,[6] his posture, the way he moved and gestured,

industrial (in·dus′trē·əl): relating to manufacturing.

impending (im·pend′iŋ): approaching.

replica (rep′li·kə): a copy.

---

2. **carbine** (kär′bīn′): short-barreled rifle used in battle.
3. **fielded** (fēl′did): answered.
4. **props** (präps): things that make the event seem real, such as guns; theatrical props.
5. **stock** (stäk): handle of a rifle.
6. **stance** (stans): a person's standing position.

was all just a hair off. It was only a game to him. And, of course, that's really all it was.

And I guess that's what bothered me. Because warfare isn't a game, and I don't think it should be glorified. I think it gives young people the idea that being a soldier is a fun occupation. And in the real world, soldiers are a breed apart. Military historian John Keegan wrote, "Soldiers are not as other men. War must be fought by men whose values and skills are a world apart—a very ancient world."

The sad truth is that our society usually looks down on soldiers, treats them with scorn[7] until they're needed. British poet Rudyard Kipling touched on this in his poem "Tommy."

> *"Then it's Tommy this, an' Tommy that, an'*
> *Tommy, 'ow's yer soul?*
> *"But it's 'Thin red line of 'eroes' when the drums*
> *begin to roll, . . ."*

There were 34,000 casualties at Chickamauga. Now, nearly 140 years after the battle, we make a festival of it. On the Union side, many of those killed were the immigrants the Lincoln actor talked about. Those soldiers, most of them, had joined for the meager[8] pay or had been drafted because they didn't have the $300 needed to buy their way out. When the realities of army life sank in, many found themselves in a place they didn't want to be, doing things they didn't want to do. It couldn't have been fun. I don't think we should make it look like fun.

The Civil War buffs did put on a good show. The sham battle had the smoke and noises of the real thing, but without the lead balls and the bloodshed. The whole point of the thing, though, seemed to be aimed toward the battle, and I'm uncomfortable watching men play at shooting and killing one another. It tends to cheapen the sacrifice of the real soldiers.

---

7. **scorn** (skôrn): extreme disrespect.
8. **meager** (mē′gər): inadequate amount.

In a Word . . .

In New York around 1920, fire and firefighting enthusiasts who were fascinated by the equipment and the actual fighting of the fires were called **buffs** after the buff-colored (yellowish brown) uniform of the New York volunteer firemen.

The day after I saw the Civil War reenactment at the park, the *Sacramento Bee* ran a front-page article on the battle staged there. The reporter interviewed one of the participants, a government attorney in real life, and ran a color photo of the fighting. A little further down on the same page was another story about soldiers. An article reported the killing of Korean civilians by American GIs during the first month of the Korean War, nearly 50 years ago.

Some are calling for the court-martial[9] of those responsible. "It's pretty simple," said a West Point law professor. "Soldiers are not allowed to fire on civilians."

---

9. **court-martial** (kôrt′ mär′shəl): military trial.

SIDELIGHT

The people who participate in Civil War reenactments disagree with the author of this selection. The following excerpt from another article tells why.

Joseph Sohm; ChromoSohm Inc./CORBIS

"Reenactors come from all over the country, so the children make friends with other children who have different backgrounds and experiences. Whether they reenact with Confederate units or Union units, they look forward to seeing one another and renewing friendships at each reenactment. It is always fun to be with people who share a special interest in the Civil War. . . .

"The Civil War was not just about battles. Children who reenact give others a broader view of the history of the 1860s. When spectators see children at a reenactment holding a fair to raise money for invalid soldiers or sewing handkerchiefs for a father who is away at battle, they are learning through living history. These young teachers and historians give us a glimpse of what it was like to live during the Civil War years."

—by Meg Galante-De Angelis in "Young Civil War Reenactors,"
Cobblestone (December 1999)

Charleston, S.C., after Sherman's march—view of ruined buildings. ❓ **Why do you think Sherman said that he was "sick and tired of war"?**

ironic (ī•rän′ik): meaning the opposite of what one would expect.

Simple maybe for the professor standing at his podium. Not so simple, though, for the frightened young draftees on the front lines who had been ordered to shoot.

An old man, an ex-GI who had been there, was interviewed for television. From the look on his face it was plain that it tortured him to think of it. "You just got to try to live with it," he said, "if you can."

It's ironic that our educated middle class likes to dress up and play soldier when there's no danger involved, but when it looks like a real-life soldier may have made a mistake we're all ready to step on him.

In the Civil War, Union Gen. William T. Sherman brought war home to the South's civilians when he led a march through Georgia and burned the city of Atlanta. After the war, he was named commanding general of the Army. When Sherman was an old man, he said, "I am tired and sick of war. Its glory is all moonshine. . . . War is hell."

✓ Reading Check

1. What event is described in this selection?

2. How does the author feel about this event? Give a quotation from the article to support your response.

3. According to the author, what mistaken idea will this event give young people?

4. Briefly summarize the newspaper article from the *Sacramento Bee* that the author uses to support his point.

5. Why does the author quote the words of William T. Sherman at the end of the article?

Cross-Curricular ACTIVITIES

■ ART/LANGUAGE ARTS

Dandy Duds Recall that, early in the Civil War, soldiers preferred bright, showy costumes to the solemn uniforms we imagine most troops wearing. Re-read the second paragraph of "Supplying the Armies" on page 119. Then, do some research on the topic of Civil War uniforms. Next, choose two uniforms that you find striking or that differ greatly from one another. Make detailed sketches of these costumes, much as a fashion designer would do. For each costume, write a paragraph describing its history (who wore it and when), its different parts, and how it was made. When you have finished, present your sketches to the class.

■ SPEECH

Women's Work In 1851, Sojourner Truth attended a women's rights convention in Akron, Ohio. Before the convention began, a group of male ministers spoke out against women's rights. Truth responded by delivering a powerful speech that is now remembered as "Ain't I a Woman?" Locate this speech or another famous speech from this period. Study the speech and decide on the body language, facial expression, and tone of voice that will best convey the message. Perform your dramatic reading for a group of classmates.

■ LANGUAGE ARTS/HISTORY

Labors of Love What were some of the ways people at home supported those who fought in the Civil War? Look back through "Supplying the Armies," taking note of some of these jobs. You might also research writers, poets, and famous people who lived during that time and find out how they contributed—Walt Whitman , Clara Barton, and Louisa May Alcott are examples. If you had lived during the war, what would you most like to have done? Create a poem or a series of journal entries written from the point of view of your imaginary young person. Describe the work you do every day, as well as your feelings about the work and the war. When you have finished, exchange what you have written with that of a partner. Each of you should make suggestions to help improve the other's work.

■ ART/DESIGN

Stamp of Greatness Choose a person or a member of a group you encountered in this chapter. What important contribution to society did this person make? Design a postage stamp that commemorates this person. You may want your stamp to show a portrait of the person, or you may want to use a symbol to express one of the person's qualities. Be sure to look at some other commemorative stamps before you begin. What words do you see on these stamps? What other elements will you need to include?

READ ON: FOR INDEPENDENT READING

■ NONFICTION

Lincoln: A Photobiography by Russell Freedman (Houghton Mifflin, 1987). Few thought Abraham Lincoln was a handsome man. When a debate opponent called him two-faced, Lincoln said, "I leave it to my audience. If I had another face, do you think I'd wear this one?" Yet he was the most photographed man of his time. Russell Freedman won the Newbery Medal for this account of Lincoln's life, told in pictures and words.

The Long Road to Gettysburg by Jim Murphy (Clarion Books, 1992). The author of *"from* What a Foolish Boy" (page 127) follows two actual teenage soldiers, one Union and one Confederate, through the bloodiest battle that has ever been fought on this continent. This book appears on the Orbis Pictus list of Honor and Notable books.

Till Victory Is Won: Black Soldiers in the Civil War by Zak Mettger (Lodestar Books, 1994). Thousands of African Americans participated in some way in the Civil War—and not all their fighting was done on the battlefield. Black soldiers had to struggle for respect, recognition, and even equal pay—against their own side! This is their story.

■ FICTION

Across Five Aprils by Irene Hunt (Follett Publishing Company, 1964) reveals how the Civil War affected more than just the fighting soldiers. In this classic novel, young Jethro Creighton is left to run the family farm when his older brothers go off to fight. Jethro never fights in or even witnesses a single battle, but the war changes his life forever.

Bull Run by Paul Fleischman (HarperCollins, 1993) is a book to read aloud. In twelve voices whose accents and points of view range widely —from that of a general to a young boy, from a mother to that of her children—Fleischman weaves the story of the first great battle of the Civil War.

Soldier's Heart: Being the Story of the Enlistment and Due Service of the Boy Charley Goddard in the First Minnesota Volunteers by Gary Paulsen (Delacorte Press, 1998), has been honored as an ALA Best Book for Young Adults. In World War I they called it shell shock. In World War II they called it battle fatigue. Today it's known as post-traumatic stress disorder. In the Civil War, though, no one knew why boys like Charley never really got over the terrible things they'd seen and done. They called the mysterious change in them "soldier's heart."

CHAPTER 5

A Nation Transformed
The Industrial Era   1877–1914

How to Spend $480,000,000—Fast

Steel tycoon Andrew Carnegie (1835–1919) was one of the wealthiest people in the world. However, Carnegie didn't think of the money as his to keep; he thought of it as his to use wisely for the common good. He thought that to die rich was to die disgraced.

He had some quick spending to do if he didn't want to die disgraced. At the age of sixty-five, he had just sold his Carnegie Steel Company for 480 million dollars.

Carnegie loved to read, so he started by paying for public libraries—2,509 of them. Then he bought organs for churches—about 8,000 in all. He paid for museums, lots of them, and hospitals, parks, and theaters. In New York City, he built what is now the Carnegie Hall for music; in Pittsburgh, he founded what is now known as Carnegie-Mellon University.

Carnegie still couldn't give his money away fast enough. He used the last 125 million dollars to set up the Carnegie Corporation. Andrew Carnegie died in 1919, but the corporation still spends money on his behalf today.

Bettmann/CORBIS

▲ Andrew Carnegie.

This Pen Comes with Batteries

Everyone's heard of Thomas Edison and his amazing inventions: the light bulb, the phonograph, the movie camera, the—electric pen?

It's not as silly as it sounds. Until Edison invented the electric pen in 1875, all business writing was done by hand, and if a copy was needed, it had to be copied by hand as well. Edison's pen was the first mechanical copier.

The pen was really a motorized stencil maker. It "wrote" on the paper by punching tiny holes in it—eight thousand holes per minute! Then a roller pushed ink through the holes onto one sheet after another, copying the writing as many times as needed.

Memorable Quote

"I came to America because I heard the streets were paved with gold. When I got here, I found out three things: First, the streets weren't paved with gold; second, they weren't paved at all; and third, I was expected to pave them."

—joke told by Italian immigrants

VOCABULARY MATTERS

Suffrage is the right to vote. American women who fought for the right to vote were called *suffragists*. British women, on the other hand, were called *suffragettes*. The word was coined in 1906 by a British reporter who substituted the ending *–ette,* meaning "tiny," as an insult. In the early twentieth century, British women, frustrated by their government's refusal to listen, expressed their views by picketing, heckling, illegal demonstrations, and even hunger strikes. In America, *suffragettes* referred to women who, like their British counterparts, turned to more aggressive tactics. Through the combined efforts of both *suffragists* and *suffragettes*, American women finally won the right to vote in 1920.

Making the Move

A traveler to a New England farm village in the early 1900s couldn't believe his eyes. The church had been abandoned. The school building was half ripped down. Only two people remained in the entire village.

Where had all the farmers gone? They had moved to the cities. In 1861, when the Civil War began, only one American in five lived in a city. By the time the United States entered World War I, though, the cities were home to half the people in the nation. More arrived every day.

Not all were American-born farmers. Anyone walking the streets of New York City might think all of Europe had come to America. People came from Hungary, Austria, Russia, Poland, Norway, and Sweden. By 1890, New York had as many Germans as the city of Hamburg, half as many Italians as Naples, and *twice* as many Irish as Dublin.

CORBIS

America Drops the Ball

It's almost twelve o'clock. People on the streets stand and crane their necks upward. High atop the mast of a nearby building, the giant ball drops. Some people check their watches, then walk away.

No cheers? No confetti? No "Happy New Year"? Probably not. This is the late 1800s, and in cities across the United States, the "time ball" drops every day. Before time balls, the cities had no standard time. The time balls solved their problem.

In 1883, the United States was divided into four time zones. Every day, four times a day, telegraph operators at the U.S. Naval Observatory in Washington, D.C., told cities across the country what time to drop the ball. When radio arrived in the 1900s, time balls weren't needed anymore. Today, the ball that drops in New York's Times Square on New Year's Eve is the only time ball left.

Despite the popular Old West stories, not all cowboys were named Hank or greeted strangers with "Howdy, partner." Read on to learn what the first cowboys were really like and about one of the traditional songs they sang.

SONG

MUSIC ●

HISTORY ●

Cielito Lindo

from *Songs of the Wild West*

Commentary by ALAN AXELROD

Arrangements by DAN FOX

▲ Vaquero.

Denver Public Library, Western History Department

pedigree (ped′i•grē′): origin; history.

The generations of easterners (and perhaps even some modern westerners) who grew up watching William S. Hart, Tom Mix, Gene Autry, Roy Rogers, and John Wayne in the movies and on television may find it difficult to see cowboys as anything other than blue-eyed men with names like McCoy, Murphy, and Jones. In fact, the pedigree of all cowboys— black, white, brown, red—is found not in the freedom of the plains but in the slavery of Spanish America.

When the cattle herds of the early Spanish missions had grown too large for the priests to manage, they trained mission Indians—who under Spanish colonial law were free, but for all practical purposes were enslaved to the mission and its surrounding ranchos—as horsemen. These early cowboys were called *vaqueros*— from the Spanish word *vaca*, meaning "cow." To this day, a cowboy who likes to wear fancy duds and ornaments is called a buckaroo, which is how *vaquero* sounded to Anglo ears.

You Need to Know...

As America grew, so did its varieties of popular music. On the western frontier, music old and new was central to daily life. Pioneers searching for a new beginning sang familiar songs to remind them of home. Cowboys riding the vast and lonely range sang lullabies to their cattle at dusk. Laborers on the railroad sang upbeat tunes to help the time go by. People from many cultures—Anglo American, American Indian, African American, and Mexican—contributed their unique styles and feelings to the music of the West. This selection will introduce you to one of these songs and to the hardworking men who found comfort in its soothing strains.

On a Mission

In the late 1700s, the Spanish government, which still controlled Mexico, joined with the Roman Catholic Church to create missions in the land that would later become the American Southwest. These missions, or settlements, served two purposes. They helped Spain maintain a stronghold in these unsettled areas. They also helped the Church spread Christianity to the native peoples. Many American Indians and Mexicans moved to the missions, where they were given food and shelter in exchange for work. Typically, the women made pottery, cared for animals, and wove cloth, while the men worked in the fields and on the ranches.

stoic (stō′ik): seeming unaffected by pain or suffering.

By the eighteenth century, most *vaqueros* were of mixed Indian and Spanish ancestry. They roped steers with a loop of braided rawhide[1] called *la reata* (the later cowboy's lariat) and wore leather leggings, called *chaparreras* (chaps) to protect themselves from razor-sharp chaparral.[2]

The "singing cowboy" of films and television could also trace his pedigree back to the Hispanic *vaquero*. While "Cielito Lindo," a traditional Spanish song, might have been too emotional for the <u>stoic</u> Anglo buckaroo, even he would have appreciated the message of its familiar chorus: "Sing and don't cry."

---

1. **rawhide** (rô′hīd′): cowhide that has not been made into leather.
2. **chaparral** (shap′ə•ral′): brush, or low bushes, that grows in the American Southwest.

Cielito Lindo

A pronunciation guide for the Spanish lyrics appears in italics.

De la Sie - rra Mo - re - na, Cie - li - to
Day lah See-ay - rah Moe - ray - nah, See-ay - lee - toe

Lin - do vie - nen ba - jan - do.
Leen - doe bee-ay - nen bah - han - doe.

Un par de o - ji - tos ne - gros, Cie - li - to
Oon pahr day oh - hee - tohs nay - grohs, See-ay - lee - to

Lin - do, de con - tra - ban - do.
Leen - doe, day cone - trah - bahn - doe.

Guitar: Capo 1st fret   *(Please turn the page.)*

Reprinted with the permission of Simon & Schuster Books for Young Readers, an imprint of Simon & Schuster Children's Publishing Division from SONGS OF THE WILD WEST Commentary by Alan Axelrod. Copyright © 1991 The Metropolitan Museum of Art.

CIELITO LINDO (Continued)

Reprinted with the permission of Simon & Schuster Books for Young Readers, an imprint of Simon & Schuster Children's Publishing Division from SONGS OF THE WILD WEST Commentary by Alan Axelrod. Copyright © 1991 The Metropolitan Museum of Art.

✓ Reading Check

1. Why did Spanish mission priests begin training Indians as horsemen?

2. What is a *vaquero*?

3. Where did the English word *buckaroo* come from?

4. What message is repeated throughout "Cielito Lindo"?

5. What is the main idea of this selection?

MEET THE *Writer*

Alan Axelrod has written books and articles on the American frontier, Colonial America, and early American writing. He has also taught English at Lake Forest College and Furman University. Today he works as an editor at the Henry Francis du Pont Winterthur Museum in Delaware.

In the following article you will see how the bicycle craze of the 1890s gave the U.S. military a bright idea—at least for a time.

The Great Bicycle Experiment

from *Cobblestone*

by TONI A. WATSON

Toward the end of the nineteenth century, the U.S. Army was looking for a way to replace the horse in military transportation. General Nelson Miles suggested the bicycle. He said that it was quiet and reliable, and, unlike the horse, it did not have to be fed and watered.

Some of the men from the Twenty-fifth Infantry, which was stationed at Fort Missoula, Montana, were chosen for this unusual experiment. Second Lieutenant James A. Moss, a white officer, commanded the unit. He was eager to test the bicycle in the rugged country of western Montana.

At first, Moss's bicycle corps consisted of one sergeant, one corporal, one musician, and five privates. They devoted three weeks to drills, practice rides, and exercises in jumping fences and fording[1] streams. They could soon climb a nine-foot fence with their bicycles in twenty seconds. In deep water, two soldiers in single file would hang a bicycle on a long pole and carry it across.

Denver Public Library, Western History Collection

▲ A young man poses with his bicycle. ❷ How is a modern bicycle different from this one?

You Need to Know...

The first bicycle, known as the draisine (drā′zēn′), was invented about 1817 by Baron Karl von Drais of Germany. This vehicle had no pedals. Instead, the rider pushed it along with his or her feet, much like a scooter with a seat. In 1839, a Scottish blacksmith added pedals to the draisine. By the late 1800s, the bicycle had been refined. Spokes, chains, and air-filled tires made the vehicles faster and more dependable. The development of industry and mass production also made it easy to produce inexpensive bicycles rapidly. By the 1890s, about four million Americans owned bicycles!

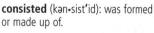

consisted (kən·sist′id): was formed or made up of.

_____

1. fording (fôrd′iŋ): crossing a river at a shallow place.

The first test ride that summer was to Lake McDonald and back. They covered 126 miles (one way) in three and a half days. During that time, the corps experienced heavy rains, strong winds, deep mud, and steep hills. Frequent tire punctures, broken pedals, and lost chains added to their problems.

Riding twenty-six-inch Spalding bicycles, the men each carried a knapsack,[2] a blanket, a shelter tent, a tin cup, and extra bicycle parts. Every other soldier had a rifle strapped <u>horizontally</u> to the left side of his bicycle. Soldiers without rifles carried revolvers and thirty rounds of ammunition. They carried as little as possible on their bodies to avoid serious injuries when they fell.

A second trip was made to Yellowstone National Park, and for the first time in history, a body of armed cyclists crossed the Great Divide of the Rocky Mountains.

For the first time in history, a body of armed cyclists crossed the Great Divide of the Rocky Mountains.

To test the bicycle and his men more thoroughly, Moss proposed an <u>expedition</u> of nineteen hundred miles from Fort Missoula to St. Louis, Missouri. He arranged to have food dropped about every one hundred miles along the way. The corps carried only a two-day supply of rations. Although this was an <u>incentive</u> to travel fifty miles a day, if the men met with difficult conditions, they would have to travel on an empty stomach.

Bike Enlightenment

In the 1890s, the popularity of "safety" bicycles soared in the United States and in Europe. Unlike its forerunner, which had a huge front wheel and a small back wheel, the safety bicycle featured two wheels of about the same size. It was easier to mount, to handle, and to stop than the earlier model. Made of stainless steel, the safety bike weighed about 43 pounds. Today, many more sizes and types are available. Mountain bikes, utility bikes, and touring bikes used for recreation and transportation weigh around 25 to 30 pounds, while the racing bicycle weighs less than 20!

horizontally (hôr'i·zänt'ə·lē): in a position parallel to the horizon; not vertically.

expedition (eks'pə·dish'ən): a journey for a specific purpose.

incentive (in·sent'iv): something that encourages someone to perform a certain task or work toward a goal.

---

2. **knapsack** (nap'sak'): a bag that is carried on the back; backpack.

Bicycles in the Army,

St. Louis, Mo. — Lieut. James A. Moss (white) of the Twenty-fifth infantry, U. S. A, (Afro-Americans, is about to undertake a special mission by order of Gen. Miles. About June 1 in command of 20 Afro-American soldiers. he will start from Fort Missoula to ride on bicycles to St. Louis, nearly 2,000 miles across the roughest, rockiest country in the United States, for the trip means crossing the main divide of the Rocky mountains. Careful preparations are now being made for the trip. Lieut. Moss' report to the war department will be used as a basis for deciding whether it would be advisable to form a bicycle corps as a feature of the army.

▲ This article appeared in the *Cleveland Gazette* on May 29, 1897. **?** **What preparations do you think Lieut. Moss made for the trip?**

On the morning of June 14, 1897, Moss and twenty-three troopers pedaled through Fort Missoula's outer gate. A doctor and reporter accompanied them. Large numbers of local citizens turned out to see them off.

The riders reached St. Louis on July 24. There they were met by a large crowd of cyclists who escorted them through the city. The Twenty-fifth Infantry Bicycle Corps had made the trip in forty days. The corps returned to Montana by train.

The bicycle was never adopted as a means of military transportation, perhaps because, as Moss noted, without puncture-proof tires, military cyclists would "dread the enemy's tacks as much as his bullets."

escorted (es·kôrt′id): accompanied to show honor or respect.

✓ Reading Check

1. Name one way in which bicycles were a better form of transportation than horses.

2. Where was the bicycle first tested by the military?

3. Name three problems experienced by the soldiers who tested the bicycles.

4. Where did the first long-distance test ride begin and end? How many miles long was the ride?

5. Why did the military never adopt bicycles?

The Industrial Revolution brought wealth to many Americans. How did the newly rich spend their money? Read on to find out.

How the Wealthy Lived

from *Cobblestone*

by HELEN WIEMAN BLEDSOE

Mrs. William K. (Alva) Vanderbilt spent a quarter of a million dollars (more than four and a quarter million dollars today) on one of her balls. The flowers alone cost eleven thousand dollars (just less than two hundred thousand dollars today). Mrs. Odgen Mills claimed she could entertain one hundred dinner guests without hiring extra household help. Oliver H.P. Belmont bedded his horses on Irish linen sheets decorated with embroidery and placed gold nameplates on their stalls. These families were some of the Gilded Age's very rich. They spent their huge incomes on elaborate mansions, lavish parties, and extensive traveling.

America's rich of the late 1800s followed a fairly rigid social calendar. They spent the fall season in New York, centered on Fifth Avenue, which was nicknamed "Millionaires' Row." The ladies spent a great amount of time paying social calls on friends. The exchange of visits at times became quite burdensome.[1] In such cases, the visitor simply left an engraved calling card that announced that she had made the obligatory stop.

Invitations for parties arrived daily throughout the fall. Gertrude Vanderbilt's diary recorded that she attended more than ninety dinners in one fall season in the 1890s.

> **You Need to Know...**
> After the Civil War, Americans turned eagerly from the horrors of wartime to the pleasures of the good life. As the industrial boom dropped large sums of money into formerly empty pockets, the upper middle class grew rapidly larger. It also grew more extravagant in its tastes. For the very rich of the Gilded Age, indulgence was the word of the day.

gilded (gild'id): covered in a thin layer of gold.

elaborate (ē·lab'ə·rit): detailed and complicated.

lavish (lav'ish): more than is needed; overly generous.

rigid (rij'id): fixed; inflexible.

obligatory (ə·blig'ə·tôr'ē): necessary; required.

1. **burdensome** (burd'n·səm): demanding; hard to put up with.

▲ Mrs. William Backhouse (Caroline) Astor. ❓ **Why was it important to receive an invitation to her annual ball?**

One party host offered cigars wrapped in hundred-dollar bills to his guests. At another event, black pearls lay hidden inside diners' oysters. The hostess of yet another party named her dog the guest of honor and presented the pet with a collar worth fifteen thousand dollars.

The party season reached its climax at Mrs. William Backhouse (Caroline) Astor's elaborate annual ball in January. . . . Then, early in the spring, these wealthy families journeyed to Europe, accompanied by servants and trunkloads of clothes. They lived in lavish hotel suites. They shopped for the latest fashions and purchased antique furniture and art.

In June, it was back to the United States for parties held at country homes and on yachts. July brought the rich to their Newport, Rhode Island, summer "cottages"—a playful name for what were actually huge estates.

At Newport house parties, men generally wore tennis or yachting clothes. The ladies mostly wore white summer dresses. They all had lunch together, often outdoors or under a tent.

The afternoon "Coach Parade" on Newport's Bellevue Avenue was a daily ritual. Ladies dressed in finery and rode up and down the street in their horse-drawn vehicles. They would wave to one another while comparing clothes, carriages, and horses.

Afternoon tea was followed by music and card playing. The women changed to elaborate tea gowns. For dinner, it was yet another dress for each female guest. A woman had to bring sixteen different outfits for a four-day weekend—so as to avoid wearing the same dress twice!

Many Newport houses had large ballrooms with gilded furniture, and enormous chandeliers. Balls began about 10 P.M., usually following a dinner party. Sometimes they were fancy, dress-up affairs, where the women came in costume. In the fall, the social whirl began all over again back in New York.

Due to their social obligations and the enormous size of their households, America's wealthiest required large staffs of a dozen or more servants. These included a personal maid for the wife, a valet (male servant) for the husband, a butler, a chef, and several other kitchen helpers, launderers, and footmen (to serve dinner and run errands). In addition, families often owned several kinds of carriages and six to ten horses, so they also employed stable hands.

Although they worked hard for their millions, these very rich Americans spent much of their time showing off their great wealth. Perhaps Mark Twain had them in mind when he first coined the phrase "the Gilded Age."

✓ Reading Check

1. During the Gilded Age, where did the wealthy spend the autumn, spring, and summer seasons?

2. Give one detail of a lavish dinner party.

3. What was the "Coach Parade"?

4. How did wealthy people manage their households?

5. Who coined the phrase "the Gilded Age"?

SIDELIGHT

"During the Gilded Age, Caroline Astor ruled New York's social elite. Her balls and parties were the events of the year for the wealthy crowd. She served expensive food on golden dishes and greeted visitors from a throne-like couch. Rich New Yorkers clamored for invitations, but many were turned away. Her guest lists were limited to four hundred, and Mrs. Astor made it clear that only 'worthwhile' people were invited.

The Astor parties were dreadfully dull, but no one cared. The socialites of the Gilded Age were desperate to be among the chosen 'Four Hundred.' Those who made the cut were thrilled; those who missed out were terribly ashamed.

Being on or off the list, however, was usually temporary, depending on Mrs. Astor's whims. She dropped and added names constantly. Friends fell in rank when they annoyed her. She replaced them with others who were more in her favor. As a result, many New Yorkers became clones of Mrs. Astor and her dictates. They agreed with her at every turn and tried not to outshine her. Being in the Four Hundred group was too important for them to risk thinking for themselves."

—"Mrs. Astor and the 'Four Hundred'" by Stephen Currie
from *Cobblestone* (April, 2000)

In 1900, a hurricane struck Galveston, Texas, killing at least eight thousand people. Read on to learn more about the deadliest natural disaster in the nation's history.

The Great Galveston Hurricane

from *Weatherwise*

by PATRICK HUGHES

debris (də•brē'): wreckage; pieces of things that have been destroyed.

"With a raging sea rolling around them, with a wind so terrific none could hope to escape its fury, with roofs being torn away and buildings crumbling . . . men, women, and children . . . huddled like rats in the structures. As buildings crumpled and crashed, hundreds were buried under debris, while thousands were thrown into the waters, some to meet instant death, others to struggle for a time in vain, and yet other thousands to escape death in miraculous and marvelous ways."

This is an eyewitness account of the Galveston hurricane of 1900, the deadliest natural disaster in U.S. history. It killed more Americans than the legendary Chicago Fire, San Francisco Earthquake, and Johnstown Flood combined, yet today is all but forgotten.

You Need to Know...

The city of Galveston, Texas, was founded in 1836 on a long, narrow island about two miles off the Texas mainland. It soon grew into a thriving port city. By 1900, it was the largest city in Texas. Galveston welcomed thousands of immigrants to the United States, becoming a kind of Ellis Island of the South. The prospering people of Galveston looked forward to the new century. They believed that the 1900s would hold only good things for their city. They were not at all prepared when the worst natural disaster ever to strike the United States completely destroyed Galveston. Even the Galveston weatherman, Isaac Cline, was taken by surprise. Without the aid of today's hi-tech radars, Cline had little idea that a killer storm was hurling itself across the Gulf of Mexico, straight toward the island. According to his memoirs, he had noted showers on the morning of September 8, 1900, "but dense clouds and heavy rain were not in evidence." As you will see in the following selection, the deadly evidence was soon to arrive.

The hurricane killed at least 8,000 people. It cut Galveston Island off from the Texas mainland and submerged it under the sea. In the City of Galveston, on the eastern end of the island, the storm killed some 6,000 men, women, and children and left 5,000 more battered and bruised. It swept away 2,636 homes—nearly half the city's total—and reduced to rubble at least 1,000 more. Not a single building escaped damage; every survivor had faced death.

Galveston had been "a city of splendid homes and broad clean streets" wrote Clarence Ousley, editor of the *Tribune*, "a city of oleanders[1] and roses and palms; a city of the finest churches, school buildings, and benevolent institutions in the South; a thriving port . . .; a seaside resort . . .; a city of great wealth and large charity."

After the hurricane, Galveston was "a city of wrecked homes and streets choked with debris sandwiched with six thousand corpses; a city . . . with the slime of the ocean on every spot and in every house; a city with only three churches standing, not a school building or benevolent institution habitable; a port with shipping stranded and wrecked many miles from the moorings . . .[2] a rolling surf three hundred feet inward from the former water line . . . lapping an area of total destruction four blocks deep and three miles long . . . a city whose very cemeteries had been emptied of their dead."

The Gathering Storm

The storm that destroyed much of Galveston and killed, maimed, or made homeless more than half its citizens was born west of the Cape Verde Islands about August 27, 1900. By September 4, it was moving northward over Cuba. It became a full-blown hurricane as it raked the Florida Keys on September 5. On Friday the 7th, the Weather Bureau in Washington notified Isaac Cline, chief of the Galveston office, that storm warnings had been extended to Galveston.

submerged (səb·mʉrjd): placed under the surface of a body of liquid.

benevolent (bə·nev′ə·lənt): kindly; characterized by doing good deeds.

habitable (hab′it·ə·bəl): able to be lived in.

maimed (māmd): severely wounded or injured; crippled.

---

1. **oleanders** (ō′lē·an′dərz): fragrant flowering shrubs that thrive in tropical climates.
2. **moorings** (mo͞or′iŋz): ropes or chains that hold a floating object in place.

That afternoon, Captain J. W. Simmons of the steamer *Pensacola,* en route from Galveston to his home port, watched the barometer fall to 28.55 inches as he struggled to stay afloat in towering seas. He had never seen the glass that low before.

At daylight Saturday morning, early rising Galvestonians went down to the beach to watch the thundering surf crash farther and farther inland. Already, breakers had smashed several beachside buildings and destroyed a streetcar trestle.[3]

At 10:10 A.M., Washington warned Cline the storm center was expected to make landfall west of Galveston, putting the city in the hurricane's right semicircle. The winds would be strongest in that area, exposing Galveston and its inhabitants to the threat of a deadly storm surge.

By noon, the wind was blowing out of the northeast at more than 30 m.p.h. and increasing steadily. The barometer was dropping rapidly, and heavy rain was falling. The Gulf of Mexico was already three to five feet deep in streets near the beach, and cottages in the eastern end of the city were breaking up. Meanwhile, the rising water of Galveston Bay had submerged the wagon bridge and train trestles connecting Galveston to the mainland and were flooding inland over the wharves on the north side of the city. It was too late to get off the island.

The Last Message

"Gulf rising rapidly; half the city now under water," Cline wired Washington at 2:30 P.M., adding the city was going under fast, and "great loss of life must result." This was the last message to get out of Galveston.

Between 4 and 5 P.M., the waters of the bay met those of the gulf, submerging the entire city. By 5:15 P.M., the wind was gusting to 100 m.p.h. and rolling up tin roofs and toppling telephone poles. Huge chunks of masonry crashed into flooded streets in the business district, while near the beach, homes were pounded to pieces by wind, water, and wave-tossed wreckage. Flying debris from

Denver Public Library, Western History Department

▲ U.S. Signal Station on the summit of Pike's Peak. Such signal stations are used to send weather reports.

❓ **Why do you think this one is on top of a mountain?**

---

3. trestle (tres′əl): a structure that holds up a raised track or bridge.

disintegrating buildings killed people in the streets, while whirling wreckage pinned others underwater to drown.

Isaac Cline stood in eight inches of water at his elevated front door about 6:30 P.M. when the racing water suddenly rose above his waist. Gulf water was now 10 feet deep in the street and 15.2 feet above sea level. The water rose another five feet in the next hour.

By 7:00 P.M., it was dark, with the wind howling at an estimated 120 m.p.h. Waterborne wreckage of other houses and a railroad trestle 1/4-mile

Courtesy of the Rosenberg Library, Galveston, Texas

▲ Galveston after the storm.

long were battering the east side of Cline's house. At 7:30 P.M. the wind shifted to the east, blowing with even greater fury, and the house fell. It carried with it about 50 people who had sought shelter there. As the house capsized, Joseph Cline grabbed the hands of his brother's older girls, Allie May (12) and Rosemary (11) and jumped through a second story window. Isaac Cline, his wife, Cora May, and his youngest daughter (six), Esther Ballew, were carried under when the house rolled over. Cline lost consciousness. When he awoke, he was above water. Esther was nearby, but Cora May was gone.

A few minutes later, Cline saw his brother and his other two children atop the floating house and joined them. For the next three hours they scrambled from one piece of wreckage to another as the house broke up. The rain fell in torrents, while the roaring wind hurled timbers and other missiles past their heads. The brothers huddled with their backs to the wind and the children in front of them, holding planks behind them to ward off the deadly flying debris that killed so many that terrible night. Even so, they sometimes were struck by heavier objects and knocked into the raging water.

The wreckage they clung to grounded about 10:30 P.M. The exhausted survivors climbed over mounds of debris

disintegrating (dis·in′tə·grāt′iŋ): falling apart.

estimated (es′tə·māt′id): judged or determined to be nearly accurate.

capsized (kap′sīzd′): turned over.

As people in distant parts of the country began using the telegraph to share news about the weather, predicting bad weather became easier. For example, reports of snow in Chicago helped easterners prepare for their own winter blast. Joseph Henry, a famous scientist of his day, became excited about the ways the telegraph could advance meteorology, the study of the weather. At the Smithsonian Institution in Washington, D.C., Henry set up a weather telegraphy (tə·leg′rə·fē) program to study American storms. Henry's efforts—including his creation of a huge, color-coded forecast map in the great hall of the Smithsonian—led to government involvement in weather reporting. By 1870, Congress had set up a national weather service to track weather as it moved west to east and to warn people of any possible dangers.

to a still-standing, two-story house and crawled in an upstairs window. Almost a month later, the body of Cora May Cline was found under the wreckage that carried her family to safety.

Tales of Survival

When her home went down, Mrs. William Henry Heideman, who was pregnant, was swept away on the roof of a wrecked cottage. The roof struck other debris and Mrs. Heideman was hurled off—only to land in a steamer trunk bobbing by on the surging water. The trunk hurtled along, bumping against driftwood and other debris, until it smashed against the massive wall of the Ursuline Convent and was pulled inside. William Henry Heideman, Jr., was born a few hours later.

Others also were plucked from passing debris and wreckage and pulled into the convent yard. James Irwin was naked when rescued. The only dry clothing in the convent was a nun's habit, so after the storm subsided, Mr. Irwin left the convent dressed as a Sister of Charity.

The rambling wooden buildings of St. Mary's Orphanage stood on the beach three miles west of the city. They housed 10 Roman Catholic Sisters of the Incarnate Word, 93 orphans, and a workman.

The water was already three feet deep by 10:00 A.M. Saturday. Later, as the storm worsened, the sisters took the children to the chapel on the first floor of the girls' building. They prayed there until the rapidly rising water drove them to the second floor. From there they watched the boys' building break up. Sometime between 7:00 and 9:00 P.M., the roof of their building collapsed. With death threatening, the sisters tied the children to their waists.

After the hurricane, only a few scattered bricks marked the site of the orphanage. Ninety bodies were found nearby—one nun still had nine small children tied to her body, while another held a child in each arm.

Only three orphans, all boys, survived. Somehow they got out of the building and onto an uprooted tree sweeping by on the rushing water.

New Horror

The dawn brought new horror. All that remained of thousands of homes and many of the people who had lived in them was a great mound of wreckage jammed with bodies the storm had piled up in a rough semicircle around the southern side of the business district. Outside this barrier, everything had been swept away.

Many bodies and many of the living were naked or near-naked, their clothes ripped off by <u>protruding</u> nails, jagged pieces of wood, broken glass, and flying debris. Hundreds of whole families had perished; almost every family had lost at least one member. As many as 10,000 survivors were homeless. Galveston Bay was clogged with human bodies, and the corpses of cows, horses, chickens, and dogs were everywhere.

protruding (prō·trōōd′iŋ): sticking out from.

Bettmann/CORBIS

▲ Building the Galveston seawall. ❓ **How does the seawall protect the city?**

By Monday, makeshift morgues[4] were jammed with corpses. The weather was hot, and the health of the living demanded immediate action. So on Tuesday, Galveston became a city of funeral pyres.[5] A dark pall of smoke hung over the island for weeks as the grim task continued.

Ironically, the hurricane itself saved many survivors—and showed them how to prevent a similar disaster in the future. The <u>barricade</u> of wreckage thrown up by the storm had acted as a breakwater or seawall, shielding the buildings and people behind it from the terrible destructive force of racing flood waters, crashing waves, and whirling wreckage. So Galveston built a seawall.

barricade (bar′i·kād′): a barrier put up quickly for protection.

A similar hurricane hit the city on the night of August 16, 1915, which closely followed the track of the 1900 storm. This time, only eight people died. Galveston had learned its lesson well. Tragically, other low-lying U.S. coastal communities may someday have to learn the same lesson.

---

4. **morgues** (môrgz): places where dead bodies are temporarily kept to be identified or examined for cause of death before burial.
5. **pyres** (pīrz): mounds of wood on which dead bodies are burned.

▲ Ruins of Galveston's Sacred Heart Church.

✓ Reading Check

1. How many people were killed by the Galveston hurricane of 1900?

2. What had the city of Galveston been like before the hurricane?

3. What were the last words wired from Galveston to the Weather Bureau in Washington?

4. How did Isaac Cline and his brother protect their children after Cline's home had collapsed?

5. How did the hurricane teach the people of Galveston to prevent another, similar disaster?

MEET THE *Writer*

In the late 1970s and early 1980s, **Patrick Hughes** worked as the managing editor of *Weatherwise* magazine. From 1992 until his death in 1999, he served the magazine as a contributing editor. Hughes wrote "The Great Galveston Hurricane" for the August 1979 edition of *Weatherwise*.

Around the turn of the century, a new musical form called ragtime began sweeping the country. The following selection tells about the Maple Leaf Club in Sedalia, Missouri, where Scott Joplin's ragtime style made him the "King of Ragtime."

from The Maple Leaf Club
from *Scott Joplin*

by KATHERINE PRESTON

▲ Scott Joplin.

Library of Congress / PRC Archive

The people who are walking east along Main Street hear a barbershop quartet singing a number of popular songs. The singing, which is not quite in tune but has a lot of spirit, ends amid a burst of applause and shouts of laughter. As the cheers and laughter begin to die down, the sounds of the night are replaced by music being played on an upright piano.

integrated (in′tə·grāt′id): open to people of all races.

A steady stream of people—both black and white—head in the direction of the music, which is coming from a club located over a feed store at 121 East Main Street. It is called the Maple Leaf Club, and it was founded just two years before, in 1898.

Although membership in the Maple Leaf Club is limited to blacks only, the clientele[1] is <u>integrated</u>. This mixing of the races might strike some visitors to Sedalia as odd, for in most

You Need to Know...

Musician Scott Joplin was the son of a former slave. He left his home state of Texas at the age of fourteen and traveled up and down the Mississippi River, playing the piano whenever he could. Finally he settled in Sedalia, Missouri, where his energetic music found favor. Within years, Joplin had found fame, too. His tune "Maple Leaf Rag," published by the owner of the store where he played, would eventually become the first piece of sheet music ever to sell over one million copies. Joplin's style, known as ragtime, had emerged after the Civil War, when black musicians began using an instrument that had been rarely used by slaves—the piano. Ragtime music combined a ragged or irregular rhythm (often played by one hand on the piano) with a regular beat (played by the other hand). In the following selection, step into the exciting musical world of the Maple Leaf Club and meet the "King of Ragtime" himself.

---

1. **clientele** (klī′ən·tel′): regular group of customers.

places in turn-of-the-century America, blacks and whites do not mix socially. However, the Maple Leaf Club has developed a reputation as one of *the* places to visit in town. It is especially recommended for people who like the new and still developing form of music called ragtime.

The source of the Maple Leaf Club's lofty reputation is readily obvious as soon as a person climbs the stairs and enters the club. For the official club pianist is none other than Scott Joplin, the indisputable ragtime king.

Despite the summer heat, the club is crowded. It is a large smoky room dominated by mirrors and a huge carved walnut bar. Gas chandeliers swing overhead. There are scores of men seated around numerous gaming tables, playing dice or poker. Groups of men also surround large green pool tables. Some of the men hold cue sticks and study the layout, while others bend over the tables, concentrating on their shots, as people chat amiably and the piano plays on.

Seated at the piano, the 31-year-old Joplin seems to be ignoring all of the commotion around him. He occasionally glances up and flashes a smile as someone yells a greeting to him from across the room. But most of the time he is serious and remarkably caught up in his music. Although he is a small, dark man who dresses quietly and neatly, he commands a lot of attention when he is at the piano.

Over the course of the evening at the Maple Leaf Club, Joplin will launch into a rousing piece of music that will have all of the people in the club tapping their feet and clapping their hands. And if he "rags" (playfully changes) a tune that everyone knows, a lot of folks will start to sing along. After this song is over, he might begin to play a brand-new piece. Then again he might improvise a piece as he goes along, playing each verse a little differently from the others but all the while incorporating the syncopated,[2] "ragged" rhythm that is the hallmark of ragtime.

lofty (lôf′tē): impressive.

indisputable (in′di•spyo͞ot′ə•bəl): unable to be challenged.

dominated (däm′ə•nāt′id): overwhelmed or overshadowed by.

amiably (ā′mē•ə•blē): in a friendly, easygoing way.

commotion (kə•mō′shən): noisy disturbance or confusion.

improvise (im′prə•vīz′): to make up or create without any preparation.

Collection of Sandy Marrone / PRC Archive

▲ The piano song sheet for the "Maple Leaf Rag." ❓ **Where did the song get its name?**

---

2. **syncopated** (siŋ′kə•pāt′id): beginning musical tones on unaccented rather than accented beats.

At least several times each night, Joplin will oblige the requests of his audience and play some of his own compositions, including "Maple Leaf Rag," which was probably named for the club. When he plays this piece, which is just beginning to achieve widespread popularity, many of his listeners will start to clap along with the music. Some might even break into an impromptu[3] dance. A number of coins will have been added to Joplin's growing pile of tips by the time he ends his rendition.

> **Over the course of the evening at the Maple Leaf Club, Joplin will launch into a rousing piece of music that will have all of the people in the club tapping their feet and clapping their hands.**

The music making continues throughout the night as people come and go. By the early-morning hours, only a few people are left in the room: musicians who have been assembling in the club over the course of the evening. Some of these musicians are visiting friends in Sedalia, others are just passing through town, and the rest are local pianists who play at other clubs in town but are finished with their work for the evening.

When the Maple Leaf Club finally closes its doors for the night, all of these musicians sit down to play with one another. Although Joplin and some of the other pianists have been working all night, they are eager to play when there are a lot of other musicians around to trade musical ideas, play for each other, and invent new ragtime melodies.

With its roots in black American folk music, ragtime was regarded at first by the American public as being low class and improper. Because it was initially played in saloons, where a tune was often matched with crude or bawdy lyrics, ragtime was not considered to be a very

---

3. **impromptu** (im·prämp′tōō): without planning; spontaneous.

Rhythm Relations

The ragtime music of the 1890s and early 1900s had a strong impact on the rhythms and moods of the jazz music that became popular during the 1920s. Both forms were rooted in African American folk music, and both originated in the South—ragtime in St. Louis, Missouri, and jazz in New Orleans, Louisiana. However, there are definite differences between the two kinds of music. Ragtime music is formally composed; that is, it is written down. It is also played mainly on the piano. Jazz music, on the other hand, is usually improvised, or made up as the musicians go along. It is also played on a wide variety of instruments, including piano, saxophone, and clarinet.

respectable (ri•spek′tə•bəl): considered acceptable and proper by society.

respectable art form. "Take that ragtime out of my house," musician Eubie Blake was told by his mother when he was a boy just learning how to play the piano.

Ragtime was also one of the first forms of music to jazz up traditional tunes. However, this practice of altering standard songs displeased many people as well. James Europe, one of the most popular black composers and bandleaders in Harlem in the early 1900s, went so far as to deny that this musical form even existed. "There never was any such music as ragtime," he maintained.

Yet many of the first ragtime composers, including Joplin, believed that the music captured the charm of the Victorian era and was full of grace. He felt that the lyrics—not the melodies—were responsible for ragtime's unpopularity in many places. He said:

> I have often sat in theaters and listened to beautiful ragtime melodies set to almost vulgar words . . . and I have wondered why some composers will continue to make people hate ragtime because the melodies are set to such bad words.
>
> I have often heard people say, after they had heard a ragtime song, "I like the music but I don't like the words." . . .
>
> If someone were to put vulgar words to a strain of one of Beethoven's beautiful symphonies, people would begin saying, "I don't like Beethoven's symphonies." So it is the unwholesome words and not the ragtime melodies that many people hate.

To turn ragtime into a popular and respectable musical form in the 20th century was not an easy task, for it meant taking the music out of the barrooms and finding an opportunity to play it before a more cultivated audience. To work toward this goal required patience, diligence, and sacrifice.

diligence (dil′ə•jens): persistence.

Well aware of the challenges that were facing him, Scott Joplin was willing to show that he was as determined as he was talented. He wanted the entire country—not just Sedalia—to discover that ragtime was a legitimate form of music . . . and that he was the ragtime king.

legitimate (lə•jit′ə•mət): recognized or approved.

✓ Reading Check

1. What was unusual about the crowd that gathered at the Maple Leaf Club?

2. When Scott Joplin played, he would often "rag" a familiar tune. What does this mean?

3. What happened at the Maple Leaf Club after it closed for the night?

4. Name two things about ragtime music that some people did not like.

5. Why did Joplin like ragtime music?

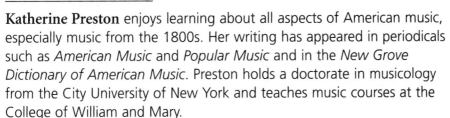

MEET THE *Writer*

Katherine Preston enjoys learning about all aspects of American music, especially music from the 1800s. Her writing has appeared in periodicals such as *American Music* and *Popular Music* and in the *New Grove Dictionary of American Music*. Preston holds a doctorate in musicology from the City University of New York and teaches music courses at the College of William and Mary.

In the years after the Civil War, the newly built transcontinental railroad ran straight through the heart of America—at the same time crushing the hearts of some Americans. The following selection explains the human cost of these "engines of industry."

The Granger Collection, New York

▲ A railroad bridge in the American West. Oil over a photograph, circa 1870.

from The Railroad Unites America

from *The Iron Horse: How Railroads Changed America*

by RICHARD WORMSER

The crews of the Union Pacific had a much easier construction job than the crews of the Central Pacific. The land was relatively flat and there were few mountains to cross. Construction began in the great prairies of the Midwest, and for most of the Irish, the land and its people were a source of wonder and astonishment. The countryside seemed flat and unending. There was not a tree or a shrub anywhere. Farther west, the crews saw the great buffalo herds that inhabited the plain. The herds were so large that when they crossed the railroad tracks they could delay a train for hours. The crews also saw coyotes, antelopes, jackrabbits, prairie dogs, grasshoppers, and rattlesnakes.

The major difficulty Dodge and his men had to face was the Native

You Need to Know...

In 1862, President Lincoln approved funds for a railroad that would connect California to the rest of the nation. During the Civil War, construction started and then stopped as the railroad companies grew busy moving troops and supplies. Finally, in 1865, the work began in earnest. Congress had given the enormous task to two railroad companies, the Union Pacific in the east and the Central Pacific in the west. General Grenville Dodge was in charge of the work for the Union Pacific, while Collis Huntington headed up operations for the Central Pacific. With the help of thousands of Chinese and European immigrants, the companies began laying track—the Union Pacific in Omaha, Nebraska, and the Central Pacific in Sacramento, California. Slowly, over vast plains, gigantic mountains, and endless deserts, the two railroad tracks snaked closer together.

Americans. (Collis Huntington solved his problems with them by giving the chiefs free passes to ride on his trains, including the locomotive. The rest of the tribe could ride for free on the freight trains.) The tribes had not been consulted about having a railroad run through what had traditionally been their hunting grounds. They had no objection to people hunting there or passing through. But the railroad was another matter. The Plains Indians—mainly the Sioux, Cheyenne, Kiowa, and Arapaho—saw clearly that the railroad was the death blow to their way of life. Iron Bull, the Crow chief, summed up the significance of the railroad for his people: "We have reached the end of our rule and a new one has come. The end of our lives, too, is near at hand. . . . Of our once powerful nation there are now but a few left . . . and we too, will soon be gone."

The truth was that the railroad developers, like the gold hunters and farmers, wanted the land of the Indian peoples. In order to convince the federal government to send in the army to wipe out the tribes, they argued that the Indians were dangerous and needed to be <u>subdued</u>, if not wiped out. But before they were defeated, the Plains Indians put up a struggle that lasted for almost thirty

subdued (səb·dōod): defeated; brought under submission.

Peter Newark's American Pictures

▲ The joining of the east and west tracks of the transcontinental railroad.
❓ Why did the tracks meet in the mountains and not on the plains below?

plundered (plun'dərd): robbed, usually as part of an attack.

years. In 1865, Red Cloud, a Sioux chief, warned of what was to come: "You destroyed the buffalo, you lied to us, you will get nothing from us but war." Two hundred miles west of Missouri, the Cheyennes, under Chief Spotted Tail, attacked and plundered a train, killed its crew, and destroyed the track. Raiding parties continually ambushed advance parties of surveyors. In the Black Hills, General Dodge himself was attacked while looking for a route through the mountains for the railroad. He barely escaped.

"You destroyed the buffalo, you lied to us, you will get nothing from us but war."

One of the most famous encounters between the Native Americans and the Union Pacific took place in 1868 at Plum Creek, Nebraska. A group of Sioux warriors waited by a railroad track for a train to come. Years later one of the members of the raiding party told the story:

The white soldiers had run us from our lodges and hunting grounds. They burned everything we had. Our blankets were ragged. Our ponies thin. We needed the white man's medicine. We thought if we could take what was inside the iron horse, we could become strong again.

The raiding party ripped up sections of the track to cause a derailment[1] and then waited in ambush for a freight train. But instead, a flatcar appeared, carrying several men who were inspecting the track. The flatcar derailed and the Indians attacked, killing two of the crew and wounding a third, Willie Thompson. Thompson pretended he was dead even as one of the Indians scalped him. Miraculously, he survived. The Sioux then continued to wait for a freight train. When it finally appeared, it crashed into the flatcar and derailed. Thompson watched

---

1. derailment (dē·rāl'mənt): the act of forcing a train off its tracks.

as the fireman and engineer were killed and the Sioux broke open the freight cars to plunder them. Thompson noticed that the Indian who had taken his scalp dropped it. After the raiders left, he got up, picked up his scalp, and waited until he was rescued. He took his scalp to a doctor, hoping that he might be able to sew it back in place. When the operation was unsuccessful, Thompson donated the scalp to the Omaha, Nebraska, public library, where it was displayed for many years as one of their prime exhibits.

The Golden Spike

On May 10, 1869, at Promontory, Utah, the east and west tracks of the transcontinental railroad were joined together. Two locomotives—one on each side of the track—stood at attention, along with a spirited crowd of about five hundred local people. While a band played triumphant music, the final spike, made of solid gold, was presented to the governor of California, who was also the president of Central Pacific Railroad. The governor attempted to hammer the spike into place but could not keep the heavy hammer from slipping off the slick metal. Finally, Jack Casement, the boss of the Union Pacific work crew, drove the golden spike home. America was now connected by rail, from sea to shining sea.

The United States Army, under General William Sherman, was finally sent in to drive the Plains Indians out of the railroad's territory. Sherman's goal was to either make peace with the tribes through treaties or destroy them militarily. More often than not, the treaties were broken by the whites. The army also wiped out a number of peaceful Indian villages, massacring men, women, and children and then reporting the event as a great battle, when in fact there had been no resistance. Colonel George Custer, who would eventually be killed by the Sioux at the battle of the Little Big Horn in 1876, led some of the most notorious massacres. In retaliation, a Cheyenne chief named Tall Bull led his Dog Soldiers, as his warriors were called, against the railroad, wrecking trains and killing their crews. The army tracked them and finally located Tall Bull's camp. They attacked, killing him and most of his followers.

The United States not only destroyed the society and culture of the Plains Indians, it also destroyed their means of survival. The buffalo was the winter source of food for most of the tribe and a major source of clothing to protect

notorious (nō·tôr′ē·əs): well known in a negative way.

massacres (mas′ə·kərz): cruel, large-scale killings of people.

retaliation (ri·tal′ē·ā′shən): the return of one harmful act with another.

▲ Railroad workers.

people from the bitter winter cold. Buffalo hunters like William "Buffalo Bill" Cody slaughtered buffalo to supply the railroad workers with food, while others massacred the herds just for the "sport." Between 1865 and 1885, some twelve million buffalo were slaughtered by white hunters, soldiers, and railroad passengers.

By 1900 the Indian wars had ended. Out of an estimated one million Native Americans who lived on this continent when the first European settlers arrived in Jamestown, Virginia, three hundred years earlier, only 300,000 were left.

✓ Reading Check

1. How did the Plains Indians feel about people hunting or traveling in their region? How did they feel about a railroad running through their land?

2. How did railroad builders convince the government to send troops to fight the Indians?

3. What happened after Willie Thompson's flatcar was derailed by Indians? Summarize the story.

4. Who led some of the worst attacks against the Indians? How did the Indians respond?

5. According to the author, how did the United States destroy the American Indians' means of survival?

MEET THE *Writer*

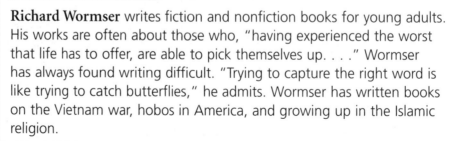

Richard Wormser writes fiction and nonfiction books for young adults. His works are often about those who, "having experienced the worst that life has to offer, are able to pick themselves up. . . ." Wormser has always found writing difficult. "Trying to capture the right word is like trying to catch butterflies," he admits. Wormser has written books on the Vietnam war, hobos in America, and growing up in the Islamic religion.

Cross-Curricular ACTIVITIES

■ HISTORY/MATHEMATICS

Off to Work We Go In the early 1900s, many people your age held full-time jobs. Today, this is illegal in the United States. Is this law still sound, or is it outdated? Poll a group of twenty-five to fifty students in your school to find out how they feel about the fact that it's illegal for them to work full time. First, decide on two or three questions to ask relating to this issue. The questions should ask for a *yes* or a *no*, a number, or a short phrase. When you are ready, conduct your poll as quickly as possible. (If you take too long, people may discuss the questions and influence the way others respond.) Afterward, tally the results. Then, create a visual, such as a bar graph, to show the results of the poll. Post the display on a bulletin board.

■ LANGUAGE ARTS/HISTORY

Full Steam Ahead? During the wars with the American Indians over the transcontinental railroad, the United States Army sent representatives to the Plains tribes who lived in the West to try to make peace treaties. Imagine that you are a reporter who has returned to the East from covering a meeting between the army and one of the Plains tribes. Write a human-interest article for your newspaper describing the way of life of the American Indians you met. Use books and Web sites to find out more about the culture of the tribe you chose: its government; the roles of men, women, and children; housing and occupations; leisure activities; and values important to the tribe. Explain how the building of the railroad will affect the tribe's way of life. If possible, use a computer to make your newspaper page look real. Include the date and the title of the newspaper at the top of the page. If possible, include copies of any photographs of the tribe that you find.

■ SCIENCE/HISTORY

My Significant Five During the Industrial Age, new inventions and the technology they introduced dramatically changed the lives of all Americans. The automobile took over the roads from the horse and carriage, electric lights replaced the glow of candles— in a few decades, a host of inventions became part of daily life. What do you think were the five most important inventions of this period? Use books and Web sites to find out about the inventors and their creations and write a report about your list of five inventions. Explain how each invention came about, tell who created it, and describe how it changed American society. Your concluding paragraph should tell why you think your top five were the most significant. Give an oral presentation of your report to your class.

■ SCIENCE/GEOGRAPHY

A Storm Is Born Weather forecasting today is much more scientific, and accurate, than it was one hundred years ago. Prepare a report explaining how today's storm-tracking technology could be used to avoid a tragedy like the Galveston hurricane. You might also research a hurricane or tornado that struck somewhere in the United States in recent years and create a report about this hurricane or tornado—where it began, how meteorologists followed it, and where it landed. Your report should include two or three written paragraphs and one or more maps or diagrams.

READ ON: FOR INDEPENDENT READING

■ NONFICTION

Bully for You, Teddy Roosevelt! by Jean Fritz (G. P. Putnam's Sons, 1991). Roosevelt never walked when he could run, and his mouth ran as fast as his legs. Somehow, between charging up San Juan Hill in Cuba and hunting lions in Africa, he found time to become the youngest-ever President of the United States.

Growing Up in Coal Country by Susan Bartoletti (Houghton Mifflin Company, 1996). The law said no boy under fourteen could work in the mines, but bosses were happy to hire a six-year-old and say he was small for his age. This Orbis Pictus Notable book explains how boys worked from seven in the morning until six at night, picking through coal until their fingers bled or matching wits with the giant rats that ruled the mines.

Full Steam Ahead: The Race to Build a Transcontinental Railroad by Rhoda Blumberg (National Geographic Society, 1996). Build a railroad all the way from New York to California? One congressman said they might as well try to build a railroad to the moon. Yet, when two rival companies started laying down tracks, one from the east and one from the west, they didn't ask whether it could be done. Their only question was, who will get farthest first? Find out the answer in this Orbis Pictus Honor book.

A Strange and Distant Shore: Indians of the Great Plains in Exile by Brent Ashabranner (Cobblehill, 1996). They'd been massacred, imprisoned, and driven from their land. When the Great Plains Indians still wouldn't give up, the United States government arrested seventy-two of their tribal leaders and sent them to an old Spanish fort in Florida. This Orbis Pictus Notable book describes how they poured their sorrow into works of art.

■ FICTION

Dragon's Gate by Laurence Yep (HarperCollins, 1993). As far as Otter and his uncle Foxfire are concerned, they're just "guests" on "Gold Mountain," earning money carving a tunnel for the American railroad so they can return as revolutionaries to the real world—China. In this Newbery Honor book, Otter soon finds that the hunger and cold, brutal overseers, and dangerous work are more than he expected.

Land of Hope by Joan Lowery Nixon (Bantam Books, 1992). Fifteen-year-old Rebekah and her shipboard friends, a Swedish girl named Kristin and an Irish girl named Rose, pass the long ocean voyage planning and dreaming of their new lives in America. However, Rebekah soon finds herself slaving seven days a week in a sweatshop. What will become of her American dream? Find out what happens to Kristin and Rose in the sequels, *Land of Promise* and *Land of Dreams*.

Words by Heart by Ouida Sebestyen (Little, Brown and Company, 1979). In this ALA Best Book for Young Adults, Lena knows she can memorize more scripture than anyone else. She'll win that contest, and for once it won't matter that hers is the first African American family ever to live in the town of Bethel Springs. In 1910, though, some people think that's one black family too many.

CHAPTER 6

American Issues
The United States from 1914 to the Present

Some People Really Know How to Live It Up

How long is the human life span? The *life span* of a species—the maximum age its members can reach—is defined by the oldest living member. For the human species, that was Madame Jeanne Calment, who died at the amazing age of 122 in 1997.

However, the average *life expectancy* for Americans—the length of time, on average, that we can expect to live—is still only around 76 years. Still, we're definitely living longer. In 1900, the average life expectancy in this country was only 47 years! When today's centenarians (people who have reached the age of 100) were children, only one person in 100,000 could expect to live to 100. Today, our chances are ten times as good. Who knows? Maybe someday our life expectancy *will* reach 122!

AP/Wide World Photos

▲ The world's oldest astronaut, John Glenn, flew a nine-day mission in space at age seventy-seven.

Cold Enough for Ya?

Colonists in the late 1700s were puzzled. What had happened to the record snowfalls and freezing temperatures they'd heard so much about from their grandparents and great-grandparents? It was believed that the American climate must have gotten milder. One suggestion was that the new cities, with their many stoves and chimneys, were warming the air.

Today some scientists say that there may be evidence to support the theory of climate warming. Smoke and gases in greater quantity than ever before are crowding the atmosphere. These gases trap heat from the sun near the earth's surface, like the glass windows of a greenhouse.

Memorable Quote

"We should all be concerned about the future because we will spend the rest of our lives there."

—from *Seed for Thought* by Charles Franklin Kettering

VOCABULARY MATTERS

New ideas and developments call for new words to describe and name them. *Clone* was used in 1970 by Alvin Toffler, in his book *Future Shock*, to name a person or animal developed from one cell of its parent, thus creating a genetically identical offspring. *Clone*'s parent word is the Greek word for "twig." Why? Because some twigs are grafted onto other plants to reproduce themselves.

AP/Wide World Photos

▲ Dolly, the world's first cloned adult mammal.

INVESTIGATE: What do *you* think the world will be like when you are an adult?

The result is global warming—a steady rise in the earth's average temperature. In fact, the ten hottest years on record occurred in the 1980s and 1990s. Debates about the issue of global warming continue, even as scientists continue to keep a sharp eye on any changes in the earth's temperature.

I'd Like a Hundred Copies of This Pig, Please

It took nearly three hundred tries, but scientists in Scotland finally cloned a sheep named Dolly. They used Dolly's DNA, or genetic code, to make another sheep with exactly the same genes. The sheep was a twin, only younger.

Why bother with cloning? One reason is to save lives. Scientists are trying to breed pigs with human-type livers, for example. These scientists believe that if animals could be cloned with just the right organs, many people who now die waiting for transplants might be saved.

Cloning can be used to help animals, too. It's hard to bring some endangered species back from the brink of extinction. Animals often won't breed in captivity, and in the wild they might die before they've had a chance to reproduce. Cloning could boost their population and give the species a better chance of survival.

Future History

In 1965, thirty of the smartest people in America got together to try to guess what the world would be like by the year 2000. Some of their predictions came true: personal computers, fax machines, and safer automobiles. Others were wildly off base: human colonies on the moon, robot maids to do all our housework, and a nuclear power generator in every home.

Other experts of the time predicted we'd all head downtown to do errands on a moving sidewalk, or in flying cars. Some said television would be "the greatest force for world enlightenment and freedom that history has ever known."

What does the future hold? How will people live, work, study, and have fun in the twenty-first century and beyond? What problems—social, environmental, political—will we solve, and what new problems will turn up? Stay tuned....

Baseball is often viewed as one of America's greatest contributions to popular culture. As with all things, though, there are many sides to the saga of baseball. Read on to find out about a little-known period in the history of the sport.

A Gentleman's Agreement

from *Shadow Ball: The History of the Negro Leagues*

by GEOFFREY C. WARD and KEN BURNS, with JIM O'CONNOR

Two Innings Ahead of Everyone Else

In 1919 the bloodiest race riots since the Civil War swept the United States. The worst took place in Chicago. It started when a black boy was stoned to death because his rubber raft floated too close to a white beach. By the time it ended, thirty-eight people were dead and over five hundred injured. For many of the blacks who had moved north to escape the harsh anti-black laws of the South, the riots confirmed their worst fears—racism was everywhere.

But as a result of the riots, African Americans began to assert themselves. Marcus Garvey, the black nationalist,[1] urged blacks to

confirmed (kən·fʉrmd'): proved that something was true.

You Need to Know...

Between 1887 and 1919, the game of baseball was governed by an unwritten code. According to this "gentleman's agreement," African Americans were not allowed to play on professional teams. Although the ban was not official, team owners, managers, and players did what they could to keep blacks out of the game. Occasionally, though, an African American would manage to make his way to the plate and play. Bud Fowler, for example, joined an all-white club in New Castle, Pennsylvania, in 1872. However, neither this club nor any of the other fourteen he played for would keep him long, and Fowler eventually left the game. By 1899, black players were completely shut out of both the major and minor leagues, but they would not be discouraged. Soon, all-black teams began to spring up around the country. The teams traveled in buses from town to town, playing wherever they found opponents. It was an exhausting life. Then, in 1919, a player named Andrew "Rube" Foster changed black baseball forever.

---

1. **nationalist** (nash'ə·nəl·ist): person who is strongly loyal to his or her own group.

look to themselves for help. "No more fears," he wrote. "No more begging and pleading." Blacks began to set up their own businesses. Few would become more successful than Rube Foster.

In the year of the riot, Foster began organizing the Negro National League. He believed that a black-owned and -operated league would keep black baseball from being controlled by whites and would give black players the opportunity to make as much money as white players. And, he said, he wanted to "do something concrete for the loyalty of the race."

There were eight teams in the league: the Kansas City Monarchs, Indianapolis ABCs, Dayton Marcos, Chicago Giants, Detroit Stars, St. Louis Giants, Cuban Giants, and Foster's own Chicago American Giants.

The owner of the Kansas City Monarchs was a white man named J. L. Wilkinson. Foster believed that all the clubs should be owned by blacks, but he agreed to let the Monarchs into the league because of Wilkinson's long, impressive history in black baseball. He had founded the barnstorming All Nations team, whose members were black, Indian, Asian, and Hispanic.

Under Rube Foster's leadership, the American Giants seldom lost a game. One year he led them to a 123–6

The Negro Leagues Baseball Museum

MCCALL DRAKE SWEATT WILKINSON DR. SMITH SPEDDEN POMPEZ FOSTER BOLDEN SANTOP WINTERS CURRIE

▲ Rube Foster (fifth from right) at the opening game of the first Negro World Series in 1924.

record. The Giants were so successful that they sometimes drew bigger crowds than the Cubs or the White Sox, Chicago's two white major league clubs.

He believed that a black-owned and -operated league would keep black baseball from being controlled by whites.

Foster, one fellow Negro leaguer recalled years later, was always "two innings ahead of everyone else." As a manager, he insisted that his teams play "smart baseball"—a fast, aggressive game built around bunts, steals, hit-and-runs, and crafty pitching.

By comparison, white baseball was a slower, quieter game. After Yankee slugger Babe Ruth belted fifty-four home runs in 1920 and brought thousands of new fans to his team, major league managers built their strategy around hitting the long ball.

No player stayed on Foster's American Giants unless he could bunt a ball into a circle drawn along one of the foul lines. Any Giant who was tagged out standing up had to pay a five-dollar fine. "You're supposed to slide," Foster told them.

The result was a fast-paced, exciting game, and the Negro National League was a huge success. In the 1923 season alone, over 400,000 fans attended league games. Foster's creation became one of the largest black-owned businesses in the country.

Three players dominated the league: Pitcher Smokey Joe Williams, who stood 6'5", threw so hard that his team had to change catchers after four or five innings because their hands would swell up from the pounding.

Bullet Joe Rogan could throw heat like Smokey Joe, but he had another weapon in his arsenal.[2] He invented the "palm ball"—a change-up that "walked up" to hitters who were waiting for his fastball. It totally baffled them.

---

2. **arsenal** (är′sə•nəl): collection of techniques.

Barnstorming

Barnstorming is a word with an interesting history. The general meaning of this word is "traveling from town to town to give exhibitions or demonstrations." The word's original definition grew from the use of barns as hangars by early aviators who flew around the countryside, stopping at small towns to give airplane rides and stunt-flying exhibitions.

---

aggressive (ə•gres′iv): active; forceful.

baffled (baf′əld): confused.

Oscar Charleston was a fierce, hard-hitting center fielder who could outrun any ball. When a young baseball writer once suggested that Charleston was "the black Ty Cobb," an old-time reporter corrected him. "Cobb," the reporter said, "is a white Oscar Charleston."

The Negro National League's success attracted the attention of a group of white businessmen who saw the profits to be made in black baseball. In 1922 they formed the Eastern Colored League, which included the Philadelphia Hilldales, Brooklyn Royal Giants, Lincoln Giants, Baltimore Black Sox, Atlantic City Bacharachs, and New York Cuban All-Stars.

The Eastern League immediately began raiding the Negro National League for its best players. This enraged Foster, and he refused to schedule a World Series that had been planned with the Eastern champion for 1923.

In 1924 Foster's business sense prevailed, and the first Negro World Series was held between the Kansas City Monarchs and the Philadelphia Hilldales. The Monarchs won in a tough ten-game series.

The emotional and financial strain of running the league—and watching his best players being lured away to the rival Eastern League—started to wear Foster down. In 1926 he suffered a nervous breakdown. One day he was

enraged (en·rājd′): angered.

prevailed (prē·vāld′): triumphed.

Baseball Roundup

Baseball is considered the all-American game. Is it really American? Some historians say no. As early as the 1600s, people in England played a game known as rounders. Like baseball, rounders involved batting a ball and circling a set of bases. In rounders, however, a fielder could throw the ball directly at a runner. If a runner was struck, or "soaked," he was out. In Colonial America, rounders was played under the names "town ball" and sometimes "base ball." By the time Alexander Cartwright wrote down the rules of baseball in 1845, "soaking" had been replaced by tagging. Today, Cartwright is considered by some to be the father of organized baseball—that is, the American form of the old British game.

Bettmann/CORBIS

found chasing imaginary fly balls in the street near his house. Finally he was sent to a mental hospital, where he died in 1930.

On the day Foster was buried, one reporter wrote that his coffin was closed "at the usual hour a ball game ends." Three thousand fans braved a cold, icy rain to attend the funeral of the man they called "the father of black baseball."

✓ Reading Check

1. Name one positive result of the race riots of 1919.

2. Who organized the Negro National League? Why?

3. How was baseball in the Negro National League different from baseball in the white leagues?

4. Who formed the Eastern Colored League? Why?

5. What happened to Rube Foster in 1926?

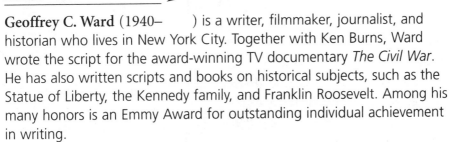

MEET THE *Writers*

Geoffrey C. Ward (1940–   ) is a writer, filmmaker, journalist, and historian who lives in New York City. Together with Ken Burns, Ward wrote the script for the award-winning TV documentary *The Civil War*. He has also written scripts and books on historical subjects, such as the Statue of Liberty, the Kennedy family, and Franklin Roosevelt. Among his many honors is an Emmy Award for outstanding individual achievement in writing.

Ken Burns's (1953–   ) Civil War documentary has been described as "a kind of video miracle." As a documentary filmmaker, Burns has created a host of spellbinding films on a range of topics—Thomas Jefferson, baseball, Lewis and Clark, New York City, and jazz. He is often praised for his ability to combine successfully the elements of image, music, voices, and sound effects. For his work, Burns has been nominated for an Academy Award.

How do powerful social movements in history begin? Find out how one person contributed to the civil rights movement.

"You're Under Arrest"

from *Rosa Parks: My Story*

by ROSA PARKS with JIM HASKINS

vacant (vā′kənt): empty.

When I got off from work that evening of December 1, I went to Court Square as usual to catch the Cleveland Avenue bus home. I didn't look to see who was driving when I got on, and by the time I recognized him, I had already paid my fare. It was the same driver who had put me off the bus back in 1943, twelve years earlier. He was still tall and heavy, with red, rough-looking skin. And he was still mean-looking. I didn't know if he had been on that route before—they switched the drivers around sometimes. I do know that most of the time if I saw him on a bus, I wouldn't get on it.

I saw a <u>vacant</u> seat in the middle section of the bus and took it. I didn't even question why there was a vacant seat even though there were quite a few people standing in the back. If I had thought about it at all, I would probably have figured maybe someone saw me get on and did not take the seat but left it vacant for

You Need to Know...

In 1945, the State of Alabama passed a law requiring all bus companies to segregate their buses—to create separate seating areas for black passengers and white passengers. Black passengers were required to sit at the back of the bus. Furthermore, if the white seats were full, black passengers were expected to surrender their seats. In Montgomery, Alabama, African Americans made up 66 percent of the bus-riding population. To most members of the Montgomery branch of the National Association for the Advancement of Colored People (NAACP), this law seemed outrageously unfair, and the group began thinking about ways to resist it. A boycott—a refusal to ride the buses—was suggested, but many black people depended on the buses and were afraid they would lose their jobs if they didn't show up. However, just as the NAACP began creating another plan, one of its members, Rosa Parks, boarded a bus. Parks might have known that her actions on that fateful bus ride would help launch a successful boycott. What she didn't know was that she would go down in history as a hero of the civil rights movement in America.

▲ Before the boycott African Americans had to sit at the back of the bus.

me. There was a man sitting next to the window and two women across the aisle.

The next stop was the Empire Theater, and some whites got on. They filled up the white seats, and one man was left standing. The driver looked back and noticed the man standing. Then he looked back at us. He said, "Let me have those front seats," because they were the front seats of the black section. Didn't anybody move. We just sat right where we were, the four of us. Then he spoke a second time: "Y'all better make it light on yourselves and let me have those seats."

The man in the window seat next to me stood up, and I moved to let him pass by me, and then I looked across the aisle and saw that the two women were also standing. I moved over to the window seat. I could not see how standing up was going to "make it light" for me. The more we gave in and complied, the worse they treated us.

I thought back to the time when I used to sit up all night and didn't sleep, and my grandfather would have his gun right by the fireplace, or if he had his one-horse wagon going anywhere, he always had his gun in the back

complied (kəm·plīd'): did as ordered.

of the wagon. People always say that I didn't give up my seat because I was tired, but that isn't true. I was not tired physically, or no more tired than I usually was at the end of a working day. I was not old, although some people have an image of me as being old then. I was forty-two. No, the only tired I was, was tired of giving in.

The driver of the bus saw me still sitting there, and he asked was I going to stand up. I said, "No." He said, "Well, I'm going to have you arrested." Then I said, "You may do that." These were the only words we said to each other. I didn't even know his name, which was James Blake, until we were in court together. He got out of the bus and stayed outside for a few minutes, waiting for the police.

As I sat there, I tried not to think about what might happen. I knew that anything was possible. I could be manhandled or beaten. I could be arrested. People have asked me if it occurred to me then that I could be the test case the NAACP had been looking for. I did not think

Other Bridges to Cross

On November 14, 1960, six-year-old Ruby Bridges also chose to stand her ground. Bridges was the first African American child to attend Frantz Elementary School in New Orleans, Louisiana. Until 1960, New Orleans had ignored the 1954 Supreme Court ruling that outlawed segregated schools. Finally, the federal government ordered the schools to comply. Bridges, escorted by federal marshals, walked calmly through a crowd of angry white protesters. The protesters screamed hateful words and threw rotten eggs, but Bridges was there to stay. Alone in her first-grade class-room for an entire year, Bridges worked with her dedicated teacher. "Kids know nothing about racism," Bridges said years later. "They're taught that by adults."

AP/Wide World Photos

▲ Ruby Bridges being protected by U.S. Marshals as she enters her new school.

about that at all. In fact if I had let myself think too deeply about what might happen to me, I might have gotten off the bus. But I chose to remain. . . .

* * * * *

My life has changed a great deal since 1955. I've done a lot more traveling than I know I would have done, and I have met a lot of people I would not have otherwise met. Some people have me believe, when they talk with me, that I have influenced their lives in many ways.

I look back now and realize that since that evening on the bus in Montgomery, Alabama, we have made a lot of progress in some ways. Young people can go to register to vote without being threatened and can vote without feeling apprehensive. There are no signs on public water fountains saying "Colored" and "White." There are big cities with black mayors, and small towns with black mayors and chiefs of police. Tom Bradley was elected the first African-American mayor of a major American city. Douglas L. Wilder was elected governor of Virginia, the first black governor of a state ever elected. And thirty years ago no one would have believed that Jesse Jackson, a black man, could run for president of the United States and get white votes in the state primary elections.

▲ Rosa Parks.

> **I look back now and realize that since that evening on the bus in Montgomery, Alabama, we have made a lot of progress in some ways.**

All those laws against <u>segregation</u> have been passed, and all that progress has been made. But a whole lot of white people's hearts have not been changed. Dr. King[1] used to talk about the fact that if a law was changed, it might not

segregation (seg´rə•gā´shən): separation of people into different groups or locations according to race.

---

1. **Dr. King:** Dr. Martin Luther King, Jr. (1929–1968), a leader in the civil rights movement who was assassinated.

resurgence (ri•sʉr′jəns): return.

violations (vī′ə•lā′shənz): actions that break or ignore laws.

change hearts but it would offer some protection. He was right. We now have some protection, but there is still much racism and racial violence.

In recent years there has been a <u>resurgence</u> of reactionary[2] attitudes. I am troubled by the recent decisions of the Supreme Court that make it harder to prove a pattern of racial discrimination in employment and by the fact that the national government does not seem very interested in pursuing <u>violations</u> of civil rights. What troubles me is that so many young people, including college students, have come out for white supremacy[3] and that there have been more and more incidents of racism and racial violence on college campuses. It has not been widespread, but still it is troublesome. It seems like we still have a long way to go.

---

2. reactionary (rē•ak′shə•ner′ē): moving or working against another event or force.

3. white supremacy (sə•prem′ə•sē): consideration of the white race as higher or better.

▲ Elizabeth Eckford tries to make her way into Little Rock's Central High School.

Sometimes I do feel pretty sad about some of the events that have taken place recently. I try to keep hope alive anyway, but that's not always the easiest thing to do. I have spent over half my life teaching love and brotherhood, and I feel that it is better to continue to try to teach or live equality and love than it would be to have hatred or prejudice. Everyone living together in peace and harmony and love . . . that's the goal that we seek, and I think that the more people there are who reach that state of mind, the better we will all be.

✓ **Reading Check**

1. Why did Rosa Parks recognize the driver of the bus?

2. What reason does Parks give for not moving from her seat?

3. According to Parks, what are three ways in which society has changed for the better since 1955?

4. Name two aspects of today's society that trouble Parks.

5. According to Parks, what is the best way to overcome racism and hatred?

MEET THE *Writers*

Rosa Parks (1913–   ) was born in Alabama. After attending college, she became one of the first women to join the NAACP. At the time of her arrest, Parks was working in the garment industry, as well as doing volunteer work for the NAACP. Since then, she has continued to work for the cause of civil rights. In 1979, Parks won the Spingarn Medal for her efforts.

Jim Haskins (1941–   ) has written over one hundred nonfiction books, many for young people. Haskins's favorite subjects are African American history, the civil rights movement, and important African American leaders. Many of his books have won awards. *Rosa Parks: My Story* won the Parents Choice picture book award in 1992 and the Hungry Mind Young Adult nonfiction award in 1993.

What happens in your life when you leave your homeland and move to another country that has a different language and culture? Let four young people tell you.

The New Immigrants
from *Junior Scholastic*

by NAOMI MARCUS

customs (kus'təmz): traditions and practices of a group of people.

Can you imagine your parents deciding to move your family halfway around the world, to a new country where you don't know the language, the customs, or the culture? What would you miss most? What would you most fear?

Millions of young immigrants who come to the U.S. must face these challenges. Who are today's immigrants? Where do they come from and why?

Today's U.S. immigrants come from a wider range of countries than ever before. According to the U.S. Census Bureau, there are nearly 23 million foreign-born residents in the U.S. They account for 8.4 percent of the total U.S. population.

You Need to Know...

An immigrant is a person who comes to a new place in order to make a home there. America is a land of immigrants. From its very beginnings, America has drawn people from all over the globe who are in search of a new life. Many U.S. citizens believe that the great mix of peoples, cultures, and customs in our country is precisely what makes it so strong. However, the life of individual immigrants can be difficult. In this excerpt, four young immigrants explain what coming to America was like for them.

residents (rez'i·dənts): people who live in a place.

At the turn of the century, huge waves of Irish, Italians, and Eastern Europeans immigrated to the U.S. Today, immigrants are again coming to the U.S. in large numbers—but most are from Asia and Latin America.

What countries send the most immigrants? U.S. government figures show that in 1994 and 1995, the largest number of immigrants came from Mexico, the Philippines, Vietnam, the Dominican Republic, China, and India. . . .

Another major change in the profile of the new immigrants: They are more likely to be fairly well-educated,

profile (prō'fīl'): overview or general picture of a person, group of people, or thing.

and more prosperous than earlier immigrants. *The New York Times* recently reported that, rather than slamming the door shut behind them, today's immigrants remain more connected to their homelands. Long-distance phone calls are cheaper than ever before. Thanks to cheap air fares, video phones, and satellite TV programming, today's immigrants can keep in closer touch with their native lands.

Today's U.S. immigrants come from a wider range of countries than ever before.

Today's immigrants come from different countries than those who came to the U.S. at the turn of the century. But they come for many of the same reasons: to flee from war, make better lives for their children, and find stability. . . . Here are their stories, in their own words:

flee (flē): escape.

stability (stə·bil′ə·tē): the state of being steady or unlikely to change.

Fleeing from Civil War

Jasmina Hamidovic, 12, left Bosnia with her parents and younger brother in 1997. Civil war was tearing her country apart.

We left [Bosnia] because the war came to our town. My parents were fired from their jobs, and soldiers came and took over our house. We went to our cousins in Zagreb [the capital of Croatia] and stayed there awhile. I tried to learn English by watching American television programs . . . with subtitles. I was kind of happy and kind of sad to hear we were going to America. We took a long bus ride, then five or six airplanes. We first went to Austria, then to Amsterdam, Chicago, Minneapolis, finally to San Francisco.

The language was the biggest difference in the U.S. I liked my new school, though at the beginning it was kind of weird. Kids have such a different attitude here. . . . My teacher said I was so polite.

I'd heard that here people kidnap kids and stuff. I was scared of going to school alone, and playing alone. Then I saw that when I go to school, no one follows me, and I got over it.

I missed my old school, my friends, my teachers, and [the river where I used to go] swimming. But I am glad that we came here. Here in the Bay Area [of San Francisco] there are almost 4,000 people from my country. We are Muslim and we celebrate our holidays together. I am glad that we came here.

Different Customs

Hardish Singh, 14, came from Punjab, India, last year. He is still learning English; Hindi is his first language.

We came because in Punjab [there are] no good jobs. [There are] more good jobs in America. When my uncle picked us up at the airport, I thought the freeways were very rushed. I never saw so many cars. The first day when I arrive, we went to a store. . . . [There was a line of people at the cash register], but I walked right up to the front of the line. I didn't know that was wrong. My father told me, then the second day no problem.

Plans to Go Back to Yemen

Akram Massar, 14, came from Yemen with his family several years ago.

We came because my father wanted us to get a better education, and to learn a new language, English. He'd been [working in America]—he wanted us with him. When I first came here, I didn't like it much; I wanted to go back home. At the airport, there was an elevator. I had never been in an elevator, I was so scared. I didn't know [that] it wouldn't fall. My father just said, "Come on."

I had a lot of crazy ideas [about this country] before I came. . . . So I was scared. Just crazy ideas. Also, when I first came here, I would cross against the red light. A lot of things I just didn't know.

In school, after I learned enough English, I would help other Arabic kids, [and] explain things to them. In my country, if you didn't do your homework, they'd hit you on the hand with a big stick! I got hit a lot on the hand,

and on the feet. But here I think a lot about my education, and I work really hard.

I play basketball now, which I learned in America. I play soccer. On my street, Mexican and Arabic peoples play soccer together. But I am going to go back to Yemen to marry. My married brother lives in Yemen, in my town, and he is building a house for our family. We send him money to help.

Reunited with Their Mother

Judith Paredes, 16, came here with her sister two years ago. They were reunited with their mother, who had moved to the U.S. five years earlier.

After our father left us, my mother came to America, alone, for a better future. She was smuggled in by coyotes (people who smuggle illegal aliens across the border from Mexico). She had to go from Peru through Panama, Costa Rica, El Salvador, and Mexico. Mom worked in a clothing

Culver Pictures, Inc.

▲ Approximately 17 million immigrants arrived in the United States between 1892 and 1943. **❓ How are the young immigrants in this selection different from those in this photo?**

factory, and a restaurant at night, to send money back to me and my sister. My mom always called us and she would cry every time. I didn't see her for five years.

When she finally told us she had legal papers and she sent us tickets to join her, I didn't believe it. When we were in the airplane I cried and cried. At the San Francisco airport, the immigration officers took us into a room for an hour while they looked at our documents. I was so scared—I thought they were going to send us back. When we came out, I saw my mom . . . and we hugged and cried.

In Peru, everyone said, "Oh, you are lucky you are going to America." I had an idea that life was easy here. But it's not. It was so hard for me—I would try to communicate with other people, but I couldn't. Other kids would make fun of me. In Peru, we have a different way of speaking— it's softer. Here, everyone shouts! I can't get used to it. Also, in Peru, everyone comes outside—to talk and visit and play together in the street. Here, people are isolated.

We go to the Catholic church and I study hard in school. I have a summer job that I really like. But I want to go back to Peru after I get my education.

✓ Reading Check

1. Name two ways that today's U.S. immigrants are different from those of the early 1900s.

2. For what reasons do many immigrants come to the United States?

3. Give a detail from one of the immigrants' stories that shows how difficult immigrants' lives can be.

4. What did Judith Paredes expect life in the United States to be like? What was it really like?

Whales—one of the most magnificent creatures in the ocean—and a girl who finds them fascinating come together in this informative and inspiring essay.

MAGAZINE ARTICLE

SCIENCE ●

from A Girl Among the Whales
from *Storyworks*

by EVE NILSON

Kennan Ward/CORBIS

▲ Humpback lifts its flukes out of the water as it takes a dive off the coast of Alaska.

marine (mə•rēn′): having to do with the sea or the ocean.

My mom is a <u>marine</u> biologist. She has spent much of her career studying humpback whales. Every summer since we were born, my brother and I have joined my mother on her research trips, spending three or four months at a time sailing through the calm waters of Alaska's Inside Passage.

This is one of the most beautiful places on earth. It is a wilderness where humpback and killer whales come to feed, bears roam the rivers full of salmon, and eagles soar over green forests and ice-covered mountains.

I feel extremely lucky to have a mom who takes me to these wonderful places. Over the years, I have had so many adventures. I have swum to freezing waterfalls and run through fields of wildflowers. I have been chased by a grizzly bear and stared at by an orca.[1] I have seen whales bigger than school buses and snow-white mountain goats clinging to cliffs over ancient glaciers. I have learned so

You Need to Know...

The humpback whale is one of the loveliest, most mysterious creatures of the sea. It can grow to 62 feet—about the length of two schoolbuses! It has very long, thin flippers; a tapered head; white skin underneath; and dark gray or black skin on the sides and back. Humpbacks travel in groups, often leaping above the surface of the water in beautiful arcs. They also communicate with each other using a complex series of screams and other sounds. The humpback can be found in every ocean of the world. Unfortunately, this graceful creature can also be found on the endangered species list. Ocean pollution is gradually destroying the humpback's habitat and killing the small sea creatures that are its food source.

---
1. orca (ôr′kə): killer whale.

©Ron Sanford/Photo Researchers, Inc.

▲ The humpback whale. ❷ **Why do humpbacks migrate to the cold waters of Alaska in the summer?**

much, and each experience makes me want to learn more.

Over the next few pages, you'll read some of my favorite wilderness stories. I hope that my experiences will inspire you to visit these places one day. I also hope you'll want to help protect these fragile wilderness areas, and the amazing creatures who live there.

A Whale Picnic

Every year I look forward to returning to Alaska because I get to see my old friends. My whale friends. Every whale looks different, and we have learned to recognize the many whales who return year after year to the feeding grounds of Alaska. There's Big Mama. She's the biggest whale I've ever seen. And she's easy to recognize because she has a tail with a deep tear at each tip. Another old friend is named Snake Eyes. His tail is white with two black dots.

Pacific humpbacks travel 5,000 miles every year. They spend part of the year in the warm waters off Hawaii (some go to Mexico). In summer, they swim up to the cold waters of Alaska. They come to Alaska to eat. And eat and eat and eat. Humpbacks eat a year's worth of food during the three or four months they're in Alaska, because they won't eat again for the rest of the year. Every day they eat tons of small fish and shrimp-like creatures called krill.

One of my mom's most important discoveries is that whales often work together to catch schools of herring and other fish. My mother calls this cooperative feeding.

When they work together, the whales are able to catch more fish than they could by themselves. One cooperative feeding technique is the bubble net. A group of whales

cooperative (kō•äp'ər•ə•tiv): working together toward a common goal.

technique (tek•nēk'): a method of doing something.

will dive below a school of fish and blow a circle of bubbles that gets larger as it rises to the surface. The ring of bubbles traps thousands of herring. The whales burst through the surface, each with an open mouth big enough to contain a small car, and each mouth full of thousands of little silver herring. It's an awesome sight.

> **The whales burst through the surface, each with an open mouth big enough to contain a small car, and each mouth full of thousands of little silver herring.**

Whales also use sounds to startle their prey. The whale's beautiful song will cause a school of herring to bundle themselves into a ball. The fish are trying to protect themselves by appearing as a single large creature. But they wind up making it easier for whales to gobble them down in one convenient gulp. . . .

The Curious Calf

A female whale usually gives birth every two or three years to a single baby. A calf weighs two tons. Every day, it drinks 120 gallons of milk from its mother. A female whale's milk is very thick, like condensed cow's milk. Whale calves grow quickly by drinking this rich milk.

One day, my mother and I were out in our little motor boat making recordings of whale songs. We were watching a whale calf play in the seaweed. We sat quietly and watched it as it playfully tossed the seaweed to and fro with its tail and pectoral[2] fins. These are the fins attached to the whale's chest. All of a sudden, the calf came over to our boat. It came right up so close to me that I could see the tiny shellfish called barnacles near its mouth. The calf was looking up at me through the water, and I stared right back. His eye was a watery white, with a big pupil. He

---

2. **pectoral** (pek′tə·rəl).

Silly Love Songs?

True, marine mammals such as dolphins and whales make "clicks" and sing "songs," but do these sounds mean that the creatures can "talk"? Some researchers don't think so—at least, not yet. They say that marine mammals probably use the sounds for survival. For example, dolphins' "clicks" make echoes that help them find food, and their whistles help them recognize each other (like names do for humans). Sounds are also used to attract mates! During mating season, male humpback whales sing long, complicated songs that are made up of a series of notes. The songs can last up to twenty minutes and are sometimes repeated.

---

condensed (kən·densd′): reduced in volume by evaporation of water content.

breached (brēchd): broke through the surface.

put his big pectoral fin over the boat. I reached out and touched him. He felt soft and rubbery.

For that moment, I really felt like we were communicating. He looked at me so trustingly, as though he knew I would never harm him. These are the kinds of moments I cherish most in Alaska. . . .

Sometimes at night, the water fills with millions of tiny marine creatures called dinoflagellates. These are like underwater fireflies that light up the water whenever they are touched by a fish. Once a whale breached nearby. As the fifty-ton whale hit the water, it made a huge shimmering splash that lit up the night sky like fireworks.

When I lie in my bunk at night, I can hear the beautiful feeding song of the humpback whales. Its eerie melody stays with me all year long, and seems to call me back year after year to sail with the whales in Alaska.

✔ Reading Check

1. Why does the author of this selection return to Alaska every summer?

2. Why do Pacific humpback whales return to Alaska every summer?

3. The author hopes her essay will inspire her readers in what two ways?

4. The author describes a moment when she felt connected to the whale. Summarize this passage.

5. What are dinoflagellates?

MEET THE *Writer*

Eve Nilson was a thirteen-year-old schoolgirl when she wrote this original essay.

Is it possible that the tiny speck we call Earth hosts the only intelligent life in the universe? Read on to see how technology has begun to help us answer this question.

Is Anyone Else Out There?

from *The Planet Hunters: The Search for Other Worlds*

by DENNIS BRINDELL FRADIN

We are planet-based beings, and we believe that planets at just the right distance from stars with just the right conditions are the only places life can occur. So the whole story of searching for extraterrestrial life begins with finding planets around other stars beyond our Solar System.

—Planet discoverer Dr. Alex Wolszczan

What if in the twenty-first century the Planet Finder or another instrument spots a few blue-and-green worlds with oxygen atmospheres, oceans, and continents? Besides ranking as one of the most thrilling events ever, the discovery would mark the beginning of another scientific adventure, for people wouldn't be content to just *look* at Earth-like worlds. We would want to learn whether those remote planets were home to beings like ourselves.

You Need to Know...

As long as there have been humans, there have been stargazers. The ancient Chinese, Babylonians, and Egyptians charted the stars and predicted the motions of heavenly bodies. The Greek philosophers first proposed that the Earth was round. Later, the Polish astronomer Copernicus correctly suggested that the earth travels around the sun. Between the 1600s and the 1900s, scientists such as Galileo, Newton, and Einstein gradually gave us a clearer, more accurate picture of the universe. Today we know that the universe is made up of a vast number of galaxies grouped into clusters. We also know that these clusters are rushing rapidly away from one another—that the universe is expanding. We do *not* know whether the universe is limited or if it extends forever. Either way, it is unimaginably large. Are we humans all alone in it?

There are three ways for us to communicate with extraterrestrials.[1] One way would be for them to visit us. Tens of thousands of people have reported seeing alien spaceships or "flying saucers." Thousands of individuals claim to have been abducted[2] or <u>temporarily</u> kidnapped by extraterrestrials. Although a few scientists believe these claims, most remain <u>skeptical</u>, for no one has produced a convincing photograph or other proof of visits to Earth by aliens or their spacecraft.

According to most scientists, the simplest and most sensible way to make contact with extraterrestrials (assuming they exist) is to exchange radio signals with them. For about sixty years, human beings have been broadcasting FM radio programs as well as television (which also uses FM radio waves in its operation). Some of the waves are received by our radios and TV sets, but others pass through Earth's atmosphere and travel endlessly through space at the speed of light—186,000 miles per second. A TV or FM radio program that is being broadcast at this very moment will travel a distance of ten light-years in ten years, twenty-five light-years in twenty-five years, and so on. If anybody on an extrasolar[3] planet aims a radio telescope at Earth, they might detect our FM radio and TV broadcasts and distinguish them from the natural radio noise <u>emitted</u> by heavenly bodies. For one thing, signals beamed by intelligent beings are stronger than cosmic static. Also, our broadcasts are at specific frequencies,[4] while radio noise from heavenly bodies covers many frequencies <u>simultaneously</u>.

With the proper equipment, the extraterrestrials could actually listen to our FM radio shows and watch our TV programs. If in our year 1999, extraterrestrials thirty light-years from Earth <u>intercept</u> our signals, they would receive our broadcasts from 1969. They might hear reports of the landing of the first people on the Moon on July 20, 1969,

temporarily (tem′pə•rer′i•lē): for a limited period of time.

skeptical (skep′ti•kəl): doubtful.

emitted (ē•mit′tid): sent out; transmitted.

simultaneously (sī′məl•tā′nē•əs•lē): happening at the same time.

intercept (in′tər•sept′): to stop or catch on the way from one place to another.

---

1. **extraterrestrials** (eks′trə•tə•res′trē•əlz): beings from other planets.
2. **abducted** (ab•dukt′id): taken away unwillingly.
3. **extrasolar** (eks′trə•sō′lər): outside of our solar system.
4. **frequencies** (frē′kwən•sēz): the numbers of energy waves sent out in a given amount of time.

or watch that year's World Series between the New York Mets and the Baltimore Orioles. In other words, somewhere in space there could be intelligent creatures who listen to our rock-and-roll music and watch such shows as *Sesame Street, I Love Lucy,* and *The Three Stooges!*

Since we broadcast radio and TV signals, it seems likely that intelligent beings on distant planets do too. Several radio telescopes are currently being used to listen for signals from distant civilizations. These projects are known to radio astronomers as SETI, which stands for the **S**earch for **E**xtra**t**errestrial **I**ntelligence.

▲ A few of the 27 radio telescopes of the Very Large Array (VLA) near Datil, New Mexico.

Pete Saloutos/The Stock Market

As of 1997, no alien signals had been detected. A difficulty with SETI searches is that there are millions of places in the sky to point our radio telescopes. It could take thousands of years to study each point in the sky long enough to detect an alien radio or TV signal. But if astronomers find a few Earth-like worlds, SETI researchers could target those locations where success seems most likely.

If we ever intercept broadcasts from another planet, we could set up a long-distance conversation with the extraterrestrials.

If we ever intercept broadcasts from another planet, we could set up a long-distance conversation with the extraterrestrials. We might teach them our language and relate basic facts about our planet. We could even beam them an encyclopedia of our knowledge, explains Dr. Mike Davis of Arecibo Observatory, the site of a SETI program called Project Serendip. The extraterrestrials might do the same for us.

Radio contact with extraterrestrials would satisfy our deep-seated yearning to prove that we have company in the Universe, claims astronomer Seth Shostak of the SETI Institute, an organization near San Francisco that is running a SETI search called Project Phoenix. "It would be scary to believe that in all of vast space, Earth is the only planet with living, thinking beings," says Shostak. "We humans need to know that we're not alone."

The possibilities of what we could learn from the extraterrestrials would be unlimited and "mind-blowing," says Dr. John Stansberry. For example, they might teach us how to end world hunger, cure cancer, and clean up our polluted planet. "Since the aliens are likely to be many thousands of years more advanced than we are, they might give us good advice on how to avoid war," says Seth Shostak. Planet hunter Dr. Daniel Whitmire adds: "We could learn information from them that would take us a million years to attain on our own. We might learn almost unimaginable science, such as the secret of immortality [living forever] for people, and how to travel to the stars."

So Near, Yet So Far

Faster spaceships might not be the only way to visit distant planets. Consider the possibility of a wormhole. Although humans are not yet able to build one, the idea is this: A black hole—a dark region in space with a tremendous gravitational pull formed by the core of a star that has broken apart—opens somewhere in our universe. It briefly connects to another universe light-years away, forming a tunnel—a wormhole. This can happen because space is sometimes curved. Imagine a strip of paper as long as a football field. If you lay it flat, the distance between the beginning and end of the paper is one hundred yards. However, if you fold the paper over on itself, the distance between the beginning and end is practically nothing. When one black hole connects with another universe, scientists speculate that it may be possible to hold open the tunnel—the wormhole—with special walls. This would allow—in theory at least—rapid travel between two distant points in space.

▲ Black hole.

Erich Schrempp/Photo Researchers, Inc.

The more difficult, yet more exciting, way to communicate with extraterrestrials is to visit them. Between 1969 and 1972 the United States landed astronauts on the Moon six times. Around the year 2018, we will visit Mars. What will we do after we explore the Solar System?

"Ultimately our goal over the centuries is to visit planets around other stars," says Dr. William Cochran. "Today it is only in the realm of science fiction, but one day we may get serious about it."

The vastness of space is a major obstacle to interstellar travel (voyages to other stars). At the fastest speed achieved by people in space as of 1997—25,000 miles per hour—it would require more than 100,000 years to reach the Sun's nearest known stellar neighbor, Proxima Centauri, and far longer for more distant destinations. Obviously, if we expect to explore other solar systems, we must build much faster spaceships.

Rocket scientists have ideas for building spacecraft that can achieve speeds of millions of miles per hour, considerably reducing the travel time. They are known by such exotic[5] names as the "fusion rocket," the "ion-propulsion spaceship," the "interstellar ramjet," the "antimatter starship," and the "laser-powered spaceship." Another idea is to launch an interstellar "space colony," a craft the size of a small town in which people would live generation after generation while journeying to another planetary system. Within the colony there would be houses, schools, parks, and farms. The travelers would live and die on the colony, until finally, after centuries, the descendants of the original space pioneers would reach their destination.

Currently there are no plans to build an interstellar space colony or any other kind of starship. This is because of another obstacle to attempting interstellar travel. Few people want to spend a tremendous amount of time, effort, and money in building a starship as long as we know of no place to visit that might have intelligent life. But if we detect Earth-like planets, that will change everything, says Dr. William Cochran. "We would have a goal—

NASA

▲ During the launch of a space shuttle, 83,000 kg of fuel is burned in 8 minutes. **❓ How will the present speed and thrust of today's spacecraft have to change if we are to visit other planets?**

---

5. **exotic** (eg·zät′ik): strange or fascinating.

to visit those planets—so it would spur our interest in building interstellar spacecraft."

Eventually, perhaps not many years from now, planet hunters will discover a few worlds that seem "just right" for life. Radio telescopes will listen for extraterrestrial broadcasts from those planets, and rocket scientists will start building spacecraft that can travel to the remote worlds. After studying several such planets, the day may come when we find one that is home to intelligent beings. Then we will have solved one of the great mysteries in science and answered a question that has been asked since the first human beings gazed up at the five "wanderers"[6]:

Is anyone else out there?

---

6. **wanderers:** The ancient Greeks referred to the five moving objects in the sky as *planetae*. The Romans named these planets Mercury, Venus, Mars, Jupiter, and Saturn.

✓ Reading Check

1. According to many scientists, what is the simplest way to contact intelligent life on other planets?

2. What does SETI stand for?

3. What could be one reason that SETI has not detected alien radio signals?

4. Name two possible benefits of making contact with extraterrestrials.

5. Name two obstacles to long-distance space travel.

MEET THE *Writer*

Dennis Brindell Fradin is the author of dozens of nonfiction books, many of them on topics in history and science. His book *Hiawatha: Messenger of Peace* was named a Notable Children's Trade Book in the Field of Social Studies. When he isn't working on a book, Mr. Fradin enjoys watching baseball—and watching the stars, too.

Cross-Curricular ACTIVITIES

■ LANGUAGE ARTS/DRAMA

Face to Face What might Rosa Parks and a civil rights leader of today say to one another? Find out about one of today's leaders. Then, write a script in which Parks and your chosen leader discuss the times in which we live. Each character should explain what he or she has done to help improve the lives of African Americans. With a partner, perform the dialogue for the class.

■ LANGUAGE ARTS

Listen and Learn Do you know someone who immigrated to the United States from another country? If not, do you know someone who is new to your school? Arrange to interview this person about his or her experiences. Before the interview, write a list of eight to ten questions you would like to ask. (Be sure the questions cannot be answered with a simple *yes* or a *no*.) Your questions should invite a description of both good and bad aspects of the change the person has undergone. If possible, tape-record the interview. Later, transcribe it—that is, write it out neatly on clean paper. Send a copy to the person you interviewed. Enclose a note explaining what you learned from the interview and what you enjoyed most about it. Get the person's permission to share the interview with the rest of your class.

■ SCIENCE

Critters Aren't Quitters What endangered species live in your state? Look in books, in magazines, or on the Internet to find information about an endangered species in your area. What forces have caused their numbers to shrink? What can the average person do to help save the species? Create a public-service brochure that brings attention to the predicament of this species. The brochure should provide interesting facts and statistics related to the species. It should also include a list of tips to help save the animal, illustrations or photographs, and the titles and authors of two or three books on the subject. Place several copies of the brochure in your classroom library.

■ VISUAL ART

Facts on Film Ken Burns, coauthor of "A Gentleman's Agreement" (page 187) is an award-winning documentary filmmaker. His many documentaries tackle a range of big subjects—baseball, the Civil War, and New York City, to name a few. Write a proposal for your own documentary based on a selection in this book. Include sketches of important scenes that you will include in the documentary. Share your proposal and sketches with the class.

■ ART/HISTORY

On the Wall As a class project, create a mural on butcher paper that illustrates the important social movements of the twentieth century. Before you begin, decide on the arrangement of these topics. You may want to arrange them chronologically, or assign them an order based on the class's evaluation of each one's importance. Your mural may be a series of separate scenes within a frame, or your total design may allow the various topics to flow together. You may wish to use images alone or include some text. After deciding on the overall design, sketch and then color your mural. Display the finished mural.

READ ON: FOR INDEPENDENT READING

■ NONFICTION

Invisible Enemies: Stories of Infectious Disease by Jeanette Farrell (Farrar Straus & Giroux, 1998). How do we treat and control these seven deadly diseases—smallpox, leprosy, bubonic plague, tuberculosis, malaria, cholera, and AIDS? Half history, half science, this 1999 ALA Best Book for Young Adults tells a story of panic and heroism, horrible mistaken "treatments," and steadfast searches for a cure.

Now Is Your Time! The African-American Struggle for Freedom by Walter Dean Myers (HarperCollins, 1991). From the first prisoners brought from Africa to Virginia in 1619, to the many heroes of the modern civil rights movement, Myers traces the African American heritage and draws lessons and inspiration from the past. An Orbis Pictus Honor Book.

Seeing Earth from Space by Patricia Lauber (Orchard Books, 1990). What's it like to be an astronaut, looking down at a tiny, fragile blue planet that humans call home? Join award-winning writer Patricia Lauber as she explores the strange and colorful world of satellite images, and find out what these images can teach us about life on Earth. An Orbis Pictus Honor Book.

Our Beckoning Borders: Illegal Immigration to America by Brent Ashabranner (Cobblehill, 1996). Why are so many people willing to break the law so they can call America their home? Why are other people so angry when they do? This book explores the human faces behind the growing problem of illegal immigration.

■ FICTION

Children of the River by Linda Crew (Delacorte Press, 1989). A good Cambodian girl doesn't date and she expects her parents to arrange her marriage. Sundara fled Cambodia with her family four years ago, and here in Oregon things just aren't the same. She knows Jonathan is special. Can her family ever accept their friendship?

Eva by Peter Dickinson (Delacorte Press, 1988). A terrible car accident is followed by a long coma. At last, to her parents' relief, thirteen-year-old Eva wakes up—in the body of a chimpanzee. The transplant was the only way to save her life. Is Eva really a human being in the body of a chimp or has she become something different—something new—and perhaps, both species' final hope?

Nothing but the Truth by Avi (Orchard Books, 1991). Has Philip Malloy been suspended for patriotism or is he a rebellious kid who needs to learn respect? The controversy spreads through Philip's high school and into the national media. Who's right? Who's wrong? A Newbery Honor Book, this novel, told in diary entries, conversations, speeches, and memos, forces readers to face these issues and decide for themselves.

There's an Owl in the Shower by Jean Craighead George (HarperCollins, 1995). Borden Watson has a rifle, and he wants revenge. Spotted owls cost his father his logging job. Now Borden's going to shoot all the spotted owls he can find. His plans are upset by a skinny, orphaned owlet named Bardy who comes to live with Borden and his family. Can Borden and his family love Bardy and still go on hating spotted owls?

Glossary

The glossary below is an alphabetical list of the underscored words found in the selections in this book. Some technical, foreign, and more obscure words in this book are not listed here, but instead are defined for you in the footnotes that accompany many of the selections.

Many words in the English language have more than one meaning. This glossary gives the meanings that apply to the words as they are used in the selections in this book.

Each word's pronunciation is given in parentheses. A guide to the pronunciation symbols appears at the bottom of each right-hand glossary page.

The following abbreviations are used:

adj. adjective   *adv.* adverb   *n.* noun   *v.* verb

abolish (ə·bäl'ish) *v.:* to do away with.

abolition (ab'ə·lish'ən) *n.:* the doing away with something.

accusation (ak·yōō·zā'shən) *n.:* formal statement finding a person guilty of wrongdoing.

acquire (ə·kwīr') *v.:* gain possession of something by one's own efforts.

adjourn (ə·jʉrn') *v.:* to close until a later time.

adrift (ə·drift') *adv.:* moving or floating in no single direction.

affirmation (af'ər·mā'shən) *n.:* a statement or declaration that something is true or right.

afflict (ə·flikt') *v.:* to cause to suffer.

aggravate (ag'rə·vāt') *v.:* to make worse.

aggressive (ə·gres'iv) *adj.:* active; forceful.

agility (ə·jil'ə·tē) *n.:* speed and gracefulness of movement.

allay (ə·lā') *v.:* to reduce; to give relief.

allocate (al'ō·kāt') *v.:* to give out in portions according to a plan.

amass (ə·mas') *v.:* to gather together.

amateur (am'ə·chər) *n.:* a person who participates in an activity for enjoyment rather than money.

amiably (ā'mē·ə·blē) *adv.:* in a friendly, easygoing way.

analytic (an'ə·lit'ik) *adj.:* able to study carefully to determine what something is or how it works.

appropriate (ə·prō'prē·it) *adj.:* suitable for a particular purpose.

archaeology (är'kē·äl'ə·jē) *n.:* a branch of science that studies past human cultures by looking at the clues they left behind.

array (ə·rā') *n.:* display; collection.

assimilate (ə·sim'ə·lāt') *v.:* to bring into; absorb.

authentic (ô·then'tik) *adj.:* real.

baffle (baf'əl) *v.:* confuse.

barricade (bar'i·kād') *n.:* a barrier put up quickly for protection.

benevolent (bə·nev'ə·lənt) *adj.:* kindly; characterized by doing good deeds.

bizarre (bi·zär') *adj.:* very surprising and incredible.

brackish (brak'ish) *adj.:* having a disagreeable taste; sickening.

breach (brēch) *v.:* to break through the surface.

capsize (kap'sīz') *v.:* to turn over.

censure (sen'shər) *n.:* blame or disapproval.

census (sen'səs) *n.:* an official count of people.

collage (kə·läzh') *n.:* a grouping of apparently unrelated parts.

commemorate (kə·mem'ə·rāt) *v.:* to remember with honor.

commend (kə·mend') *v.:* to recommend; to present as qualified.

commission (kə·mish'ən) *v.:* to give an assignment or an order.

commotion (kə·mō'shən) *n.:* noisy disturbance or confusion.

communal (kə·myōōn'əl) *adj.:* shared; related to a community.

community (kə·myōō'nə·tē) *n.:* people living in a group apart from general society.

complexion (kəm·plek'shən) *n.:* the appearance of the skin, especially the face.

comply (kəm·plī') *v.:* to do as ordered.

condense (kən·dens') *adj.:* reduce in volume by evaporating part of the water content.

confirm (kən·fʉrm') *v.:* to prove that something is true.

consist (kən·sist') *v.:* to be formed or made up of.

consternation (kän'stər·nā'shən) *n.:* alarm; dismay; bewilderment.

contagious (kən·tā'jəs) *adj.:* able to spread from one person to another.

contemplative (kən·tem'plə·tiv) *adj.:* thoughtful.

contraband (kän'trə·band') *n.:* goods or people moved illegally from one state or country to another.

cooperative (kō·äp'ər·ə·tiv) *adj.:* working toward a common goal.

corrode (kə·rōd') *v.:* to rust; wear away.

crisis (krī'sis) *n.:* a period of great difficulty.

critical (krit'i·kəl) *adj.:* important.

---

at, āte, cär; ten, ēve; is, īce; gō, côrn, lʊʊk, yʊʊ *as in* pure, tōōl, yōō *as in* you, oil, out; up, fʉr; ə *for unstressed vowels, as* a *in* adult *or* u *in* focus, 'l *as in* rattle, 'n *as in* flatten, g *as in* go, j *as in* jump, hw *as in* why, chin, she, think, *there*, zh *as in* measure, ŋ *as in* wing

criticize (krit′ə•sīz′) *v.:* to make a disapproving judgment.

crucial (krōō′shəl) *adj.:* extremely important.

custom (kus′təm) *n.:* tradition and practice of a group of people.

debris (də•brē′) *n.:* wreckage; pieces of things that have been destroyed.

deceased (dē•sēst′) *n.:* dead.

decimate (des′ə•māt′) *v.:* to destroy; kill.

dedication (ded′i•kā′shən) *n.:* a setting apart for a special reason.

defiance (dē•fī′əns) *n.:* daring rebellion.

demoralize (dē•môr′ə•līz′) *v.:* to corrupt; to change for the worse.

denounce (dē•nouns′) *v.:* to condemn as wicked or wrong.

diligence (dil′ə•jens) *n.:* persistence.

disintegrate (dis•in′tə•grāt′) *v.:* to fall apart.

distraction (di•strak′shən) *n.:* a state of mental agitation and disturbance.

divert (də•vʉrt′) *v.:* to turn in a different direction.

dominate (däm′ə•nāt) *v.:* to overwhelm or overshadow.

durable (dʊr′ə•bəl) *adj.:* long lasting despite hard use.

dwindle (dwin′dəl) *v.:* to become less full.

economy (i•kän′ə•mē) *n.:* use or management of money.

efficiency (e•fish′ən•sē) *n.:* capability to do something with the least amount of effort and waste.

elaborate (ē•lab′ə•rit) *adj.:* detailed and complicated.

eliminate (ē•lim′ə•nāt) *v.:* get rid of.

emancipation (ē•man′sə•pā′shən) *n.:* freedom from slavery.

embark (em•bärk′) *v.:* to begin a journey or project.

embody (em•bäd′ē) *v.:* to represent; give form to.

emigrant (em′i•grənt) *n.:* person who moves out of one country or region into another.

emit (ē•mit′) *v.:* to send out; transmit.

encompass (en•kum′pəs) *v.:* to surround on all sides.

enduring (en•dʊr′iŋ) *adj.:* lasting.

enigmatic (en′ig•mat′ik) *adj.:* puzzling; mysterious.

enrage (en•rāj′) *v.:* to anger.

epidemic (ep′ə•dem′ik) *n.:* an outbreak of a disease that spreads quickly among many people in a given area.

erode (ē•rōd′) *v.:* to wear away.

escort (es•kôrt′) *v.:* to accompany to show honor or respect.

establish (ə•stab′lish) *v.:* to set up.

estimate (es′tə•māt′) *v.:* to judge or to determine to be nearly accurate.

expedition (eks′pə•dish′ən) *n.:* a journey for a specific purpose.

exploit (eks′ploit′) *n.:* act of bravery.

extract (ek•strakt′) *v.:* to take out.

famine (fam′in) *n.:* widespread shortage of food.

fetid (fet′id) *adj.:* having a foul or rotten smell.

financial (fī•nan′shəl) *adj.:* relating to money.

flee (flē) *v.:* to escape.

flog (fläg) *v.:* to beat with a stick or whip.

flyers (flī′ərs) *n.:* usually spelled *fliers;* copies of a single printed sheet circulated over a wide area.

frenzied (fren′zēd) *adj.:* frantic; in a hurried manner.

genius (jēn′yəs) *n.:* the intellectual and creative powers of human beings.

geology (jē•äl′ə•jē) *n.:* study of the nature and history of the earth.

gild (gild) *v.:* cover in a thin layer of gold.

habitable (hab′it•ə•bəl) *adj.:* able to be lived in.

horizontally (hôr′i•zänt′ə•lē) *adv.:* in a position parallel to the horizon; not vertically.

immaculate (i•mak′yə•lit) *adv.:* perfect.

immerse (i•mʉrs′) *v.:* to dip completely into.

immune (i•myōōn′) *adj.:* unable to contract a disease.

impending (im•pend′iŋ) *adj.:* approaching.

implicate (im′pli•kāt) *v.:* to involve in or connect with.

impractical (im•prak′ti•kəl) *adj.:* not suitable or useful.

impressive (im•pres′iv) *adj.:* producing a strong effect.

improvise (im′prə•vīz′) *v.:* to make up or create without any preparation.

inadvertently (in′ad•vʉrt′′nt•lē) *adv.:* accidentally; thoughtlessly.

incentive (in•sent′iv) *n.:* something that encourages someone to perform a certain task or work toward a goal.

indictment (in•dīt′mənt) *n.:* accusation.

indisputable (in′di•spyōōt′ə•bəl) *adj.:* unable to be challenged.

industrial (in•dus′trē•əl) *adj.:* manufacturing.

industry (in′dəs•trē) *n.:* hard work.

inferior (in•fir′ē•ər) *adj.:* lower in rank or class.

initial (i•nish′əl) *adj.:* first.

inspire (in•spīr′) *v.:* to cause a desire.

install (in•stôl′) *v.:* to secure in the correct position to be used.

integrate (in′tə•grāt′) *v.:* to open to people of all races.

intercept (in′tər•sept′) *v.:* to stop or catch on the way from one place to another.

intervening (in′tər•vēn′iŋ)) *adj.:* coming between.

inventiveness (in•ven′tiv•nis) *n.:* the quality of being able to make something that did not exist before.

ironic (ī•rän′ik) *adj.:* meaning the opposite of what one would expect.

lavish (lav′ish) *adj.:* more than is needed; overly generous.

legacy (leg′ə•sē) *n.:* something passed down from one person or group to the next.

legitimate (lə•jit′ə•mət) *adj.:* recognized or approved.

lofty (lôf′tē) *adj.:* impressive.

lot (lät) *n.:* a person′s situation in life.

lure (lʊr) *v.:* to attract; tempt.

maim (mām) *v.:* to severely wound or injure; to cripple.

maneuver (mə•nōō′vər) *n.:* a planned move.

marine (mə•rēn′) *adj.:* having to do with the sea or the ocean.

massacre (mas′ə•kər) *n.:* cruel, large-scale killing of people.

mayhem (mā′hem) *n.:* purposeful injury of another person; deliberate violence.

menacingly (men′əs•iŋ•lē) *adv.:* in a threatening manner.

merge (mʉrj) *v.:* to combine; unite.

modify (mäd′ə•fī) *v.:* to change or alter.

multitude (mul′ti•tōōd′) *n.:* a great many.

notorious (nō•tôr′ē•əs) *adj.:* well known in a negative way.

obligatory (ə·blig′ə·tôr′ē) *adj.:* necessary; required.

obstacle (äb′stə·kəl) *n.:* something that stands in the way.

orator (ôr′ət·ər) *n.:* public speaker.

organic (ôr·gan′ik) *adj.:* of or related to a living thing.

ornate (ôr·nāt′) *adj.:* excessively showy or decorated.

particle (pärt′i·kəl) *n.:* very small piece.

pedigree (ped′i·grē′) *n.:* origin; history.

petition (pə·tish′ən) *n.:* formal request.

phase (fāz) *n.:* stage.

plunder (plun′dər) *v.:* to rob, usually as part of an attack.

policy (päl′ə·sē) *n.:* course of action by a government.

pool (pōōl) *v.:* bring together for a common goal.

prejudice (prej′ə·dis) *n.:* intolerance; discrimination.

prevail (prē·vāl′) *v.:* to triumph.

procession (prō·sesh′ən) *n.:* a group of people moving forward together in an orderly way.

proclaim (prō·klām′) *v.:* to state or declare publicly.

profile (prō′fīl′) *n.:* overview or general picture of a person, group of people, or thing.

prophecy (präf′ə·sē) *n.:* a prediction about a future event believed to be given to a person by God.

prosperous (präs′pər·əs) *adj.:* yielding wealth.

protruding (prō·trōōd′iŋ) *adj.:* sticking out from.

random (ran′dəm) *adj.:* without plan or organization.

ratify (rat′ə·fī) *v.:* to approve.

rebel (ri·bel′) *v.:* to go against authority.

refurbish (ri·fʉr′bish) *v.:* to fix up; make new again.

reliable (ri·lī′ə·bəl) *adj.:* sure; stable.

replica (rep′li·kə) *n.:* a copy.

resident (rez′i·dənt) *n.:* person who lives in a place.

respectable (ri·spek′tə·bəl) *adj.:* considered acceptable and proper by society.

restrictive (ri·strik′tiv) *adj.:* limiting.

resurgence (ri·sʉr′jəns) *n.:* return.

retaliation (ri·tal′ē·ā′shən) *n.:* the return of one harmful act with another.

reunion (rē·yōōn′yən) *n.:* a meeting of people who have been separated from one another.

reverence (rev′ə·rəns) *n.:* high regard; respect.

revive (ri·vīv′) *v.:* to remember; to bring to mind.

rigid (rij′id) *adj.:* fixed; inflexible.

sacred (sā′krid) *adj.:* believed to be holy.

scourge (skʉrj) *v.:* punish; make to suffer.

segregate (seg′rə·gāt′) *v.:* to divide from the main area or group.

segregation (seg′rə·gā′shən) *n.:* separation of people into different groups or locations according to race.

servitude (sʉr′və·tōōd′) *n.:* labor or service.

silhouette (sil′ə·wet′) *n.:* an outline.

simultaneously (sī′məl·tā′nē·əs·lē) *adv.:* happening at the same time.

skeptical (skep′ti·kəl)) *adj.:* doubtful.

skirmish (skʉr′mish) *n.:* a minor fight or conflict.

specimen (spes′ə·mən) *n.:* example; a representative of a larger group.

sponsor (spän′sər) *v.:* to organize; support.

stability (stə·bil′ə·tē) *n.:* the state of being steady or unlikely to change.

stamina (stam′ə·nə) *n.:* staying power.

statistic (stə·tis′tik) *n.:* fact or data collected as a number and arranged so as to give information.

status (stat′əs) *n.:* rank; position.

stereotype (ster′ē·ə·tīp′) *n.:* oversimplified idea or belief about a group of people.

stoic (stō′ik) *adj.:* seeming unaffected by pain or suffering.

strategy (strat′ə·jē) *n.:* plan of action.

subdue (səb·dōō′) *v.:* to defeat; bring under submission.

submerge (səb·mʉrj′) *v.:* to place under the surface of a body of liquid.

subsistence (səb·sis′·təns) *n.:* existence; life.

supernatural (sōō′pər·nach′ər·əl) *adj.:* relating to the world beyond time and space; spiritual.

surveyor (sər·vā′ər) *n.:* a person who measures the size and shape of a piece of land.

sustain (sə·stān′) *v.:* to keep up or maintain.

taunt (tônt) *v.:* to ridicule; make fun of.

technique (tek·nēk′) *n.:* a method of doing something.

temporarily (tem′pə·rer′i·lē) *adv.:* for a limited period of time.

torment (tôr′ment′) *v.:* to cause physical or emotional pain; torture.

treacherous (trech′ər·əs) *adj.:* dangerous.

tyrannical (tə·ran′i·kəl) *adj.:* cruel and unjust.

vacant (vā′kənt) *adj.:* empty.

vehemently (vē′ə·mənt·lē) *adv.:* forcefully; with intensity.

verdant (vʉr′dənt) *adj.:* green.

verify (ver′ə·fī′) *v.:* to show the truth of.

violation (vī′ə·lā′shən) *n.:* action that breaks or ignores a law.

virus (vī′rəs) *n.:* a disease caused by a tiny living particle that reproduces inside cells.

voracious (vô·rā′shəs) *adj.:* having an enormous appetite for something.

---

at, āte, cär; ten, ēve; is, īce; gō, côrn, lʊʊk, yʊʊ *as in pure,* tōōl, yōō *as in you,* oil, out; up, fʉr; ə *for unstressed vowels, as* a *in adult or* u *in focus,* 'l *as in rattle,* 'n *as in flatten,* g *as in go,* j *as in jump,* hw *as in why,* chin, she, think, *th*ere, zh *as in measure,* ŋ *as in wing*

Acknowledgments

For permission to reprint copyrighted material, grateful acknowledgment is made to the following sources:

Barron's Educational Series, Inc.: From *Sojourner Truth and the Struggle for Freedom* by Edward Beecher Claflin. Copyright © 1987 by Eisen, Durwood & Co.

Rhoda Blumberg: "The Young Witch Hunters" by Rhoda Blumberg from *Muse*, vol. 3, no. 8, October 1999. Copyright © 1999 by Rhoda Blumberg.

Chelsea House Publishers, a division of Main Line Book Co.: From *The Mexican Americans* by Julie Catalano. Copyright © 1996 by Chelsea House Publishers, a division of Main Line Book Co. "The Maple Leaf Club" from *Scott Joplin* by Katherine Preston. Copyright © 1988 by Chelsea House Publishers, a division of Main Line Book Co. "Benjamin Banneker" from *Pioneers of Discovery*, edited by Richard Rennert. Copyright © 1994 by Chelsea House Publishers, a division of Main Line Book Co.

Clarion Books/Houghton Mifflin Co.: "What a Foolish Boy" from *The Boys' War* by Jim Murphy. Copyright © 1990 by Jim Murphy. All rights reserved.

Cobblestone Publishing Company, 30 Grove Street, Suite C, Peterborough, NH 03458: "Lacrosse Yesterday and Today" by Stanley A. Freed from *Cobblestone: Indians of the Northeast Coast*, November 1994. Copyright © 1994 by Cobblestone Publishing Company. All rights reserved. "July 19, 1848: The Birthplace of Women's Rights" by Howard Mansfield from *Cobblestone: Famous Dates*, January 1995. Copyright © 1995 by Cobblestone Publishing Company. All rights reserved. "A Proud Tradition" by John P. Langellier and "The Great Bicycle Experiment" by Toni A. Watson from *Cobblestone: Buffalo Soldiers*, February 1995. Copyright © 1995 by Cobblestone Publishing Company. All rights reserved. "A Quaker Commitment to Education" by Judith Foster Geary from *Cobblestone: African American Education: A Proud Heritage*, February 1998. Copyright © 1998 by Cobblestone Publishing Company. All rights reserved. From "Living History: Young Civil War Reenactors" by Meg Galante-DeAngelis from *Cobblestone: Children in The Civil War*, December 1999. Copyright © 1999 by Cobblestone Publishing Company. All rights reserved. "How the Wealthy Lived" by Helen Wieman Bledsoe and "Mrs. Astor and the 'Four Hundred'" by Stephen Currie from *Cobblestone: The Gilded Age*, April 2000. Copyright © 2000 by Cobblestone Publishing Company. All rights reserved.

College of William and Mary on behalf of Peggy Shaw: "Droughts Played Major Role in Jamestown, 'Lost Colony' Tragedies" by Peggy Shaw from *The William and Mary News*, April 23, 1998. Copyright © 1998 by The William and Mary News, College of William and Mary.

Cowboys & Indians Magazine: From "The Trail of Tears" by John Wadsworth from *Cowboys & Indians*, January 2000. Copyright © 2000 by Cowboys & Indians Magazine.

Dial Books for Young Readers, an imprint of Penguin Putnam Books for Young Readers, a division of Penguin Putnam Inc.: From *Rosa Parks: My Story* by Rosa Parks with Jim Haskins. Copyright © 1992 by Rosa Parks.

Farrar, Straus and Giroux, LLC: From "Smallpox" from *Invisible Enemies: Stories of Infectious Disease* by Jeanette Farrell. Copyright © 1998 by Jeanette Farrell.

Grolier Publishing Company: "Thomas Jefferson" from *Science in Colonial America* by Brendan January. Copyright © 1999 by Franklin Watts, a division of Grolier Publishing. From *Benjamin Franklin: The New American* by Milton Meltzer. Copyright © 1988 by Milton Meltzer.

Highlights for Children, Inc., Columbus, OH: From "A Few Appropriate Remarks" by Nancy Norton Mattila from *Highlights for Children*, February 1999. Copyright © 1999 by Highlights for Children, Inc.

Holiday House, Inc.: From *The Oregon Trail* by Leonard Everett Fisher. Copyright © 1990 by Leonard Everett Fisher. All rights reserved. "Your Rights and Mine" from *Give Me Liberty! The Story of the Declaration of Independence* by Russell Freedman. Copyright © 2000 by Russell Freedman. All rights reserved.

Henry Holt and Company, LLC: From *Breaking Ground, Breaking Silence* by Joyce Hansen and Gary McGowan. Copyright © 1998 by Joyce Hansen and Gary McGowan. "The Women of the American Revolution" from *Who Were the Founding Fathers?* by Steven H. Jaffe. Copyright © 1996 by Steven H. Jaffe.

Alfred A. Knopf Children's Books, a division of Random House, Inc.: From *The Kidnapped Prince: The Life of Olaudah Equiano*, adapted by Ann Cameron. Copyright © 1995 by Ann Cameron. "A Gentleman's Agreement" from *Shadow Ball: The History of the Negro Leagues* by Geoffrey C. Ward and Ken Burns with Jim O'Connor. Copyright © 1994 by Baseball Licensing International, Inc.

Little, Brown and Company Inc.: "Gold Mountain" from *The Gold Rush* by Liza Ketchum. Copyright © 1996 by The West Project.

Lodestar Books, an affiliate of Dutton Children's Books, an imprint of Penguin Putnam Books for Young Readers, a division of Penguin Putnam Inc.: "Supplying the Armies" from *A Separate Battle: Women and the Civil War* by Ina Chang. Copyright © 1991 by Laing Communications, Inc.

Los Angeles Times: "Reenactment of War Is Far Too Civil" by Jon Love from *Los Angeles Times*, November 9, 1999. Copyright © 1999 by Los Angeles Times.

Margaret K. McElderry Books, an imprint of Simon & Schuster Children's Publishing Division: From *The Planet Hunters: The Search for Other Worlds* by Dennis Brindell Fradin. Copyright © 1997 by Dennis Brindell Fradin.

The Millbrook Press: From "The Time of Most Distress" from *William Bradford: Rock of Plymouth* by Kieran Doherty. Copyright © 1999 by Kieran Doherty. All rights reserved.

National Geographic Society: "When I Was a Kid" by Sandra Fenichel Asher from *National Geographic World*, November 1998. Copyright © 1998 by National Geographic Society. From "Into the Unknown: The Incredible Adventures of Lewis and Clark" by Margaret McKelway from *National Geographic World*, July 1999. Copyright © 1999 by National Geographic Society.

Scholastic Inc.: From "The New Immigrants" by Naomi Marcus from *Junior Scholastic*, September 21, 1998. Copyright © 1998 by Scholastic Inc. From "A Girl Among the Whales" by Eve Nilson from *Storyworks*, vol. 7, issue 1, September 1999. Copyright © 1999 by Scholastic Inc.

Simon & Schuster Books for Young Readers, an imprint of Simon & Schuster Children's Publishing Division: "Cielito Lindo" from *Songs of the Wild West*, commentary by Alan Axelrod, arrangements by Dan Fox. Copyright © 1991 by The Metropolitan Museum of Art.

Walker and Company, Inc.: "The Railroad Unites America" from *The Iron Horse: How Railroads Changed America* by Richard Wormser. Copyright © 1993 by Richard Wormser.

Sources Cited:
Quotation by Scott Burnam from "Lacrosse: For Some It's More Than a Game" from *e-lacrosse.com*. Published online by Tonabricks, 1997-2001.